Careers in
Industrial Research
& De

Careers in Industrial Research & Development

J. H. Saunders
Monsanto Textiles Company
Pensacola, Florida

MARCEL DEKKER, INC.   New York   1974

607.2
Sa 8c
92049
Feb. 1975

MARCEL DEKKER, INC.
305 East 45 Street, New York, New York 10017

Library of Congress Catalog Card Number   73-82193
ISBN :   0-8247-6099-9

Current printing (last digit) :
10 9 8 7 6 5 4 3 2 1

Printed in the United States of America

CONTENTS

FOREWORD

During the past thirty years I've had the pleasure of trying to explain to my young graduating students the nature and scope of career possibilities in the various areas of professional life that they may enter.

How helpful it would have been if this book, Careers in Industrial Research and Development, had been available to my students and the many other students throughout the world! In it they could find first-hand what professional life in industrial research and development is like, for this book goes into much greater detail than the university counselor or faculty member can in the short time that he speaks with his students. Dr. Saunders answers many, many questions about the organization of the industrial research and development laboratory, how technical programs are selected and carried out, where the young graduate will fit in the organization during different stages of his professional life, the opportunity for using his innate creativity, and where the R&D organization fits into the entire corporation.

I hope that someone will soon prepare companion books in which mine and other students can find information on careers in industrial process design, operation, technical service, and other types of professional effort after graduation.

This book will receive a wide welcome and acceptance by both the academic and the industrial worlds.

John J. McKetta
The University of Texas
Austin, Texas

PREFACE

"What's industrial R & D like? How is research different from development? I've heard so many things about industry, but really know so little about it--how can I find out if I'd like it? What do they really do, and even more important, why?"

These are questions frequently raised by graduating students in science and engineering as they begin to consider their future careers. Some of the same questions, and many more, are still asked by employees after a few years of employment in industry. I have asked these questions in earlier years, too, and more recently have asked myself why industry doesn't do better at explaining what it really does and why. The next logical step was to try to collect in a reasonably short volume some of the key information related to these questions. In so doing I have tried to answer as many as possible for the students of science and engineering who wonder what a job in industry may be like. In addition, I have tried to provide answers for those who have been in industry for a few years and still are confused by what is done and by the reasons--apparent or imagined-- for doing it.

The scope of the book includes the major activities in industrial R & D other than experimentation and the direct use of scientific knowledge. These are taught to an extensive degree in the universities, and it is assumed that the reader is already prepared for continuing this phase of his lifelong education. The content of the book is directed more toward the people-related aspects of R & D, with emphasis on planning, communicating, and doing, on understanding what is done and why. Some elements of philosophy, sociology, and economics are necessary parts of the story.

The similarity between various aspects of industrial R & D and one's private life is touched upon lightly numerous times. The object of this is twofold: to show that guiding principles and many techniques are equally appropriate for both, and to emphasize that it is life in its entirety which is important--one's vocation cannot really be isolated from the rest of his life but must be integrated with it.

There are problems in any job in industry, just as in any of life's activities. It is believed that industrial problems have been recognized fairly here, along with the very real pleasures of industrial R & D. Ways of dealing with the problems and maximizing the pleasures are offered. Critics of industry may feel that the author's views on these points are too optimistic. If this is so, there are two reasons. First, one must be something of an optimist to stay in research of any kind for twenty-five years. In addition, the author has been fortunate in knowing and working with groups of people who have justified the views given here.

Some of the ideas and opinions expressed here may be judged to be useless by the young engineer or scientist. Probably a few of them are for any specific person. It is also likely that some further consideration, and especially some experience, will improve the understanding and feeling for validity of those ideas which at first seem out of place or of a different time. In any case, these ideas and opinions represent an attempt to translate experience in a way which I hope will prove helpful to many who are at the thresholds of their professional careers.

Within the scope of this book no distinction has been made or intended among race, sex, religion or other subdivisions of people. For simplicity only a single pronoun has often been used, e.g., "he," rather than "he and/or she." Differences do exist among races, sexes, and religions; many of these help keep the world an interesting place. Large differences also exist within any subdivision. A theme which this book emphasizes is that each person is an individual with some talents and limitations, with certain opportunities and problems. Each should be encouraged and guided to the extent possible to make the best of his own situation.

Many people have been influential in the preparation of this book. The thoughts expressed here have been developed in a large part as a result of contacts with many outstanding people in the fields of science and engineering, particularly D. H. Chadwick, T. H. Cleveland, A. M. Gemassmer, E. E. Hardy, R. L. Jenkins, C. S. Marvel, F. S. Riordan, Jr., and my father, C. W. Saunders. In addition, I have been privileged to have had the general guidance of three other outstanding leaders, C. A. Hochwalt, M. C. Throdahl and J. R. Wilson.

Special appreciation is given also to R. L. Ballman, M. A. Blatz, F. S. Riordan, Jr., J. H. Saunders, Jr., F. M. Silver, and J. H. Southern, who read the manuscript and made many helpful suggestions, to T. C. Turner for comments on Chapter 7, and to S. M. Tarter for his very helpful review of Chapter 9. I also wish to

thank the management of the Monsanto Company for its encouragement
in preparing and publishing this book.

The coming generations of scientists and engineers face new and
more difficult problems than their predecessors. Although technology
steadily becomes more complex, the major challenge does not lie in
the achievement of purely technical solutions, but in the relationships
between groups of people and in the wise use of technology as a tool
for the benefit of people. These problems can be met soonest and in
the best way if the mutual understanding among universities, industry,
government, and people at large is greatly improved. The author
hopes that this book is one of many which can help improve that
understanding.

J. H. Saunders

Careers in
Industrial Research
& Development

Chapter 1

A PRELIMINARY VIEW OF
INDUSTRIAL RESEARCH AND DEVELOPMENT

INTRODUCTION

Industrial research and development, in a broad sense, are concerned with acquiring desirable knowledge, demonstrating its usefulness, obtaining a high yield from human efforts, and generating a profit for the organization which sponsors the efforts. Very often the scientist or engineer needs several years of experience before he can fully understand the importance of all these features and their many ramifications and before he truly feels at home with them. In particular, the college graduate with no previous industrial experience may encounter difficulties in understanding and appreciating the manner in which industrial research and development are conducted.

The young technical man entering industry will usually have an appreciation for the academic methods of acquiring knowledge and conducting research. The depth of his appreciation will vary with the individual's academic degree, of course. In any case, he will often have developed a somewhat idealistic enthusiasm for the acquisition of knowledge for its own sake. This enthusiasm should never be lost! It is the first and one of the most important fundamental characteristics of the successful technical person. Having developed this enthusiasm, he is now ready to add an understanding of other basic characteristics of the well-rounded, vitally important participant in the world of science and technology.

The acquisition of desirable knowledge was listed as one of the first concerns of industrial research and development. This is not unexpected, since in truth this should be an essential feature of any research, academic or otherwise. While the development of knowledge for its own sake is both stimulating and educational, the rewards of personal pleasure, professional reputation, income, human benefit,

1

and national security are not realized until the usefulness of the knowledge gained is apparent. In academic research, the criteria of usefulness should be to aid in teaching, to develop better understanding of known or suspected phenomena, and to explore new areas of knowledge. In industry, the criteria include discovery and development of new products which ultimately will be useful to people and can be sold for a profit, discovery and development of new or improved processes for those products, generation of better understandings of known or suspected phenomena of importance to the company, and exploration of new areas of knowledge which are or may be of interest to the company. In industry every possible effort is made to visualize the usefulness of the work before it is done. Thus in industrial research and development one will find the selection of projects governed largely by the company's areas of interest and the necessity to generate a profit from the money spent by the laboratory.

The second concern of industrial efforts listed was the demonstration of usefulness of the knowledge gained. From the student's viewpoint, the academic world is concerned largely with acquiring selected information in his chosen field. The lectures, laboratory training, and research are all oriented toward the training of the individual. The ultimate usefulness of the information is often vague to the student; this consideration receives very little emphasis compared to that placed on learning. Similarly, any demonstration of the information gained is not a major consideration, beyond the level of learning by experimenting in the laboratory, usually on a small scale, and of written or oral tests. Upon completion of his formal education, the technical person finds that knowledge is of limited value until its usefulness is demonstrated to those who may benefit from it. One may "build a better mousetrap," but little has really been gained until the new ease of catching mice has been demonstrated to those who have an abundance of the pests! The suitable demonstration of technical knowledge may include design, construction, and operation of a pilot unit, which will perform the desired operation on an intermediate scale, and later the design, construction, and operation of a successful commercial scale unit. A suitable demonstration might also be a clear verbal report, giving essential technical information in a manner such that interested, even nontechnical, people can understand it fully, appreciate its significance, and realize what should be done as a result of the information gained.

A high yield from human efforts is a goal common to many activities in an industrial civilization. Research and development are not exceptions. While every individual in an organization will usually agree quite sincerely with this objective, many stumbling blocks continually arise. Poor selections of projects, failure to clearly identify objectives, inadequate coordination of programs, and poor human relations are among the most frequently encountered factors leading to a less than desired yield from the efforts expended. (These same factors, interpreted in a broad sense, are probably the most frequent causes of poor results in other areas of human activity, too.) Of these factors, the difficulties inherent in human relations are often the most resistant to solution.

The factor which most clearly places industrial research and development in a unique category in the world of science and technology is the necessity to generate a dollar profit. All research should be designed to yield a profit, if one considers "profit" broadly as a positive difference between the value of the results achieved (products, service, knowledge, national security, students trained, or dollars) and the cost of the effort and materials required to obtain those results. In the industrial world this profit must be primarily in dollars. In government sponsored, or institutional, or university research, the profit is measured largely in other terms.

It is the object of this book to aid the yound technical man or woman in understanding and enjoying the challenging and rewarding world of industrial science and technology. Primary emphasis is placed on efforts to explain what is done and why, in research and development, rather than on specific technical knowledge, an area which is adequately covered by universities, a variety of postgraduate training programs, and a host of excellent books. In this introductory chapter, let us briefly consider some of the major questions about industrial R & D which confront a student and a young employee. Subsequent chapters will attempt to answer in greater depth the questions raised here.

WHAT IS RESEARCH? WHAT IS DEVELOPMENT?

The terms "research" and "development" are used jointly in the title of this book, intentionally. The distinction between the two is rarely complete, and indeed, overlap is usually desirable. The following discussion will try to indicate in general terms, however, what is usually meant by the two terms when they are used separately in industry.

Both research and development in industry are dedicated to innovation, i.e., the introduction of something new (new at least within the organization which is introducing it to its customers), including the improvement of existing products and processes. Often smaller companies do not make any distinction at all, having all of their laboratory and pilot plant activities within a "research department" or within a "development department."

"Research" is usually concerned more with early stages of the innovation, which might include one or more of the following steps: discovery in the laboratory, demonstration of feasibility (Can the discovery be repeated, with results somewhere close to useful target levels of product quality and economics?), preliminary demonstration of a method of achieving the discovery (a process or a product), and preliminary evaluation of the product, if one is involved. The research stage, as indicated, is usually conducted on a small scale (grams, a few pounds or kilograms) in the laboratory, with a few people involved. This stage is relatively inexpensive and is the suitable stage for exploring ideas and evaluating new or modified products or processes. Research may also involve experimentation designed to help understand a phenomenon, but again usually on a relatively small scale. There are obvious exceptions to this repeated mention of small scale, of course, most notably in the size and cost of certain research equipment in many fundamental studies in physics.

"Development" is usually the technical phase of innovation lying between research and production in the time scale of that innovation. Experiments are often on a larger-than-laboratory scale, progressing perhaps through "pilot plant," "semi-works," and "full production" stages. Larger equipment, larger quantities of materials, larger teams of people, collection of much more detailed data, and much higher costs are involved relative to the scale of "research." Discoveries of new products, processes, and concepts are made in development work, as well as in research. In practice, development often tends to be less fundamental in its approach than does research.

In the best technical programs there is no sharp distinction between research and development. One stage phases smoothly into another, with cooperative programs and close communication. In order to improve the chances of achieving this cooperation, both research and development are often handled by the same department, or if by separate departments, then both departments usually report to the same director. More discussion of types of research and development, selection of programs, and other aspects of these two functions will appear frequently in later chapters.

A point of confusion sometimes arises in terminology in that the term "development" is often used in connection with "developing" a market for a new product. Some companies call this "market development," or "commercial development," or simply "development." This activity involves the study of markets or potential markets, the planning of the introduction of new products into those markets, and close liaison with both customers and one's own R & D teams. This function does not itself involve an experimental program, though it usually does call on an R & D department to give experimental assistance. In the remainder of this book the term "development" will be used to refer to an experimental function, not to a marketing function.

WHAT THE COLLEGE GRADUATE EXPECTS OF
AN INDUSTRIAL JOB

The job expectations of college graduates seem to vary considerably in some respects. In other respects students seem to hope for many of the same things. Those who have read suitable articles in the news journals of the professional societies have improved their concepts of what to expect. In many cases the experience of professors, and the time spent in counseling, have obviously shaped the student's expectations. Some discussion of realistic expectations may be helpful.

Most students appear to want to be challenged, both to use what they know and to learn more. This desire is completely reasonable, and most industries consciously try to meet it. There have, however, been many cases where the technical person has been used on jobs requiring much less than his full ability. It appears that one should not expect to have an assignment taxing his full capacity all the time-- there are not usually that many jobs of such a category to give to everyone all the time. The partially slack times provide an excellent opportunity for extra study and participation in technical societies and outside affairs. They provide an always needed chance to broaden oneself. Unfortunately, too many people do not use these opportunities and grow a little stale.

Another general desire is to have a job which has some meaning and significance, both intellectually and socially. This is an area in which industry is frequently considered to be lacking. An understanding of the significance of industrial work is of sufficient importance to merit a separate section, presented later in this chapter under the title "Why do it?"

In these days an applicant to industry usually assumes that he will have "good working conditions," including some laboratory space for experimental work and some desk space for study, writing, thinking (there is usually too little of that), and debate (this seems to flourish well enough). Air conditioning seems to be the rule, as is a considerable amount of excellent equipment. (With the wonders of NMR, IR, UV, GC, et al., the simplicity of a mixed melting point has sometimes been forgotten!) Access to a library is expected, as is mental stimulation from seminar series, presented by coworkers and outsiders. These are, indeed, normally found. Working time is usually forty hours per week, with occasional needs for extra working time in emergency situations (without overtime pay).

Other opportunities for technical growth are usually found. Most companies encourage at least several of the following: attendance at technical meetings at company expense (perhaps every one to three years, depending on the individual's rank and the state of the budget), membership in technical societies, publication of technical papers when the company's confidential information is not involved, and a range of short training or refresher courses.

Just as he has functioned as a professional in many ways such as continuing a study program at home and working overtime without extra pay in emergencies, so he may expect to be treated as a professional in numerous ways. In cases of occasional emergencies at home or for other urgent personal reasons he may expect time off without loss of pay and personal help from his associates if he needs it. In cases of severe and long illness he will find formal provisions for medical leave with pay for extended periods.

In the area of more material compensation, the salary figures are at least reasonably good--generally better than in university or government laboratories. Actual figures in different areas of science and engineering are published more or less yearly by the technical news journals and are available to all. In addition companies generally provide excellent medical and hospitalization policies for the individual and his family, at a fraction of the actual cost, as well as life insurance policies equal to or as much as two-and-one-half-times his annual salary. Vacation policies normally give a minimum of two weeks vacation with pay after completion of a full "vacation year" of work, with the vacation period increasing with the number of years of employment. Three weeks after five years service, eventually

rising to four to six weeks is not unusual. One may add to this enough
holidays to equal more than a week's working time. Retirement plans
of one sort or another are the rule, often with no contribution by the
employee.

Many have argued that electricians and bricklayers can make more
money than young scientists or engineers. In special situations, such
as full time employment plus considerable overtime, a few bricklayers and electricians probably have done so. If one wants to make
the most money he can, however, he should not go into research or
development! But if one wishes to earn an enjoyable living and obtain
fulfillment more from the quality of his work and the interesting
people he is with, than from monetary reward, he should have no
hesitancy about industrial R & D.

Not all of this collection of expectations should really be counted
on at each and every company. However, nearly all companies will
have most of these, at least, and usually a few which are not listed.
A student can generally satisfy himself on the issues which seem
important to him by discussing them with a representative of the
company's personnel department and also a technical employee of
the company, preferably one in the department for which he is being
considered. While a company's policies may be uniform from department to department, the way in which those policies are applied may
vary somewhat according to the attitude of the department director.
(Opportunities for such discussions will be outlined in the chapter
on getting a job.)

This group of expectations seems impressive when collected in
one place. The other side of the coin is that the company expects
the individual to do his best in helping solve the company's problems;
to grow in ability, experience, and performance; and to be a constructive member of the company's team of problem solvers. It is hoped
that the remaining chapters of the book will help greatly in understanding just what a company expects.

WHY DO IT?

One of the important questions which science and engineering
students ask themselves, usually many times, is "What do I want to
do?" The related question normally follows, "Do I want a job in
industrial research and development?" This is a valid question which

should be answered only after much consideration. If at all possible the student should discuss it with people who have industrial experience. Some of the desirable aspects of an industrial position are outlined below.

Industrial R & D provides a job--a way of making a living, of paying one's own way. A salary in industrial R & D is such that, with good management of money and excepting catastrophes, one can pay for food, clothing, shelter, education, medical services and transportation for himself and his loved ones. He can afford some recreation and luxuries, increasing as his earning power increases. Savings can be slowly accumulated for emergencies and for college education. Contributions can be made to others who are less fortunate. A fair share of taxes can be paid, contributing not only to the continuity of a remarkable political system but also to the health, education, employment, and general welfare of low income families in our country. These alone justify personal pride in one's work. They are not unique to R & D, of course.

In addition to providing work for the individual, successful R & D creates jobs for others. Our synthetic fiber plants, for instance, employ thousands of people. These plants and these jobs are built on the good R & D results of earlier years. If we do our work well today we will create new jobs for people tomorrow.

Some people simply enjoy solving problems. To them the nature of the problem may not be as important as the difficulty of it. There are still plenty of problems, big and little, to be solved in industry.

Making a contribution to man's total knowledge is rewarding to many. Industrial careers offer this opportunity, although usually not to such an extent as one may find in selected universities and in a few research institutes. Nevertheless, industrial research has made outstanding contributions to our fundamental knowledge in such diverse fields as catalysis, adhesion, the relationships between the structure of materials and their properties, nucleation, energy transfer mechanisms, and medicine, to list a few.

There is a rather widespread desire among scholarly people to make some contribution to society. If one wishes to consider what his chances may be for achieving this in industry, why not ask first what some of the basic needs of people are? At one time we would have listed food, clothing, and shelter. Today we would probably add medical service, education, transportation, and communication. A little thought shows quickly that industry contributes greatly to all of these. In fact, we find many single companies in the United States, each of which make major contributions in nearly all of these areas.

One might also ask himself what are some of the greatest long range social problems. We could list nutritional deficiencies (a need for more and better food, combined with better distribution, storage and handling systems); better medical service for low income people; new and cleaner fuels or energy sources; new, better, and lower cost materials of construction; low cost housing; a clean environment; better mass transportation systems; and population control. Industry is and will continue playing a large role in solving these problems.

A point which is sometimes not readily considered is that good industrial R & D contributes greatly to the economic strength and hence to the political stability of the United States. In order to maintain jobs and have low unemployment rates, our industries must compete successfully with those in other countries which pay much lower wage rates. To be competitive we must produce materials that are at least as good, preferably better, and must have processes which are capable of greater productivity per employee. Good R & D are essential for both product quality and process efficiency. If the R & D fails, our competitive position will deteriorate and unemployment will grow. One does not have to recall the "great depression" of the 1930s to know the anguish and turmoil which result from major unemployment.

If one wishes to see the usefulness of his efforts he probably has a better chance to do this in the industrial laboratory than in most other types. Industrial research projects are usually designed to be useful in one to five years--an unattractive feature to some. But if one has a successful project in industry, he has a good chance of seeing the utilization of it.

An industrial position also has a good feature in common with other positions: it provides an opportunity to make life more pleasant and meaningful for others working with you. A real contribution that anyone can make in any position is to take advantage of this opportunity.

To this author, a position in industrial R & D offers many opportunities for personal fulfillment to people with a wide range of desires. There are also limitations and frustrations. Indeed, no human effort of merit is free from discouraging problems, and industry is no exception. One major problem area comes simply from the fact that a company is made up of people, and it tries to do business with other people. One may encounter a full spectrum of problems which automatically come from working with people. Here one finds a fascinating challenge, and will also be rewarded with events and relationships worthy of long memory.

A particular aspect of the "people problems" of which big companies are sometimes guilty is making the individual feel "lost in the crowd." This feeling need not exist, even in very large companies. Good management, with emphasis on participative planning of work and good communications, can overcome it. It is a hazard in all large organizations, however, whether industry, government, military, or other organizations. The individual's own approach to the job can also have a great deal to do with how much he is isolated or is a participative member of the organization.

Another major problem area is that in an industrial position one is expected to focus his interests and activities fairly closely to the interests of his employer. Thus a synthetic rubber producer may not appreciate a young chemist's desire to check out an attractive idea for promoting the ecological breakdown of DDT. Frequently some time is required before the college graduate sees that there is just as much fun in being an expert in some area of interest to his employer as there was at school, doing research in his professor's field.

Some attractive and some limiting features of industrial R & D have been described briefly. One should consider these in the context of two additional points. First, not all projects are successful. Indeed, only a small percentage of exploratory research efforts are, in the final analysis, directly useful. Since development programs are usually built on those which have already shown a successful rating through research, a higher percentage of these programs will be classed as useful. Working on a project which "does not make it" can be discouraging, of course. In such cases the other opportunities not directly tied to the success of the project are still operable, however.

The second point is one which bothers many people at one time or another. This is simply the difficulty of seeing the importance of one's own contribution in the overall picture. For example, the analytical chemist could become bored with analyzing the gases evolved from the thermal decomposition of a range of plastics. And the engineer could wonder if it is really important to have precise accuracy of metering two liquid components in making certain foamed plastics. In reality these are key steps in the development of foam-insulated building panels with superior heat and flame resistance, which will undoubtedly play a very significant part in the development of better, cheaper, low cost housing.

Each person naturally feels that he wants to make a large contribution to his goal. Often much experience and introspection are required before one realizes that large contributions really are the sum of many small ones, and it falls to most of us to make the small ones. The small contributions which each of us make do add up, though time, usually years, is required before big progress is apparent.

CHANGE AND CONSISTENCY

    The world of industrial R & D is a world which is obviously deeply involved with technology. It is equally obvious that technology is and has been changing very rapidly. It is not surprising then that one hears many concerned statements about obsolescence of knowledge and education, and even of the individual. While there is much that is true in these statements, they are frequently exaggerated and the merit of many permanent values is overlooked.

    Claims have been made that a person's technical education becomes obsolete in ten years, more or less, depending on the enthusiasm of the speaker. A more realistic statement, however, is that one's knowledge of R & D will be obsolete, competitively, in ten years or so if he stops his study program when he leaves the university.

    Most of us will find that the basic mathematics and physical laws as taught twenty-five years ago are still essentially valid. Some new knowledge and some new ramifications have been learned, and some new vocabulary has replaced the old in a few cases. In chemistry one still finds that an alcohol reacts with a carboxylic acid to give an ester. The explanation of the reaction may now involve more than first or second order kinetics, electronegative or electropositive substituent effects, and steric hindrance--one may even discuss molecular orbitals. New catalysts have been found. But however we describe it, the reaction still goes the same way now as it did years ago.

    Changes are indeed being made rapidly. New knowledge, new techniques and equipment, including analytical methods, the use of computers, tools such as the laser, an understanding of the conservation of orbital symmetry in chemical reactions, are appearing from time to time. A top quality technical person must certainly maintain a study program throughout his career if he is to keep that quality in his own performance. Relatively little of what was learned

in school will become obsolete, however. Instead, it is a strong
foundation upon which one can add new structures of learning and
achievement.

While these changes are steadily being made, the need for other,
more basic things will stay much the same. In this category we may
list such things as individual traits of honesty, intellectual curiosity,
willingness to work, generosity, courage, patience, judgment, desire
to accomplish useful goals, pride in excellence, ability to work constructively with people, concern for the welfare of others, ability to
lead people. One could list others, of course.

Those who are concerned with the rapidly changing world--whether
of industrial science or other--would do well to analyze which factors
are changing and which are not. The more superficial things are
changing rapidly--our tools, our terminology, our descriptions of
phenomena. Basic knowledge grows more slowly. The real fundamentals of our lives, including the real keys to success in our
careers, are even more stable.

AN OPINION

The world of industrial research and development is indeed a
complex one--it offers both challenge and opportunity. Like other
human efforts, if is not free from discouraging problems and
frustrations. At the same time, however, industrial R & D offers
challenges of high order in the combined fields of science, engineering, human relations, economics, and social progress. Opportunities
are available for personal satisfaction in the creation of products and
services which will serve and benefit people, the creation of jobs
which will provide employment for more people, and for the satisfaction of one's own desire for creative expression. Furthermore,
one can expect to see the useful results of his efforts. Material
benefits are available, too, of course.

A person's life is usually most meaningful and rewarding when it
approaches (but need not fully reach) "equilibrium" or harmony
between his own abilities and desires, on the one hand, and the
desires and facilities of the organization with and for which he works,
or lives, on the other. An understanding of himself, and also that of
the organization, will then be most helpful in achieving a harmonious
life, regardless of his occupation or activity.

Industrial R & D, as is inherent in the name, has industry as its sponsor. An understanding of the needs and functions of one's own industry will provide an essential basis for understanding industrial R & D. Industry in the United States does and must serve a variety of functions. It creates and sells products or services which people need and/or are willing to buy. At the same time it creates and maintains jobs for people. Industry is steadily expanding its role in serving the community and nation in additional ways. Throughout all this, industry must make a profit in order to exist and fulfill the functions outlined. Many say that industry exists only to make a profit. The analogy here is close to that of man's need for food. Do we eat to live, or live to eat? In part, at least, it may depend on one's individual attitude. The opportunity exists for one to live in accord with either feeling.

To be in harmony with its sponsor, industrial R & D must be concerned in the large majority of its efforts with the creation and development of those new products and services which its sponsoring company can or will be able to sell at a profit. Such innovation is highly challenging because of very able competition from existing products and from other R & D organizations, and also because economics adds another primary variable which is absent in much other research.

In the varieties of innovation needed by industry, there is opportunity for people of a broad range of abilities and desires. Excellence which can be oriented at least approximately parallel to the course of the sponsor is highly desired and well rewarded in personal satisfaction gained as well as in the availability of difficult technical problems, suitable facilities and organization, and salary. Advancement, recognition, and encounter with increasingly important problems are available whether one wishes to emphasize primarily his scientific and technical abilities, or whether he wishes to add administration to his scope of activities. The administrator need not forsake his scientific knowledge, though some choose to do so.

The world of industrial R & D has sometimes been called a "labyrinth." With proper understanding of himself and the needs of his organization, the direction of one's efforts will be no more complex and frustrating than in any other rather sophisticated activity, and one will have an excellent opportunity of doing the best he can with what he has. The degree to which one achieves this is, in the end, the real mark of his "success."

Chapter 2

WHAT IS AN INDUSTRIAL ORGANIZATION?

The university graduate, or any other person considering an
industrial job for the first time, may wonder just what the industrial
organization for which he may work is like. He will have encountered
a range of descriptions, some in legal terms, some in economic
language, and some in emotional phrases. It may be that none of
these really gives him the information that will help him understand
the organization which may be paying his salary. Certainly the best
possible understanding will help him decide whether he may find the
deep enjoyment which can come from a really fortunate match of
personal interests and abilities with job requirements. This chapter
makes no real attempt to cover the legal ramifications of company
and corporation structures and touches only lightly on economics.
The emphasis is more on the personal or human viewpoint, with the
object again of understanding better what a company does, why it
does some of the things it does, and its relationship to people.

TERMINOLOGY

One often hears references to such terms as "industry,"
"company," and "corporation," with these terms sometimes used
synonymously. In this sense an industry such as the "chemical
industry" is usually more or less the entire collection of companies
and corporations engaged in making and selling chemicals. The
"rubber industry," the "steel industry," and others are similar
groupings of companies and corporations whose primary commercial
interests are in the indicated categories. The "manufacturing
industry" is even larger, including companies and corporations producing and selling manufactured goods, and hence would include the

chemical industry, the automotive industry, the electronics industry, and many others. It is the broad grouping called the manufacturing industry that we are primarily concerned with in this discussion of industrial research and development.

Many, but not all, companies are "incorporated" and hence are corporations. The most important distinctions between a corporation and a company which is not incorporated are legal, such as a definition of who is financially responsible in case of business failure. These legal points need not concern us for the purposes of this discussion, and the terms company and corporation will be used interchangeably insofar as the relationships to people are concerned.

The manufacturing industry has been changing greatly over the years, with changes in nearly all aspects. The types of materials produced obviously have changed, with many once popular items no longer being produced (e.g., horse-drawn buggies, coal-burning railroad steam engines, streetcars, etc.) and many relatively new ones being popular (jet airplanes, television sets, transistor radios, for example). Working conditions have changed greatly, with much shorter working hours, cleaner and safer working areas, and more automation becoming standard. The percentage of the population directly employed by this industry has remained nearly constant, while large increases are apparent in government employment and in the service industry, as shown in Table 1 (1). In 1968 the manufacturing industry in the United States employed about 19,740,000 people, 29% of the total working force and about 10% of the population of the country. Thus 10% of our population provided the manufactured goods made in this country, constituting a large part of all the manufactured goods consumed in this country, plus some for export. Some of our country's major trends in employment in recent years can be seen from the data in Table 1.

EXPENSES, INCOME, AND PROFIT

Each company and corporation in this manufacturing industry is really a group of people organized and working so as to achieve certain goals. These goals normally include the manufacture and sale of certain types of goods--or in some cases, service--and the making of a profit on these operations. In our economic system the making of a profit is essential for the survival of the company as a

TABLE 1 Population and Employees in Various Fields of Work in the United States[a]

Year	Population	Construction	Manufacturing	Agriculture	Service	Government
				Employees in		
1950	148,665	2,333	15,241	8,036	5,382	6,026
1960	179,323	2,885	16,796	5,837	7,423	8,353
1968	199,860	3,259	19,740	3,817	10,504	12,202

[a]Population and employment figures are in thousands.

unit whose functions are controlled by the owners and employees.

The company naturally has to have a considerable amount of money in order to start its operation and to continue to function. In the case of some small companies and a very few larger ones, a few individuals will have enough money to start the company. Having supplied the money for the necessary buildings, equipment, raw materials, salaries for employees, etc., they are the owners. The operation of the company, it is hoped, will produce enough income that improvements, expansion, and continued operation can be paid for from the sale of the goods produced. In many cases the owners must borrow money from time to time to supplement the income. Naturally those called upon to lend money will not want to do so unless they think the company will continue to function satisfactorily and make enough profit to pay back the loans, with interest.

In most cases, especially with the larger companies, the money provided by the original owners and the money borrowed from banks are not sufficient to pay for the expensive plants, laboratories and other requirements. To raise more money, the corporation may sell "stock" to the public. A person can buy one, ten, one hundred, or more "shares" of stock in such a corporation. In so doing, he becomes a partial owner, in proportion to the total of all shares of stock issued by the company. In buying the stock the individual expects to get a fraction of the profits from the company each year, called "dividends." The amount of his dividend will be in proportion to the number of shares of stock he holds and may also be affected by the amount of profit which the company makes. In general, the value of a share of stock is expected to increase over many years if the company performs well and increases its profits by selling high quality products which its customers are willing to buy. While the value of a share of stock usually fluctuates according to many factors other than the performance of the individual company, over the long range those companies which are able to maintain an acceptable profit level are considered to be good investments, from the combination of dividends paid plus an increase in the market value of the stock.

Individuals owning stock are "capitalists" in that they have provided some of the money, "capital," required to operate the company. In 1970 there were about 30,000,000 people in the United States who owned stock in companies (2), and at least three times that many who were indirect owners, for example through their purchase of life insurance from companies which themselves owned stock.

A question naturally arises concerning an acceptable profit level

for a particular company. What is too much, and what is too little?
From the investor's viewpoint, he can, at various times, get about
3% to 6% interest on his money if he simply puts it in a savings
account in a bank, 4% to 5% interest on government bonds, and sometimes as high as 8% to 9% on certain other types of bonds. It is
reasonable that he would expect his combination of dividends plus
increase in stock value over the years to be somewhat more attractive than these interest rates, since there is more risk involved in
the purchase of stock in a company (the stock value can go down, and
so can the dividend rate). This gives one clue as to what the average
investor feels is an acceptable profit level for a company.

Let's take a look at a profit statement from a hypothetical company, just to see more clearly how its profit is related to the rest
of the money used in the business. Some of the most significant
figures are shown in Table 2.

We can see that this is a large company; with a payroll of
$300,000,000 it probably employs about 35,000 people. The cost of
doing business is very high, $900,000,000. Its money for operation
has originally come from a combination of loans and the sale of
stock, with nearly 17,000,000 shares of stock being held by investors.

TABLE 2 Financial Highlights of a Hypothetical Company (in dollars)

Earnings per share of stock		3.00
Cash dividends paid per share		1.80
Income from sales		1,000,000,000
Cost of doing business		
Raw materials, fuel, supplies, etc.	500,000,000	
Wages and salaries to employees	300,000,000	
Depreciation, depletion, etc.	80,000,000	
Interest on bank loans	20,000,000	
Total		900,000,000
Gross profit		100,000,000
Taxes		50,000,000
Net profit		50,000,000
Cash dividends paid		30,000,000
Retained for future growth		20,000,000

Fortunately, its operations bring in enough money to pay the costs of doing business, to pay $20,000,000 interest on its bank loans, and have $100,000,000 left as "gross profit." This profit is divided essentially in three ways. About half goes directly to the government as taxes. The remaining half is called "net profit," some of which goes to the stockholders as dividends, and some is retained in the company to be used for growth in new areas and to improve its operations. Its net profit (after tax) was 5% of its sales. A typical value for the stock might be about fifteen times earnings, or $45.00 per share. Thus the stockholder, in getting $1.80 dividend per share, received 4% on his investment.

These numbers, although hypothetical, are not unusual. The dividends for most companies will usually be in the range of about 2% to 5% of the cost of the stock. Net income, as a percent of sales, in the chemical industry has been in the range of about 3% to 8% for most companies. For General Motors, the largest industrial corporation in the United States in 1970, it was about 3.2% of sales. Many companies have at least one dollar of investment in buildings, land, and equipment for each dollar of sales, and in some of the technically more sophisticated firms there may be about two dollars invested for each dollar of sale annually. Thus the profit, expressed as a percent of the investment, may be as low as half that expressed as a percent of sale. Some actual 1970 data for several large companies are shown in Table 3 (3).

A study of most companies will show that the net profit, while it may be large in total dollars, is usually rather small when expressed as a percent of sales or of the investment in the company. Since the total number of dollars is large, however, it may be worth further consideration of what the profit is used for.

Taxes, largely Federal income tax, take about one half of the gross profit of a company. Federal income taxes from all industry totalled 28.7 billion dollars in 1968, accounting for 21% of the total Federal income (1). (Most of the rest, 44%, came from personal income tax, and 22.5% from Social Security taxes, half of which is paid by employers.) State and local taxes paid by companies account for a high percentage of the money available to state and local governments, too.

Of the remaining, or net, income, usually more than half goes to the owners of the stock as dividends. The stockholders pay income tax on these dividends, much as they do on any other type of income. So again, a considerable part of the net income eventually goes to pay taxes. The rest of the dividend naturally is used by a stockholder

TABLE 3 1970 Profits of Several United States Companies

Company	Total sales[a]	Net profit[a]	Profit, % of sale	Return on investment (%)
DuPont	$3,664	$328.7	9.0	5.1
Monsanto	1,995	77.9	3.9	2.2
Celanese	1,037	51.0	4.9	2.4
Allied Chemical	1,249	43.1	3.4	1.6
Eastman Kodak	2,785	403.7	14.5	9.7
Phillips	2,304	117.1	5.1	2.6

[a]Sales and earnings in millions of dollars.

in any way he judges to be desirable for his needs and interests.

As noted before, a part of the net income is usually retained by the company and used in any of several ways to help insure that it can continue as a sound, efficiently producing organization.

As can be seen from these simple considerations, well over half of the profit of the average company is paid as taxes, either by the company itself or by the stockholders. Universities are among the many groups which are glad to receive financial aid from the government. Indeed our educational system as a whole depends largely on the taxes paid by industries and individuals. The expenditure for public schools in this country in 1966 was $26,248,000,000, and has been growing steadily, essentially all from taxes. In the same year the expenditure for our colleges and universities was $12,509,000,000, with the major part coming from taxes. Similarly, a total welfare program (all types) of $87,758,000,000 in 1966, and $112,400,000,000 in 1968, was financed by local, state, and Federal governments, all of whom derive their income essentially from taxes (1). Thus the profit which is made by industry is of direct benefit to a large percentage of our population, even though many do not realize it.

One misconception which seems to occur from time to time is that the "captains of industry" get the profits of their companies.

In the case of a personally owned company this is true, but there are
very few personally owned companies of large size. The officers of
a company, the president, vice presidents, etc., are paid salaries,
and in years when the company does well financially they usually get
bonuses in addition. These payments are part of the operating expenses of the company and were included in the "wages and salaries"
entry in Table 2. The profits are divided as has already been indicated, and an officer of the company will share in the profit to whatever extent he owns stock in the company. If he owns 10,000 shares
of stock in our hypothetical company (Table 2) he would receive
$18,000 in dividends, out of the $30,000,000 paid as dividends. (To
own that much stock he would have invested about $450,000 in the
company in the form of stock purchases.)

In our society a company must make a profit, at least on the
average over a period of years, in order to survive. If it does not
do so, why should anyone be willing to lend it money or invest in its
stock? And if it has no profit, that means simply that its expenses
are larger than its income. The net result is that it cannot continue
to pay the wages of its employees and the costs of its raw materials.
Such a company fails, i.e., ceases to exist, and the jobs which it
had provided cease to exist. The individual can scarcely appreciate
the importance of the failure of his company until he is faced with
unemployment. In addition, company failure usually means that the
individual loses the insurance policies and the pension program which
the company had provided. These can be very expensive to replace,
especially for one of advanced age.

Based on preceding discussions, profit may be seen as an essential feature for a company's survival in our society. It is also
essential in more purely socialist countries, though in those countries
the governments usually take much more of the profit to pay for the
expenses of running the governments. In communist countries the
governments take all the profit. We have also seen that our government, through corporate income taxes and personal income taxes,
takes well over half of a company's profit to help pay for the costs of
government programs. One major difference between our capitalistic
society and socialistic or communistic societies, lies in this treatment of profit. While the differences slowly become less--we drift
toward socialism, and even communism gradually utilizes our system
for reward for personal effort--the differences still exist to a considerable degree. Our society's operation includes use of the
principle that one should be rewarded materially according to the
productivity of his efforts. It is on this fundamental belief that a

company is allowed to keep part of its profits and that the company distributes part of the profits to the stockholders.

Our practice of rewarding one materially according to the productivity of his efforts is based on one of the fundamental incentives for human effort. If people feel that they are not rewarded in some suitable way for their efforts, most soon lose the will to make more than a bare minimum effort. The "suitable reward" certainly may involve more than material returns--it may include the pleasure which comes with doing a difficult task well, personal recognition, and the pleasures associated with power. One of the major driving forces is often the feeling that one can do a better job of directing affairs than is being done. These nonmaterial incentives usually outweigh the financial rewards, as long as the financial aspects are reasonable in proportion to the scope of the job. Perhaps this can be understood more easily if one looks at our income tax tables. Calculation shows that one making about $40,000 per year from salary, bonus, dividends, and other sources, with normal taxable deductions, will contribute about 50% of his next raise to the government! The income tax rate currently goes progressively to 70% (1970 rates). Thus it is fortunate that material profit is not the only incentive for doing large and difficult jobs well.

WHAT DOES A COMPANY DO?

As has been stated before, companies produce and sell goods and/or services which people need and/or want and are willing to buy at a price that will yield the company a profit. This pattern of action has certainly been a major part of the shaping of our society. As such it has made some remarkable contributions and has generated some unforeseen problems. It is impractical to try to enumerate all of the contributions and problems, but illustrations will be given of both.

The products and services sold by companies for the most part are tested according to standards which in time are quite rigorous and discriminating: acceptance by the public on the basis of cost versus performance. While it is true that "super salesmanship" sometimes appears to promote useless or inferior items with success, such products do not usually survive for long. A combination of judgment by the public as to what it wants, competition from domestic and foreign producers, and legal requirements maintains an ever-changing commercial environment that favors those products which perform the best service at the most reasonable price available.

The products or services which the public wants naturally change with time and with the ever-changing spectrum of problems which face us. At one time or another such products as horse-drawn plows, buggies, streetcars, and coal-burning locomotives were in demand. When those wants existed, industries supplied the products. When the desire for those products declined and essentially disappeared, the companies supplying them either changed to other products or went out of business. The same pattern of change continues as public wants and needs change.

At one time it was considered that improvements in the quality of individuals' lives would be made by shortening the work week; by providing more leisure time; by reducing or eliminating diseases such as poliomyelitis, cholera, yellow fever, typhus, scarlet fever, and others; by providing cultural opportunities for many more people via radio, records, and television; and by generating enough flow of money (profits, taxes) to provide education for the masses. In each of these areas, and in many others, industries have supplied the material goods, the medicines, the more efficient working conditions, and a large share of the taxes to reach or make progress toward all of these desires. With many such changes behind us, the public mind naturally seeks other changes which also should improve the quality of life.

The feeding of the people of the earth has always been a problem, and continues as one of our major issues for the future. The food supply is considered adequate today in thirty industrialized nations in the temperate northern area of the world, where 900 million people live. But 1,900 million other people live in less developed countries, with inadequate food supplies (4). The keys to success in the industrialized countries include the development of efficient farm machinery, insecticides and herbicides, new strains of seeds which yield larger crops, and especially fertilizer. It has been estimated that half of the world's population is now being fed by the extra food yield resulting from the use of industrial fertilizer. The productive trends which have been demonstrated in the industrialized nations need certain improvements to protect our environment, and need to be extended to more countries which are deficient in food. One aspect of the progress which must still be made is the estimate that $30,000,000,000,000 to $60,000,000,000,000 of losses in food were sustained in the 1960s in the world due to pests (4).

Food and health are fairly obvious areas where one can appreciate the benefits of industry's performance. Clothing is another basic need of people. But one might ask why is it important to have a synthetic fiber industry? Wouldn't we be just as well off with cotton, linen, silk, and wool? Analysis has shown, however, that there is not enough farm land to grow sufficient natural fibers to clothe the world's population (5). Today about 50% of the world's fiber is man-made. The synthetics also have advantages in usually giving more cloth per pound than natural fibers, and in giving longer wear. The percentage supplied by natural fibers will likely decrease, as available land is needed more and more for food crops.

A careful analysis of most industrial operations will show that industry's products are bought by people for some reason which is at least fairly good. In some cases the products are classed as "essential" to life and in many cases they are considered to make life more pleasant. In general, most people are not inclined to waste a high percentage of their money, and it follows that most of the products they buy have some real value to those people.

There are certainly examples of industries' selling materials with scant, if any, real value in the products. Such products do not usually last long, and companies which rely largely on them do not, either.

While most of the material pleasures of our daily lives, and indeed most of our means of survival, have come from our industries' products, we have at the same time generated some serious problems by our industrial activities. To a large extent these problems have come about because of limited foresight and short range, rather than long range planning. It is unfortunate that our major groups of people--whether they be in government, universities, or industry-- have not, with a few notable exceptions, been gifted with outstanding foresight and planning. There are, however, enough remarkable examples of man's good foresight and planning to give more hope for the future. Part of the problem of planning is simply to recognize the real necessity for it. This necessity is certainly becoming clear to an ever increasing number of the world's business, educational, and political leaders. With examples behind us, showing what man can do in this area when he tries, there is certainly hope for the future. Some outstanding examples of past effort include the United States Constitution and the Marshall Plan for the redevelopment of Europe after World War II.

Of more limited scope, but awesome in its detail, the technical problems solved, and its speed of success was the United States plan

to reach the moon. While many argue about the value of the result,
we can certainly learn from that successful approach to solving
difficult problems. Key features included a clearly stated goal,
understood by all who were working toward it; adequate funding; hard,
continuous, and intelligent work by dedicated men and women; and
nearly consistent, constructive effort by those involved (there were
a few strikes to mar this record). If we contrast this with our approach toward major social problems such as unemployment, welfare,
or ghettos, doesn't it suggest improvements which we can make?

One of the most obvious problems at this time, which is attribut-
able in part to industry, is pollution. The seriousness of the problem
is now sufficiently clear that there is every reason to believe it will
be brought under control within a few years. Some improvements
are already apparent, and major ones will be visible in 1975-1980.
The effort will be expensive and some time will be necessary. While
estimates are probably not very reliable at this time, one study in
1970 proposed that $9.7 billion will be required to clean up industrial
pollution, and $51.3 billion to bring sewage, garbage, and other
domestic wastes under control (6). (The estimates will doubtless
grow as we learn more about the problems.) Industry is responding
to the need and must continue to do so at a faster rate.

The situation regarding industrial spending for pollution control
illustrates rather clearly an area where proper industrial action
must be guided by good legal action. Consider the possible case of
two competitors, each making 10,000,000 pounds of the same product
each year, and each polluting the air and water equally. A study
shows that $500,000 will be required each year to eliminate the
pollution from each company. If the first company elects to spend
the half million dollars each year, while the second does not, its
gross profit will be reduced by that half million dollars annually
compared to the second company. In more difficult times, when
each is not able to sell its full plant production, the second company
has a further advantage. It can reduce its selling price $0.05 per
pound below that of its competition and still have essentially equal
profit per pound. Naturally at the lower price it will sell its plant
capacity, and the well meaning company which controlled its pollution
will sell much less than its plant capacity. Operating at reduced
capacity raises the manufacturing cost still more and this company
may soon be bankrupt.

While this illustration is oversimplified, since most companies
are not producing a single product in a given plant and two competitors do not normally have exactly the same situation, the illustration

is quite valid. The issues are not usually so clearly drawn, however. Some companies do take a lead in controlling pollution while others delay as long as possible, even when laws have not been forcing the leaders to make their improvements. In these real life situations the difficulties illustrated by the example do certainly exist.

The only really workable solution to this type inequity is to pass laws requiring all plants to control their pollution at an acceptable level. Industry and government must work together far more effectively in the future in order to clean up our environment and keep it at a clean, acceptable level. (We should not expect "zero pollution," whatever that is. Man himself produces carbon dioxide--isn't that a pollutant? We must reach a sufficiently low level of pollution that we do not seriously harm natural ecological balances.)

Pollution will not be under adequate control if industry eliminates its pollution completely, of course. All other groups must also control their own pollutions. Indeed, the area of control for all is a major opportunity for industry to apply its "unit operations" of filtration, flotation, distillation, combustion, and condensation to solve new problems which the people desperately need to bring under control. Such an approach was the subject of an editorial by E. J. Bock, former president of Monsanto (7). There is every reason to expect that industry will meet this challenge, opportunity, and need, just as it has met other clear needs in the past.

A more subtle problem, and a more difficult one to solve than pollution, is the deterioration of personal meaning in routine jobs in much industrial production. This is not usually a significant problem in R & D, but does happen in much "assembly line" production. We badly need to find a way to change such routine jobs so that the individual feels and has more personal involvement and pride in his work. R & D may be able to help, by devising production methods which in the total evaluation are as productive or economical as assembly line methods but which permit an individual to identify with a larger, distinct portion of the product, if not the whole item. It seems highly probable that such an approach would do much to increase personal pride in the job and in the product, would reduce absenteeism, increase the amount of effort each day, and improve the average product quality. These advances could do much to help compensate for some loss of efficiency in production (usually calculated on the basis of consistent quality, attendance, and effort, which in fact are not achieved).

A still more difficult problem which has been the outgrowth of our technology, and primarily of our industrial technology, is that

in our society man now has more freedom than he has been able to
utilize constructively. In the times when a person used all his energy
just to provide food, clothing, shelter, and protection so he could
stay alive, his problems were very real but were also simpler. But
times change. Once no one had butter. Then only those with cows
had butter. In 1914 an average employee worked one hour and thirty-
seven minutes to earn enough to buy a pound of butter which someone
else had made. In 1970 only nineteen minutes' work was required
(in spite of inflation) (8). Furthermore, most people now prefer a
"synthetic spread" at one-third to one-half the cost of butter, which
reportedly gives fewer problems due to cholesterol.

Just as real earning power has increased, in terms of what the
average worker's earnings will buy, his working hours have shortened.
The typical work week is now in the range of 35-44 hours, and there
is a growing trend toward a four day week. (This could be one of the
best approaches toward reducing unemployment.) While more leisure
time has created whole new service industries and new demands for
manufactured goods in the areas of hobbies, sports, and travel, there
is a question whether man's ability to enjoy life more has kept pace
with his increased leisure.

More insidious, in some ways, is the fact that a small percentage
of the population can now produce the goods needed by all, and also
enough income, so that many are developing the feeling that they are
free not to work at all. A few who are nonproductive can be supported
by those who work, but no satisfactory society can be maintained
unless most do their share of the work. Our greatly increased freedom from want must, in some way, be balanced by an increased
sense of responsibility and desire to use our time and efforts
constructively. Just to illustrate, think what a change we could
make in the appearance of our country if each able-bodied person
contributed two hours of work each week toward cleaning up his
community!

In addition to the major and rather specific problem areas
described, there is the more general feeling that the quality of our
manufactured goods is not as good, on the average, as it should be.
The reasons for quality problems are many. There has doubtless
been a small percentage of the situations where a manufacturer
knowingly sold inferior goods. By far the greatest number of quality
problems have much more complex backgrounds. Nearly all companies have definite and continuing programs to insure that their
products meet quality standards. (Standards are higher for more
expensive types, naturally.) No one has found a way to guarantee

"zero defects" as yet, however. Limitations in the designer's ability, the worker's performance, the machinery's performance, individual judgments, misunderstandings between producer and buyer all contribute. R & D can and does help this range of problems some- what (but will never eliminate it) by finding better products to do a given job and by improving processes or developing better processes which are more nearly "foolproof."

In addition to this discussion of what a company does, a particu- larly interesting bulletin has appeared, giving a range of views under the title "Social Responsibilities of Business Corporations" (2). It is well worth reading if one wishes additional data and viewpoints.

AN ASSESSMENT

Companies are composed of groups of people trying to work together toward profitable goals. We should expect to find in them both the good and the bad features which are characteristic of the performance of people. This mixture is also to be found in all other activities, including government, universities, military, and private, nonprofit organizations. While it may be prejudice on the part of the author, the range of personal and business ethics displayed by R & D organizations is usually among the best to be found.

Industrial organizations are heavily dependent on technology, and the two are often classed together, whether it is the season to praise them for making our lives easier and more secure, providing more leisure, and raising our material standard of living, or whether it is the season to damn them for pollution and too much materialism. C. P. Snow has given a very carefully considered answer to those who have tended to reject industrial technology (9):

> It is all very well for one, as a personal choice, to reject
> industrialization--do a modern Walden, if you like, and if you
> go without much food, see most of your children die in infancy,
> despise the comforts of literacy, accept twenty years off your
> own life, then I respect you for the strength of your aesthetic
> revulsion. But I don't respect you in the slightest if, even
> passively, you try to impose the same choice on others who are
> not free to choose. In fact, we know what their choice would be.
> For, with singular unanimity, in any country where they have

had the chance, the poor have walked off the land into the
factories as fast as the factories could take them.

A LOOK AT THE FUTURE

The most significant trend for the future of technology, of technology based industries, and one of the most significant for our
people is going to be the simple realization that technology is a tool,
a very powerful tool, to use in solving many of mankind's problems.
It follows that we must use this tool far more wisely in the future
than we have in the past.

Technology will be useful primarily in solving those problems
which depend to a large extent on material goods. Regarding pollution, for example, we seem to have three alternatives: continue as
we are, stop all processes and activities which cause pollution, or
develop processes which will provide the goods and services which
we need without significantly polluting our environment. The last is
surely the obvious choice. Its success depends upon the establishment of clear goals, fair laws requiring all to bring their pollution
under control, suitable law enforcement, large amounts of money
to pay for the improvements, and dedicated people using technology
as the tool to do the job. The job can be done.

Technology is clearly an essential tool to use in solving problems
of food production and distribution, of population control via production of birth control devices, of low-cost housing, of better transportation systems, of new fuel and power systems, and of insuring
a continuing supply of suitable construction materials, to name a few
major ones. Please note that it is just an essential tool, however,
and a tool cannot do the job alone. Good people must work together,
in many disciplines and at many levels, using technology and other
tools to solve problems such as these. Clearly, technology-based
companies will play a major role. They undoubtedly will find ways
to utilize already familiar technology steps such as synthesis, distillation, filtration, precipitation, pyrolysis, and combustion to help
solve these problems. This will be done in such a way that those
companies which combine the foresight, broad judgment, basic
technical skills, and innovative ability to use those skills in solving
problems which may be new to their own "marketing area," will provide the technical service which is needed, at a profit to the company.

It must be realized, however, that technology and those generating it cannot alone solve even the material-related problems which face our society. A simple point will illustrate this. Our farm surpluses pile up in government warehouses, our maritime fleet is steadily decreasing for lack of shipping business, and large-scale starvation continues to occur in certain other countries. The technology to solve this starvation problem is here now, but the diplomatic and political contributions, which are clearly just as necessary, have not yet been made.

Furthermore, we must not fall into the trap of thinking that technology is a suitable tool to even apply to all of our problems. Society's greatest, most fundamental problems are in the areas of man's relation to man and man's relation to his God, if one is inclined to take his reasoning that far. How can we reach the ideal of "love thy neighbor as thyself"? Clearly we must look to religions and philosophies to guide us in our human relations, in our establishment of values, and to tell us how we really want to lead our lives. As we know where we want to go, we can use technology as a tool to help us get there.

As we look to the future and try to put technology in perspective, we can project that technology and technical companies will be judged increasingly by their total impact on society. This is to be expected, of course. We are in the habit already of judging our political structure by its total impact. Industry is rapidly reaching this state. The educational system, in time, will also be judged this way.

In the past a company was judged largely by the quality and quantity of goods it produced, by its selling prices, by the profit it made (based largely on return on investment), and by its actions within its own property boundaries (treatment of employees, etc.). Little attention was paid to the effect on the environment, and there was little organized, purposeful attempt to reach a judgment relative to social problems. The consumers themselves, on an unplanned basis, exerted some control, of course--if they did not want a company's products they did not buy them, and that form of control was quickly effective. But vision for the future rarely entered into this type control.

We now realize that this rather short range pursuit of what the consumer wanted and was willing to buy has some serious limitations. The interdependence of people throughout the world is becoming increasingly clear (though it is certainly not yet clear enough to all), and the need for long-range planning and cooperation is also becoming more obvious. We must have antipollution efforts on a worldwide

basis, as an example. If one country with a serious malaria problem
pollutes the world's water system with a very powerful insecticide it
may solve its own malaria crisis, but may do long-term damage to
the whole world's water system.

As we work to ease today's social problems, will our new technology generated for those purposes just create new and equally bad
problems for the future? Probably we will create some new problems.
But we must try to keep all--the old and the new--well below the
crisis level. It is too much to expect that problems will be
eliminated--man will always find ways to create problems if nature
doesn't supply him with enough! One of our most promising approaches toward avoiding crisis-scale problems from new technology
is called "technology assessment." The technical aspects of this will
be treated in more detail in Chapter 5 on technical programs. The
social interactions may be appropriate for discussion here, however.

Technology assessment is simply an attempt to judge ahead of
time the benefits and the undesirable consequences, and to recognize
areas of lack of knowledge, associated with the introduction of a
new product or process. Answers should be given as completely as
possible, and lack of knowledge recognized, regarding questions
relating the innovation to the future availability of raw materials, to
possibilities of product recycling, to pollution, to the consumption
of power, to the effect on social patterns such as housing, employment, and health, and to what benefits the innovation would provide.
Would any harmful results be reversible within a short time? Is
there a better way? The probable benefits should be weighed against
the probable dangers, before a decision is made to go ahead with
full-scale commercial uses. Very often in such a study it will
become clear that more information is needed to reach a judgment,
so that more research is required.

Industries have been doing assessments of new products and
processes for many years, but usually just feasibility, safety of
operation, and economic attractiveness. These assessments are
now beginning to be broadened to include the wider range of criteria
indicated above. Pollution control is receiving highest priority in
this broader approach, but the other aspects must be included too.

A company will conduct as thorough assessments as it judges
reasonable before proposing the commercial use of new products
or processes. The assessments will not stop at this point, however.
Especially with innovations of major potential social impact, other
groups, including scientific societies, conservation groups, and
especially the Federal government, will quickly become involved.

Since many innovations may have national or even international effects, we must expect the Federal government to take a leading role in making assessments. Industries will need to cooperate openly and fully in these studies.

We see some examples of this trend toward technology assessment in the 1970-1971 period, perhaps most notably in judgments regarding the desirability of building supersonic transport planes, and the selection of "safe" detergents. This trend undoubtedly will continue and will have a major effect on shaping the course of new product development.

One result of the assessment programs will be to slow the rate of new product introduction in this country. If done properly, this can be good, in that we should be able to avoid some serious problems which otherwise would occur. If the assessment approach results in a drastic depressing effect on new developments, based more on emotion than fact, we will have created a serious problem. We will then find that it badly handicaps us in our balance of world trade if one or more other industrial countries emerges as the major source of desirable new products. Our economy and our standard of living will then suffer accordingly. The proper use of technology assessment thus emerges as one of the difficult and exceedingly important challenges for our manufacturing industry, for our government, and actually for all people.

The recognition of broad social problems, the opportunities for industry to provide the goods and some of the services necessary to solve those problems, and the need for broad assessments of technical innovations show a clear need for the manufacturing industry to plan much more closely with other segments of our society. Dr. C. A. Hochwalt, former Monsanto Vice President for Research, urged the Society of Chemical Industry to join with social scientists to form a new "life environment systems industry." This industry would integrate both scientific and humanistic values in its products and services. Such a total systems approach could go far beyond the concepts of biodegradability and recycling of products which are receiving the most enthusiasm today as our best answers to man's environmental plight (10).

This view of the future of our technology-based industries obviously indicates a much broader scope of planning and judgment than has been characteristic in the past. We may rightfully hope that the young people joining industry will be helpful in bringing about such changes and will also develop themselves through the years so that they can actually do it far better than has been done before.

REFERENCES

1. Statistical Abstract of the United States, 1969, U. S. Dept. of Commerce, pp. 115, 124, 215, 274, 377.
2. "Social Responsibilities of Business Corporations," Committee for Economic Development, New York, 1971.
3. L. S. Liang, Textile Industries, Aug., 1971, p. 54.
4. The Unesco Courier, June, 1971, p. 8.
5. D. F. Othmer, Trans. N. Y. Acad. Sci., 32, 287 (1970).
6. W. H. Lycan, The Chemist, Dec., 1970, p. 415.
7. E. J. Bock, Chem. Eng. News, Nov. 9, 1970, p. 5.
8. "A Better Life for You," National Research Bureau, Inc., Chicago, 1970.
9. C. P. Snow, The Two Cultures: and a Second Look, Macmillan, Toronto, 1964.
10. C. A. Hochwalt, medalist address, Society of Chemical Industry, American Section, New York, 1971; see Chem. Eng. News, Oct. 11, 1971, p. 29.

Chapter 3

THE ORGANIZATION AND STAFFING OF
AN INDUSTRIAL LABORATORY

An industrial laboratory must serve as a successful member of
the team which is its company. To do so, it must be suitably organized within itself and also with respect to the other departments of
the company, so that the experimental problems necessary to the
future welfare of the company are identified and are adequately
solved, and the information gained is used with commercial success.
This team approach to departmental and company organization has
been one of the major strengths of the manufacturing industry in the
United States and has contributed greatly to our ability to compete
in world markets with other countries which have much lower pay
rates for the working people. Other countries are now learning the
same techniques, and Japan in particular has gone beyond us in
extending this cooperative approach to the combination of industry,
financial organizations, and the government. Our own ability to
organize, plan, and cooperate still leaves much room for
improvement.

COMPANY ORGANIZATION

No single organizational structure is ideal for all situations.
The needs of a company may vary widely, depending for example on
size, maturity, diversity of products, types of markets to which it
sells, and the number of geographical locations involved. Also, the
structure and staff most suitable to the formation and early growth
of a company may not be as suitable for a more established, stable
organization. A flexible approach should be taken toward organization, and it should be changed when needs and circumstances indicate
an improvement can be made.

One often finds some similarities between the structure of a small company and that of a large one--the large company may have several operating divisions, each with a structure somewhat like that of a small company, and each operating with considerable independence. Illustrative organization charts are shown in Figures 1 and 2.

A company that would find the structure in Figure 1 suitable would be a firm with two different production locations, which is large enough to justify separate technical and marketing departments as shown. Such a company might have several hundred to one thousand or more employees. In addition to the departments shown, small staff departments covering such areas as accounting, personnel, and law might report to one or another of the vice presidents.

A brief explanation of the function of each department will help clarify the requirements of the R & D department.

The field sales department is responsible for selling the company's products. As such, it is concerned with the number and types of products available for sale, the quality of the products, the promptness of shipments, and all company contacts with customers. At the same time, in its frequent discussions with customers, it is the first line of intelligence in knowing what new products the customers can use and discerning how effectively competitive materials are being used.

The market development department is charged simultaneously with developing markets for new products which the company can produce and with helping to identify improvements in those products which can make them more suitable for use. In some companies this department also has responsibility for developing new markets for existing products. This section must work closely with field sales in making customer contacts, with manufacturing regarding scheduling of production and product quality in new product areas, with R & D on the identification of new products which can be sold profitably and hence are work producing, as well as on achieving the necessary quality and on demonstrating for potential customers ways of using new products.

The manufacturing groups obviously are the ones that produce the company's goods. They depend on R & D for the generation of new products and for processes for producing them, on engineering for the design of their plants, and on marketing to sell their products at some price greater than the cost of manufacture.

The engineering department normally provides designs of plants, works with the construction group or company during the construction of a plant, and may assist in the initial operation of a new plant.

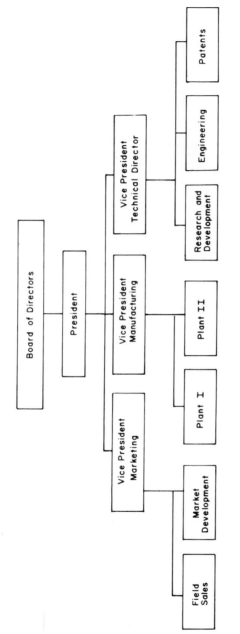

FIGURE 1 Illustrative organization, small to moderate-size company.

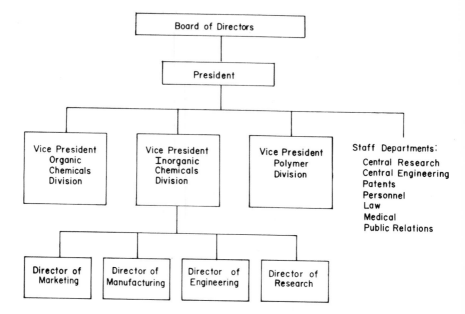

FIGURE 2   Illustrative organization of a larger company with several
operating divisions.

It may also provide similar services for modifications to existing
plants. In the course of performing these functions it works closely
with R & D during the development of a process so that the final
process is one which can be operated satisfactorily, using reliable
equipment at the smallest possible cost for the equipment and with
the greatest ease of production. Engineering also works closely
with the production staff, using its practical experience to help
insure that any new plant design is the best possible.

The patent department has the responsibility of obtaining patents
which are as strong as possible, covering processes which the company uses, products which it makes, and often uses for those products
as well. In these areas it works closely with R & D, which is the
most frequent source of patentable inventions. In some cases the
patent group may even be a part of the R & D department. In addition,
the patent department insures that the company is not infringing
someone else's patent, negotiates licenses under other people's
patents, and licenses for other people such as customers to use
selected patents held by the company. Research often serves as a
consultant to the patent department for these negotiations.

The previous discussion makes it readily apparent that the R & D groups must work effectively with all other departments. The identification of the technical problems of the company is clearly an area where all departments can and should participate. The solving of those problems assigned to R & D is largely the responsibility of that department, but others can and should help. Cooperation with engineering especially, and also with production, will help insure that the best commercially successful processes are developed. Help from marketing and from customers will be of great assistance in being sure that the products developed are of the type and quality which the customer can use and will pay for. The patent department can offer guidance with regard to the patentability of a product or process, or whether someone else already has a patent which must be licensed.

In both smaller and larger companies the same need for close organization and cooperation is present. Such cooperation is often easier in smaller companies because of the greater ease of communication. Larger companies try to achieve the same ease of communication by dividing into several different units or divisions, each acting much like a small company. A typical organization was shown in Figure 2.

In the case of the larger company, those people engaged in all phases of business associated with some logical group of products, such as inorganic chemicals, may be organized in much the same way as was described for the smaller company. Each such division may have its own R & D and engineering departments to solve current technical problems and work on products for the clearly foreseen future. These aspects of R & D in a large division may easily require a department of 100 to 400 people. Partly because of an increase in organizational problems in very large departments, the company may prefer a completely separate "central research department" which is responsible primarily for the longer range technical problems of the company. These may include the development of completely new products, radically different methods of producing the company's products, or development of a better understanding of some particular area of the company's operations. Some projects may be transferred from this laboratory to one of the divisional laboratories when those projects are scheduled for commercialization in the near future.

Isolation of this central research laboratory from the day-to-day problems of the operating divisions has several advantages. The solution of long-range problems is usually best achieved when a program can be planned for a period of several years and altered only as the changing status of that project makes it appropriate, not as unrelated outside pressures fluctuate. Both a separation by organizational structure and by location can help make this continuity of program possible. This isolation also removes the natural, healthy sense of urgency which exists in laboratories that are directly responsive to market needs. Consequently the management of such a laboratory must be constantly alert to maintaining its own sense of urgency so that targets for accomplishment are not set too low and so that individuals and groups do not become stale. Close communication and joint planning with the divisional research laboratories are essential if a product or process originating in the central department is to be transferred smoothly and efficiently to a manufacturing division.

In some companies the divisional R & D groups are located at manufacturing plant sites. This proximity is very convenient for scaling up processes from the pilot plant to plant-scale use. Personnel from the laboratory have the opportunity to know the production personnel and problems much better than if a geographical barrier existed. At the same time, this close association makes it very easy for a production man with a problem to call his friend in R & D for help, sometimes interrupting and slowing the laboratory's program. Partly to provide greater continuity of R & D programs, some companies prefer to have all R & D at one location, away from manufacturing sites.

The concentration of all R & D into one area has some advantages in the more economical establishment of large libraries, shop facilities, analytical services, and computer centers. Indeed, some of the larger companies have established beautiful campus-like areas of which any university would be proud.

From the individual's viewpoint, it is fortunate that a variety of company sizes, laboratory locations, and laboratory organizations is available. One can work toward the type which suits his personal preferences. In any case, excellent work can be and is done in all types, and very rewarding careers can be found in each.

LABORATORY ORGANIZATION

An industrial R & D laboratory must share in the identification of the technical problems of the company and their assignment to

R & D, engineering, manufacturing, or other groups. It must solve
those problems assigned to it and, insofar as possible, insure that
the results are used with commercial success.

The real purpose of having an organization, as distinguished from
a group of unorganized people, is simply to provide conditions such
that the department's problems are solved and the results are used
in the best way possible. The organization must be such that high
caliber personnel are attracted to it and are pleased to be a part of
it. In addition, it must create and maintain conditions such that
these people can work with maximum effectiveness on the company's
behalf. These requirements are applicable whether the entire R & D
program is conducted by one small department or whether the efforts
are spread among several different laboratories.

In order to achieve these essentials of good organization, a number
of functions should be performed, including the following:

1. Participation in top level planning, playing a major role in
   guiding the company in technical matters. This should include
   the short- and long-range technical objectives of the company,
   with emphasis on the discovery and development of new
   products. This function is usually performed by the director(s)
   of R & D or by a vice president for R & D.
2. Insurance of the necessary direction, control, and completion
   of technical projects assigned to the laboratory. This feature
   is normally a joint effort of the director, assistant directors,
   and group leaders.
3. Provision for clearly identified channels of communication
   with other departments and insuring the communication.
   This activity should involve several levels in the department.
4. Definition of the responsibilities and authorities of all key
   members of the department.
5. Provision for adequate communication within the department.
6. Serving as a selective "filter," screening the suggestions,
   requests, criticisms, and pressures from all outside sources,
   selecting those which are constructive and useful, relaying
   them to the proper individuals, and rejecting those which
   are not helpful. It is in this area particularly where the
   organizational structure can help the progress of the company's programs by minimizing undesirable diversions,
   petty politics, and red tape. This filtering process must
   be in good balance with the helpful communication which is
   essential with other departments, of course.

7. Inclusion of adequate services on a routine basis so that a
minimum of time by the technical staff is required on such
services. These may include the library, analytical and
testing, storeroom, shipping and receiving, purchasing,
building and equipment maintenance, etc. In larger organizations such services are frequently placed under a good
administrator who may not necessarily have a strong technical background.

The organizational approach which most frequently seems to give
the desired results in the United States is that based on a group
structure. An R & D "group" may be a team of people working on
closely related problems, frequently composed of four to ten members reporting to a "group leader." Some of the members may be
senior technical personnel with considerable experience, some may
be inexperienced, and some may be laboratory assistants. The
group may be product-oriented, e.g., studying ways of synthesizing
a family of compounds, such as aromatic amines. The group
alternatively may be technique-oriented, such as a group of
specialists in instrumental analyses.

A department frequently will have one or more groups concerned
with each major product or family of products which the company
produces, as well as groups specializing in techniques of major
interest to the company. This group structure offers many advantages.
It provides a good method for developing extensive knowledge and
experts in every area of major interest to the company. Unless
groups are quite small or turnover of personnel is unusually rapid,
good continuity of knowledge and experience are to be expected with
this system. The older members of the group usually provide the
best training possible for young people just beginning their careers.
Direction of the group's efforts is excellent training in the administration of scientific and technical programs. In addition, if used
properly, the group structure will provide training and experience
in the use of the team approach to solving problems, a major source
of the strength of United States industry.

The number of groups in a department will vary directly with the
size of the department, of course. In small departments all group
leaders may report to the director. In larger organizations several
group leaders may report to an assistant director, and several of
these may report to the director.

In addition to the groups, some individuals may be outstanding
technically and have little interest in administrative affairs. Such
people are given special recognition in many companies, may be

given titles such as "scientist" or "technologist," and may have the
same standing as a group leader. These individuals sometimes
prefer to conduct their research alone or with one or two helpers.
In some cases they may work in conjunction with a group, or in
others may report to an assistant director or director. More specific descriptions of responsibilities of these and other positions
will be given later in this chapter.

A typical R & D organization for a department of about 100 to 200
people might be equivalent to that shown in Figure 3. Smaller and
larger departments might vary simply by having fewer or more
sections, respectively. In the larger departments an additional
level, "associate director," might appear between the director and
assistant directors.

The director of such a department would most likely report to a
vice president of a company or to an assistant general manager of a
division of a large company.

Not all companies use the same title to describe a particular
function, of course. In addition to those shown, other titles such
as "manager," "senior group leader," "section leader," and "senior
scientist" may appear. The organizational structure shown, however,
is a basic type; and one will usually find close similarities between
this and the one actually encountered, even though titles and the
number of sections may vary. Further clarification may be given
later by outlining some of the functions of each of the positions
indicated.

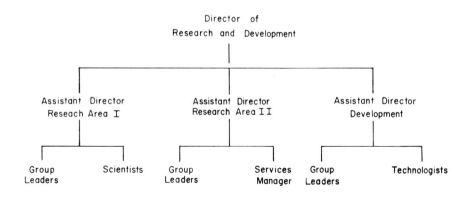

FIGURE 3 Typical organization for a moderate size R & D department.

The organization described thus far is one based on a departmental structure. In some special cases an organization may be set up in a product-oriented structure, crossing the usual departmental lines. In such a case everyone in the company directly associated with the product may report to the product director in a "task force" manner. In this situation R & D personnel may report to their department director for administrative matters, but at the same time be responsible to the product director for the selection of technical projects, approval of time schedules for achieving their targets, progress reviews, and liaison with others working on different projects related to the same product.

The task force approach is considered by some to give the most efficient coordination of interdepartmental efforts and is sometimes put into effect when a product's commercial progress is seriously behind schedule. It does have the advantage that all groups working on a product--R & D, engineering, production, market development, and field sales--can be knit into a closely cooperating organization in this way when the same groups, reporting to separate department directors, have not been able to work together effectively.

Probably the most successful use of the task force approach has been in some of the highly complex aerospace programs where many and very different types of experts must work together, on as tight a schedule as possible. Often many subcontractors are involved in such a program, and their activities must be closely coordinated if targets are to be met on time. The use of a single product director (he might have a variety of titles) to pull together efficiently all aspects of such a program clearly seems to be the best approach in such a situation.

A weakness of the task force structure is that each working member has two bosses, his product director and his department director. Conflicts of interest and hurt feelings will invariably develop unless everyone is willing to subordinate personal feelings to task force objectives even more than in a normal situation.

In some cases the task force approach is used as a last resort in a company to correct an unsatisfactory situation, where the individual departments could be working together adequately but are not. These cases represent failure of one or more of the departmental managers to perform their jobs adequately, especially in the area of cooperation.

A somewhat different view of the types of R & D organizations, and the types of companies supporting them, has been described well by Reiss (1). He divided companies according to their main interests in research, such as phenomena-oriented research, product-oriented, "scientific fire-fighting," and others. His article is suggested for interesting supplemental reading.

THE DEPARTMENTAL STAFF

Any successful department should include a spectrum of abilities, with at least a moderate percentage of the staff being outstanding in their fields. While it is unlikely that there would be general agreement on what this percentage should be, it might be in the range of 10% to 25% of the staff. One important aspect is the number of good people who can be led, inspired, and kept usefully busy by one outstanding person. Other aspects include the rate of turnover of leaders, the anticipated rate of growth of the department, and the type of work to be done. In most situations, the real talent will be diluted too thinly with less than 10% and will not be utilized efficiently with more than about 25% of the staff really outstanding. (Few departments ever have to worry about having more than 25% in this class. It is sometimes a fallacy of interviewing and hiring policies, however, to look for outstanding personnel only.) In any case, this group is the real key to success and of course is the most difficult to find. It should be recognized by the entire company that its future welfare depends on finding and keeping such a group. The corporate attitude, as well as that of the department itself, must be such as to attract and hold these essential people.

The top leadership positions in the department must be filled with highly capable people. The director is the first key to the success of the department. An ideal director should be that rare combination of talents, education, experience, and interests: a scientist or engineer of stature, a capable administrator, a sound businessman, and a successful salesman. A strong technical background combined with real achievement will aid him greatly in winning the respect and cooperation of his staff; in assessing the competence of individuals on the staff; in evaluating proposals, programs, and results; and in understanding the "atmosphere" which is important for attracting and keeping top quality personnel. The administrative ability is necessary for the organization of the department's efforts, for cooperation with other departments, for proper programming and follow-through on programs, and for maintaining a smoothly, efficiently operating unit. The director must exercise good business judgment in guiding the company and his department into areas where profits can be realized, as well as in conducting technical programs in these areas with a maximum return for the effort expended. He must be a good salesman, presenting the true worth of his proposals for future programs and of his department's current efforts so that the rest of the company correctly judges that it does indeed get what is needed from R & D. He may on occasions be the company's best salesman in dealing with customers on technical matters. His combination of achievements and ability to present them will aid greatly in establishing a record and reputation of technical excellence for his company, a valuable feature in such widely separated areas as customer relations and recruiting new personnel.

It frequently happens that no one person is available with all of the attributes of the ideal director. The best person available may be quite strong in two or three of the major areas but not strong in one or two others. These weaknesses may be offset by having assistant directors who supply the missing strength, so that the team of director plus assistant directors provides the full spectrum of abilities which is necessary.

The director of R & D is primarily responsible for participating with other directors of the company in selecting the technical objectives of the company, for planning the long-range and short-range technical programs of R & D to help achieve those objectives, for budgeting the R & D effort, for guiding the technical efforts of his department, for the staffing of his department, for the continual training of his people, and for interdepartmental communication.

An assistant director of R & D is normally responsible for directing the efforts of several groups in the department. He takes a major part in program planning and in reviewing progress, in communicating with other departments, and in training the personnel reporting to him, especially the group leaders. He assists the director in the administrative guidance of the department and frequently handles special assignments of major scope. At least one of the assistant directors should have the potential to become the director in time.

The group leader combines technical strength, a thorough knowledge of the R & D portion of an important area of the company's business, and administrative talent. He should be an inspiring leader of a group which might range in size from about three to ten people. He must be able to take a major part in planning the detailed

programs needed to achieve the objectives in his segment of the
department's program, must insure that his people know what is
expected of them and that they receive the guidance necessary for
the expected performance, must insure the satisfactory completion
of his group's projects, and must communicate the results as may
be appropriate. He is also responsible for the safety of the members
of his group. If it is possible to make a simple summary of the
basis on which his performance will be judged, it is that the group
obtains the results necessary for the commercial solution of his
assigned problems and communicates those results properly.

The group leader position is usually the first in the administrative
route of advancement. The transition from being a good technical
man, who must solve his own problems, to a good technical administrator is not always easy. As an administrator it is now his job to
get others to solve his problems for him, which requires considerable
reorientation of thought. This and other considerations will be discussed more fully in the next chapter, in sections on personnel
development and promotions.

The staff working with the group leader may include strong,
experienced personnel with titles such as research specialist, senior
chemist, or senior engineer; less experienced individuals with titles
such as chemist or engineer; and nontechnical personnel. The senior
chemists, engineers, physicists, etc., should be able to work independently, with only occasional guidance, and should have originality
and good judgment in planning and evaluating experiments. Such a
person might have a B.S. or M.S. degree plus several years of
experience, or perhaps a Ph.D. with one or two years of experience.
The research specialists have more experience and expert knowledge
and can work with even more independence.

New B.S. or M.S. graduates will usually enter an R & D group
with a technical classification of "chemist," "engineer," or the like,
according to their fields of training. In some companies the classification "assistant chemist" might also be used for one just entering
the profession. In most cases such young people will be assigned to
work closely with more experienced personnel. The new employee's
primary assignment in his first six to twelve months will usually be
to learn the science or technology on which his group's projects are
based. He will participate in a project in the group, studying, conducting experiments, and reporting his results. It is generally
expected that he will need considerable guidance in planning,
execution, and interpretation.

It is from the members of such a group that the leaders of the

future will come. Some members will show both technical and
administrative skill and will advance to group leader and on to
become a director. Other equally valuable members will develop
into very strong technical experts but may have little interest in
dealing with administrative problems. Such experts are highly
desired and are recognized accordingly. Many companies utilize
some progressive series of titles and appropriately increasing
salary ranges to reward these specialists. Such a series of titles
might include "scientist" and "senior scientist," for example. A
person reaching the top rank in this type of progression is usually
of such stature that he has a national reputation for excellence in
his field.

The scientists and senior scientists are concerned with solving
difficult technical problems and are not bothered with administrative
details. They also act as consultants to other members of the
department and to other departments. Younger men are frequently
assigned to work directly with them, which is an excellent opportunity
for younger staff members to learn advanced techniques and to participate in research that is often much like doctoral or postdoctoral
research in a university.

The nontechnical members of the department working in the
experimental activities are often called "laboratory assistants," for
the less experienced members, and "laboratory technicians," for
the more advanced personnel. Well-trained assistants and technicians
can perform many laboratory and pilot plant operations as well as or
better than those holding college degrees, especially in the more
routine areas. The laboratory assistant usually will have at least
a high school degree or its equivalent, while the technician may
have several years of college, perhaps even a degree in a field not
directly related to the company's interests, or a number of years
experience as a laboratory assistant.

The laboratory assistant normally follows specific directions
and procedures provided by a technical person or in some cases by
an advanced laboratory technician. The laboratory technician has a
thorough knowledge of general procedures in one or more specific
areas of activity (e.g., electronics, analytical chemistry, pilot
plant research, etc.). He should be able to accept an outline of an
experiment and do it well. He should be capable of recognizing some
deviations from the expected results. In addition, an outstanding
technician may serve as a leader for other assistants and technicians.

In general, one can consider that the main activities in R & D are
involved with planning; with obtaining, using, and communicating

data; and with personnel hiring and training. An activity profile for each of the types of R & D positions discussed might well look somewhat like that shown in Figure 4, where the length of the line under an activity heading indicates the relative distribution of responsibility for each R & D position. For example, the responsibility for planning is greatest with the director, and becomes progressively less as one moves down the table. The same is generally true for personnel problems. Others in the organization may have a higher portion of their responsibilities in the category of obtaining, interpreting, and communicating data, however.

The department must, of course, be staffed to meet its immediate requirements, but management must also keep in mind the staffing and training of personnel for future needs. The problems of today will best be met by a combination of directors, group leaders, scientists, and group members oriented toward certain products or toward solving certain types of problems. It is to be expected that these products and problems will change with time, so additions to the staff will be desirable to bring in new talents. At the same time the personnel who make up the department must participate in more or less constant training programs in order to keep up with new knowledge and techniques. Without such training programs obsolescence will quickly become apparent.

Some of the changes in personnel can be predicted with accuracy. Some of the group members will advance to become group leaders or scientists, some of the group leaders will advance to become assistant directors, and some assistant directors will reach the director level. Some members of the department will conclude that they are better suited for other activities within the company and will transfer to engineering, production, marketing, patent, or other departments. Indeed, the training of personnel for other departments is usually a standard function of R & D. A few people will leave the company to take advantage of job offers which promise to be that "once in a lifetime" chance. Others who for some reason do not perform well will leave, to become associated with other organizations whose aims and practices are more closely aligned with their own. Some personnel will stay with the department indefinitely, making a permanent career of R & D. The staffing and training of the department must try to maintain the proper balance among all of these factors and anticipate any expected growth.

Satisfactory staffing of a department depends upon finding a considerable number of potential employees, making a careful study to see which applicants best match the company's requirements, and

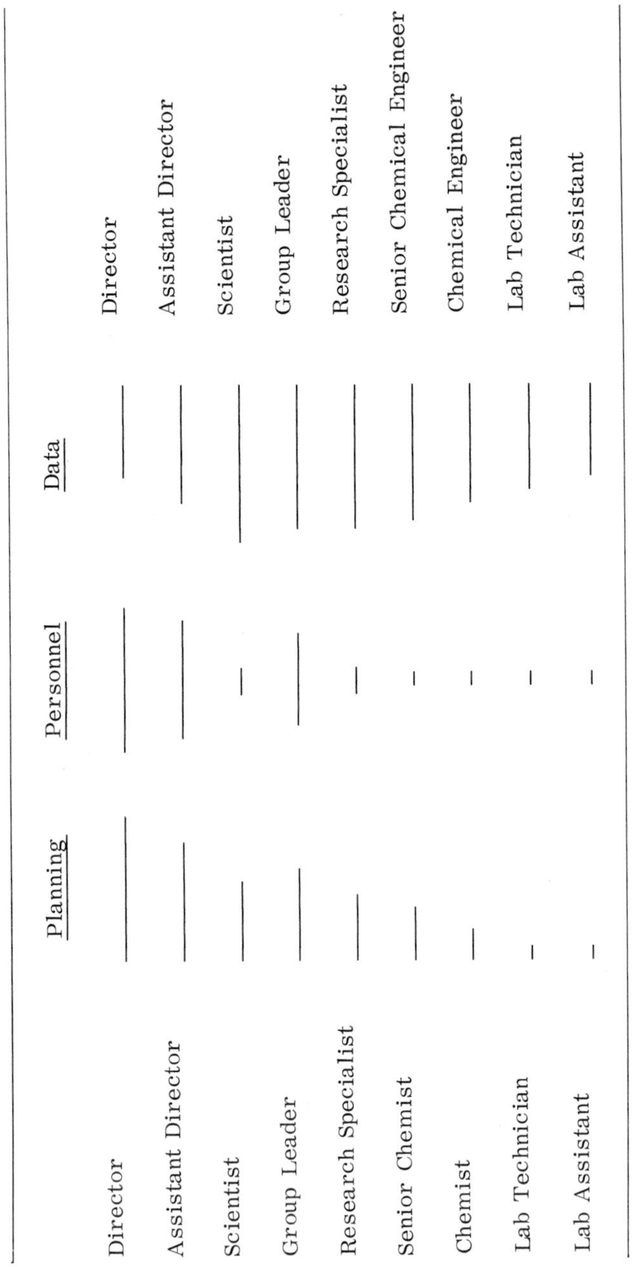

FIGURE 4 Activity profiles of typical R & D classifications.

attracting those to join the company. Various aspects of approaches
toward hiring new employees, promotion of individuals, and terminations are discussed in the next chapter. It seems appropriate to
conclude this chapter with an outline of the variability of job openings
and some of the reasons for this variability.

THE AVAILABILITY OF JOBS

It is no surprise to any technical student in the early 1970s that the
availability of jobs in R & D fluctuates greatly. The number of job
openings is simply the difference between the demand for R & D work
and the number of people already so engaged. Because of the rather
long training period required, it is difficult to achieve rapid changes
in the numbers of graduates available to join R & D programs. On
the other hand, the demand for such programs can change very
rapidly, in a matter of a few months. Until our leaders in government and in industry can achieve much better long-range planning of
technical needs, we can expect to continue to see occasional sharp
changes in the demand for technical talent. The difficulty of keeping
the demand, subject to short time fluctuations, in balance with the
supply, controlled largely by long training periods, leads either to
a scarcity of technical people or to a scarcity of job openings for
new graduates.

The job problem in the 1970s is not new, though that is scarcely
a consolation to those facing the problem. Industrial reductions in
R & D were made in the late 1940s, again in the latter 1950s, and in
1969-1970. In each case these have coincided with periods of reduction in business. At least in the first two cases, the personnel reductions were soon followed by increased rates of hiring. It is certainly
appropriate to search for a better way of managing the need for and
utilization of technical skills in the country.

The cut-back in R & D in the 1969-1970 period did not come as a
surprise to a few careful observers, who predicted it as early as the
mid-1960s. The reason, in retrospect, was simple. With the
launching of the Russian satellite "Sputnik I" in 1957, the United
States realized it was behind the Russians in this area of technology,
and mounted a program to catch up. The so-called "missile gap,"
with the Russians presumably ahead, was an issue in the 1960 presidential elections. The national goal of placing a man on the moon by

1970 and returning him safely to earth climaxed the national approach
to aerospace technology. The aerospace programs led the way in
creating an unprecedented demand for technical people. The increasing Vietnam involvement and an increase in civilian-oriented manufacturing all reinforced this demand. Our educational system
responded, with much government money available, and expanded
its capacity to train young people in technical areas. The demand,
the glamour of space programs, and rapidly rising starting salaries
helped attract young people to this area of study. The rate of growth
in output of engineering and science graduates in the 1958-1970 period
was remarkable. Technology, along with R & D, was nationally
popular. But such a rate of growth could not have continued indefinitely, or eventually everyone would have been a scientist or engineer.
In fact, the leveling-off in demand was beginning to be apparent before
1970. The data in Table 1 illustrate these trends (2).

In the period 1965-1970 a number of changes occurred, all contributing to the tight job market in 1970-1971. More than at any
time in the last thirty years, many, if not most, groups of people
in our country began to question their own activities and especially
the activities of others. This was exemplified by the widespread
use of such terms as "credibility gap." Technical programs were no
exception. The wisdom of R & D expenditures came under scrutiny
by company management, by government leaders, and by vocal critics
of our society. The new attitude was apparent just in the title of an
article appearing in the January, 1965, issue of Fortune magazine,
"Harnessing the R & D Monster." During this five-year period the
prestige of R & D deteriorated greatly. Some of this was perhaps an
emotional backlash and some was justified by previous inefficiencies
in many well-financed R & D programs. Some of the change resulted
from shifts in the broad consensus concerning national goals such as
the moon program and involvement in the Vietnam conflict.

Along with these changing attitudes, and partly as a result of
them, the United States began to "wind down" its military activities
in Asia and to reduce its efforts in aerospace areas. These changes
resulted in a considerable reduction in technical programs by the
end of 1969, extending into 1970. In times of "normal" business
expansion, the manufacturing industry oriented toward civilian
products could have hired many more of the technical people released
from the military and space programs and still have had a moderate
number of openings available for college graduates. Unfortunately,
there was no such business expansion at that time. Instead, the
situation was made worse by a decided reduction in industrial profits,

TABLE 1 Trends in R & D Funding, Training, and Employment

	1955	1960	1965	1969	1970
After-tax profit, $B[a] (all manufacturing corporations)	15.1	15.2	27.5	33.2[b]	28.6[b]
Total United States R & D, $B[a]	6.3	13.7	20.4	26.2[b]	26.9[b]
Federal funds		7.6	14.6	15.6[b]	15.3[b]
Industry funds	2.5	4.4	6.4	9.8[b]	10.8[b]
Defense-space related, %	48.4	54.7	53.6	45.2[b]	42.1[b]
Technical employment					
Private industry		~780,000	913,000	1,055,000[b]	
Federal government		153,400	~190,000	210,300[b]	
Ph.D. graduates, science		6,276	10,528		17,822

[a]$B: dollars in billions
[b]1969 figures were listed as "preliminary," 1970 figures as "estimated" and are probably too high. A more recent report indicates corporate R & D funds totaled $10.1 billion in 1970 (3).

which led most industries to "tighten their belts, " shutting down their less profitable businesses, and laying off varying numbers of employees.

Some of the changes in the performance of consumer-oriented companies from 1965 (4) to 1970 (5) can be seen in the data shown in Table 2. Many found themselves working to produce and sell much more goods in 1970 but making less profit than in 1965. Even more important than the changes themselves was the rapidly downward trend in profits. Rather than wait for the trend to continue into a state of crisis, many companies began economizing and stopping the production of goods which no longer contributed adequately to their profits. While the changes were not made in the best way possible in every case, to have done nothing would almost surely have led to financial chaos, with far worse unemployment.

Some may question whether vigorous economizing was really necessary. In times of business recession, does such action on the part of management do more than keep the profit level at 4% of sales, rather than 3%, and preserve the jobs of the managers? In some cases this may be the net result, but one has to realize that complete failure of a business is indeed possible and will happen if profits sink too low. In 1970 there were 966 business failures involving companies with valuations of $100,000 or more, compared to 345 in 1965, in the mining and manufacturing industries (2).

Some of the factors which led to the downward trend in profits in the consumer-oriented businesses were related to our trading position relative to that of foreign countries in Europe and especially Japan. The average total hourly labor cost per worker in the United States in 1970 was $4.18, compared to $2.27 for Germany, $1.60 for Great Britain, and $0.95 for Japan (6). Our relative production efficiency by itself is simply not able to offset such a large difference in wages. By 1970 foreign products accounted for 90% of home radios, 70% of all sweaters, 95% of the motorcycles, 50% of nails and staples, and 90% of baseball mitts sold in this country, to illustrate the range of businesses which were in trouble (5). It is not surprising that company managements felt they must find ways to economize.

When companies decide to economize they usually fire or lay off those people they judge to be least productive. They also may stop production of unprofitable products, thus eliminating the jobs associated with those products. Such actions have frequently reduced the employment by a given company in the range of about 2%-10%.

In the 1970-1971 period many companies reached a point where their managements felt it necessary to hold expenses down by

TABLE 2 Sales and Income Performance of Illustrative Companies, 1965–1970

	1965			1970		
	Sales[a]	Net income[a]	$/share	Sales[a]	Net income[a]	$/share
Allied Chemical Corporation	1,121	84	3.14	1,248	43	1.56
Celanese Corp.	862	65	5.10	1,037	51	3.51
Crown Zellerbach Corporation	709	47	3.03	955	42	1.77
Goodyear Tire & Rubber Company	2,226	109	3.06	3,195	129	1.78
International Minerals & Chemical Corp.	263	20	3.19	506	4.5	0.22
Sherwin–Williams Company	345	19	3.66	526	15	2.52
Union Carbide Corporation	2,064	227	3.76	3,026	157	2.60

[a]Sales and net income figures are in millions of dollars.

requiring a zero growth rate in their employment until business definitely improved. Such companies hired only enough college graduates to replace employees lost by retirement and normal attrition. With the policy limitations imposed, to have hired more young people would have required firing older employees who were performing satisfactorily. Few, if any, companies chose to do that.

Many business leaders feel that our economy and our world trade situation will improve but the improvement will be slower than that following some earlier recessions. This improvement will again bring an increase in the availability of jobs. It seems probable that we will not have a strong surge in technical employment, comparable to the "Sputnik era," unless we again suddenly find ourselves in what may be judged a national crisis which can best be solved by expanding technology. This could happen if the antitechnology forces, strong in the early 1970's, cause us to fall too far behind other key countries, either militarily or economically.

Our best hope of reducing these fluctuations in employment seems to lie in the area of better long-range planning on a national scale, with the Federal government playing a major role. To illustrate, if we wish to reduce our aerospace effort and increase our programs in better ground transportation, it would be possible to plan both changes so that one phases into the other. With some lead time in planning, people leaving the aerospace programs could have an opportunity for some retraining to bring their skills more into line with those needed for ground transportation systems. Some lead time also would be needed to build up the program on ground transportation. Contracts in aerospace can be cut overnight, so that there is no more money to employ the people on those programs. But programs in new fields cannot be created and staffed efficiently overnight.

Better long-range planning by industrial managers can also reduce the fluctuations in their own hiring practices. A continual pruning of unprofitable business areas, and a continual weeding out of unproductive personnel on an individual basis are far preferable to saving these unpleasant tasks for times of recession, when the impact is more drastic. These, combined with earlier recognition of downward business trends, more reliance on attrition, and more faith that business will again turn up can do much to eliminate mass layoffs and temporary lapses in the hiring of new personnel.

In spite of these economic difficulties in the early 1970s, and the resultant limitations on new job openings, R & D is and will continue to be a major business itself in the United States. An eight to ten billion dollar expenditure by industry (Table 1) is still a very large activity. While Federal R & D funds may stay below the peak spending year of 1968, they will undoubtedly continue at a very high level.

REFERENCES

1. H. Reiss, Chem. Eng. News, June 29, 1970, p. 18.
2. Statistical Abstracts of the United States, 1971, U.S. Department of Commerce, pp. 473-475, 508-513.
3. Chem. Eng. News, Jan. 3, 1972, p. 10.
4. Chem. Eng. News, Sept. 5, 1966, pp. 17A-31A.
5. Chem. Eng. News, Sept. 6, 1971, pp. 42A-52A.
6. Industry Week, Oct. 4, 1971, pp. S-1 - S-32.

Chapter 4

GETTING A JOB AND MAKING THE MOST OF IT

Just as graduation from a university is a major achievement in
one's career, obtaining the right job is also a very significant step
in the continuation of that career. The ease of finding the "right"
job, and indeed the ease of finding any job, may vary considerably
from year to year. In times of job scarcity it becomes especially
apparent that this step is a time of judgment by others, the potential
employers. The extent to which one has prepared himself suddenly
may be far more important than the student considered in his early
college years. Even in times of job scarcities, the well qualified
usually have at least one job offer. In times of plentiful jobs, the
well qualified have a wide choice. It is hoped that this chapter will
acquaint the student with some of the typical approaches and considerations which many companies use in finding and selecting those to
whom job offers will be made. In reading this chapter, the student
may find some useful guides as to how to present himself so that his
good qualities are readily apparent. In addition, some suggestions
are made which may aid the student in evaluating a prospective
employer, to increase the probability that the first job will be one
which will satisfy both the employee and the employer. Finally,
some thoughts on making the most of a job are offered, both as a
possible guide for earning promotions and as a guide for personal
enjoyment.

COMPANY RECRUITING

When companies are in a position to seek new technical employees
several routes toward finding suitable candidates may be followed.
The search for new personnel may include interviewing potential

college graduates, advertising in trade journals, providing job descriptions to employment agencies, inquiring among friends, and studying unsolicited inquiries from those seeking new jobs.

College interviewing frequently provides the first opportunity for a student to start an acquaintance with the industrial world. Usually one, two, or three representatives of a company will visit the college or university, making contacts with the student placement office and the department of interest, such as engineering, chemistry, physics, or mathematics. This visiting team may describe the company and its activities to some of the professors and to those students who want to interview the company representatives. These student interviews are usually short, each lasting about thirty minutes. In such a period the student can form a very preliminary opinion as to whether or not the company offers what he wants in a job, and the interviewers can judge whether or not the student may match one of the company's openings. Offers are rarely, if ever, made to the student at this stage, but will follow more extensive interviews at one of the company's locations.

The interviewing records from the college visit, all answers to the company's advertisements, resumes submitted by employment agencies, and resumes from all other sources are studied to see which are the most likely candidates to really make a successful career with the company. References may be checked at this stage as an aid in making these selections or may be checked later, just before making an offer. Those who are selected are then invited to visit one of the company's locations for further interviews, at the company's expense. Those who are not invited by a particular company should not feel hurt--this may merely indicate that their talents, though real, are not the ones needed by that company at that particular time.

A standard form of interview at the company's location, which offers advantages to both applicant and company, is known as the "panel interview." The interviewee may spend a full day at the laboratory of interest, during which time he will meet members of the personnel department, will be given a general description of the company's products and activities, its benefit programs covering insurance, pensions, and vacation policy, will be given a tour of the laboratory, and will meet four to six members of the R & D staff. Many companies invite Ph.D. candidates or other advanced interviewees to present a technical seminar on some subject of the interviewee's choice. This seminar provides an excellent opportunity for the speaker to show that he has thorough knowledge of at least one

technical subject of importance and to project his personality to the
audience. He will also have a chance to visit for one half hour or
more with several members of the staff, the "interview panel."
These people will usually be experienced employees who can describe
in detail several technical areas of the company's program and can
discuss policies and practices of interest to the interviewee. The
group leader to whom the candidate will report if he accepts the job
under consideration and an assistant director or director will normally be on the panel. In such a day of interviewing the candidate
has a very good chance to see the physical facilities and meet a
cross section of the people. He can ask important questions of
several people at different levels, getting answers representing a
variety of viewpoints. Based on these discussions and observations,
the national reputation of the company, a review of some recent
publications from the laboratory, and opinions of professors or other
knowledgeable friends, the candidate should be able to decide if the
laboratory offers the current position and the possibilities for future
development which he wants. This aspect of job selection is considered in more detail in the next section.

For the interview, even without a seminar, the candidate should
make several preparations. He should be prepared to discuss at
least briefly some technical problem with which he is personally
familiar. This should be described clearly when asked, without
hesitation and with enthusiasm and interest. The subject should be
one which has no question of security. Discussion of university
research or previous industrial research which has been published
is appropriate, but care should be taken to avoid previous industrial
research which has not been released for publication or discussion.
The candidate should understand the significance of the work he
expects to describe and be able to explain why he has been interested
in the subject. In addition, the interviewee should decide ahead of
time what features of the potential job are important to him and
formulate intelligent questions to obtain the answers he wants. At
all times he should be courteous, alert, and interested in what is
going on around him. He should present himself as he truly is and
should never represent himself as being different from his true
nature.

A company will usually be concerned with the individual's technical knowledge, his ability to use it, and his possibilities for
growing into even more responsible scientific or administrative
positions. Judgment will be based on such factors as courses taken,
grades, references, work experience, and opinions resulting from

the panel interviews. It is normally expected that the individual can fit into the department reasonably well, though everyone is not expected to be an extrovert and a good mixer. One certainly need not be a "conformist" in most R & D organizations. It is also true, however, that most jobs require at least a moderate degree of cooperation with other people, and apparent indications of unusual difficulties in this respect will certainly be a negative factor.

If one wishes to interview seriously for a job in industry, he will obviously be seeking acceptance by a "peer group" which will be somewhat different from his contemporaries at school. The new group will have an older average age, will have adjusted to the responsibilities of self support and in most cases to family life and to community activities, and will be taxpayers. While the interviewee does not have to follow exactly the same standards of appearance and conduct as the interviewers, drastic differences will be cause for concern by the interviewers. The few students who may prefer to be drastically different in external appearance may rightly say, "Why should outward appearances be important? Why shouldn't I be accepted for what I am?" The interviewers may also ask themselves, "What is this interviewee really like? To what extent do his outward appearances reflect his true nature? Why does he feel it desirable to give such an unusual outward impression? What is he trying to prove?" One concern which usually (though not always) has been valid is that a person who is sloppy in his own appearance is sloppy in his work habits, for example.

In overall hiring patterns a company usually seeks a range of individual types. Some new employees should have good leadership potential and others are desired who will make careers based on sound technical achievements. It is usually expected that some will start in R & D and as their knowledge broadens will desire to move to other departments such as sales, engineering, or production. It is recognized that not all new graduates will know exactly what they want to be doing five years later and that many will in time prefer to leave the area of R & D.

Every company hopes to have most or all new employees be "above average," however difficult that term may be to define. The company's assessment of "above average" may not coincide with the grade average in school, however. A "straight A" Ph. D. is not a good candidate at all for some jobs and correctly would be judged "below average" in such considerations. Companies will try to reach what they judge to be "above average" matches of the individual to the particular job in question. They will also usually try to reserve

some of their new openings for people who show clear promise of
being outstanding.

Some examples of matching the individual to the job requirement
may be helpful. These should be considered as illustrative and are
not without exception. Career research positions have strong
emphasis on the acquisition of knowledge and experimental data.
Assignments calling for contacts with customers require less depth
of technical knowledge but place a stronger emphasis on ease of
getting along with a wide range of people of only brief acquaintance.
Production-oriented jobs, whether in manufacturing, engineering,
or development, require less originality than does research, but
place a greater emphasis on the mechanical performance of equipment, guiding a team of nontechnical coworkers, and on meeting
detailed schedules. The business aspects of making money are more
a part of the daily life of production and marketing people than of
those in R & D. The range of talents needed in an overall R & D
department will be clearer after one has completed this book.

Job offers are sometimes made on the day of the interview but
more often are received by mail one to three weeks later. The
courteous person will acknowledge the offer, and if he cannot give a
definite answer then, will indicate an approximate time for reaching
a decision.

No interviewing system is perfect, and both individuals and companies sometimes find they have misjudged a situation. One can
usually tell within six months to two years if the individual and
company do have a mutually attractive future. After such a period,
if all reasonable efforts have been made and the two are clearly a
mismatch, it is to everyone's advantage to part. (Terminations are
discussed in more detail in the last section.)

EVALUATING THE COMPANY

It is not unusual at some middle or advanced stage in one's
career to reach a state of frustration and to blame much of it on the
individual's lack of ability to influence his own course through life.
Each person does, indeed, have many limitations as to what he can
do or achieve. At the same time, many fail to recognize or utilize
the real choices which are available to them. By the time one is
graduating from a university and seeking a job, some of his key

choices are behind him. These include his choice of a field of study and how constructively he used his time and opportunities. (He can still change his mind regarding a field of work, but he will have to utilize valuable years, effort, and money to make a major change at this point.) One of many key choices now faces him in selecting his job, and he should give himself every reasonable opportunity to make a choice which will be satisfactory to him in the years ahead.

The student should ask himself at least a year before needing to make a job decision, "What kind of job do I want?" This question should be considered even earlier by those who expect to get M.S. or Ph.D. degrees. The "open mind" approach which any technically oriented person is encouraged to develop is just as appropriate in career planning as in technical problem solving. One does well to prepare himself for the problem of getting the right job in much the same way as he prepares himself for solving his problems in his university courses: analyze the situation thoroughly, study a considerable range of available information, formulate his own ideas to provide several suitable alternate paths to a solution, select the most attractive and pursue it, and fall back on alternate approaches if necessary.

The student will be greatly aided in analyzing job requirements relative to his own interests and abilities if he can actually work for short times in several types of jobs during his school years. Summer jobs in industry and at least some teaching assistance at the university can be very informative. Discussions with professors, friends, and relatives who have had experience in industry are highly desirable. Participating in several interviews with company representatives at the campus and reading articles on various types of employment will also help. The annual "careers" issue of Chemical and Engineering News is well worth reading.

When one reaches the stage of interviewing at a company location he should already have formulated some general ideas of what he wants for a vocation and should be prepared with questions to ask at the interview. He should also have read a little about the company in question, such as the annual report of the company (available at most school placement offices and available on request from the company's personnel office) for at least the two preceding years.

If there is any choice at all in the availability of jobs, the individual will do well to consider those companies which have a proven record of technical success in an area close to the individual's interest. Some companies wish to enter fields which are new to them, and hence will be offering jobs in areas where they have not

demonstrated success. On the average such positions will have a
higher risk from the security viewpoint, but some also offer an
unusual challenge and opportunity. One should at least learn enough
to know the situation in this regard. In any case, an inquiry concerning the stability of the company is appropriate. It is also desirable
to know how the company has handled layoffs in difficult times.

One should evaluate the company's real commitment to R & D, if
one wants a career in such work. Getting the information already
indicated will provide a partial answer. It will also help to inquire
who in the company establishes the R & D goals. If this is done
entirely by marketing, the company is not really dedicated to long-
range technical programs. The later chapter on selecting R & D
programs will explain this point more fully. One may also want to
ask if the company has an established route of advancement for those
who prefer nonadministrative, highly technical careers. If the company does not provide such a route, its commitment to high quality
research is doubtful.

Another key area to evaluate is the actual role the technical
employee with zero to three years experience plays. How much
freedom and how much guidance does he have? These should be in
good balance--an answer of "complete freedom" should be considered
either misleading or indicative of an inefficient organization.
Questions should be asked to establish if the new employee will have
well qualified guidance in learning the company's expert knowledge
in the assigned area, if he will be given enough information to understand the significance of his assignment, will have direct contact
with others who will use the information he generates, and will participate in planning his technical approach to solving his problems.
Other questions and a tour of the laboratory can establish the quality
of the physical facilities, library, and equipment, as well as the
ease of obtaining new equipment.

Opportunities for professional growth should also be explored.
Are company training programs--e.g., in problem analysis, experimental design, or management techniques--offered? Are academic
courses available from nearby colleges or special lecturers? Is
there a seminar program? Is participation in professional societies
encouraged? Do some of the staff actually participate in these things?

The personnel representative will be the correct one to ask about
"fringe benefits": insurance policies including life and medical coverage, pensions, vacation policy, arrangements concerning moving to
the location if a job offer is accepted, assistance in finding housing,
etc.

Obtaining information of the kinds indicated can help considerably
in deciding whether a particular company offers the employment which
will match the individual's interests. Finding such a company is
certainly one of many key events in a successful, satisfying career
and life. There is no way to guarantee that one's first job will be
the correct step in this stage of one's career. If one tries intelli-
gently to make a good initial job selection but for some reason beyond
his control it does not prove to be a good choice, he should look for a
change within a small number of years. The experience gained on
the first job should certainly help greatly in making a better decision
on the next one.

A few students will be doubtful of the desirability of an industrial
job. Certainly, industry is not the best place for everyone. We need
excellent teachers and research scientists in our universities, and a
considerable number of students may find a better match of the individual and job at a university. Those who are dedicated to teaching
as their prime interest should prefer the university. Those who feel
that they will be challenged only by academic research, rather than
industrial research, would do well to explore the two areas more
fully, however. In particular, one should ask himself what research
ideas he himself has that are really worth pursuing. If the answer
is really strongly positive, then he may be equally suited to academic
and industrial research. If the ideas are mere extensions of his
thesis, or if they are intriguing but not of major significance, then
he should consider his preference more carefully. In such a case
he may be misleading himself to think that he will not find equal or
greater challenge in the industrial laboratory. One major difference
between the two types of research is that in a university one should
build his research reputation largely from the quality of his own
ideas, while in industry one builds on his own ideas plus the need
to solve major problems which are identified by others. Many who
think only academic research is interesting feel this way because it
is the only kind with which they are familiar. A careful analysis of
industrial positions, along lines mentioned above and indicated in
the first chapter, can help greatly in evaluating them.

PERSONAL DEVELOPMENT ON THE JOB

When a person starts a new job he has two responsibilities which
overlap considerably: performing the specific job assignment and

continuing his own development. Those who do only the former
abdicate much of the control which they can exert over their own
future. Those who do both well will reap the largest professional
rewards.

Working on a specific technical project is one of the best ways
for a new employee to learn the details of a part of the company's
technology and learn about one or more of its products. Performing
the immediate job well should receive top priority. One should put
extra effort into his job so that he becomes an expert on the subject
of his work. As his job assignments change during his first few
years of work, he has the opportunity to broaden and deepen his
knowledge and experience far beyond his college education.

At the same time that one is working to become expert in the
areas of his R & D projects, he should give second but active priority
to additional study on subjects which are not an immediate requirement of the daily job but which are related. He should also continue
reading in his major field of college study, to keep his education up
to date there, too.

One who follows this combined approach will never become obsolete and will be qualified to take on new and more difficult assignments
when the opportunities arise. In addition, people who take this
approach will soon be recognized as being highly desirable for many
types of assignments, and the opportunities are more likely to come
to them than if they had followed a less rigorous approach. In this
way one can certainly help create his own "luck" and also be prepared to make the most of it when it comes.

Even if one is not fully satisfied with his first job, he will be far
better off if he still does the best he can with it. At the same time
he should look carefully to see if there is another group or section
in the same company which has jobs more to his liking. When given
an opportunity to express his feelings about his work, he can suggest
to his superior that he would like to be considered for an opening in
the group which seems more desirable. He will have no chance of
a transfer if he is performing poorly; any chance will certainly be
somewhat in proportion to the excellence of his work and his overall
qualifications.

The young technical employee is well advised to seek assignments
of several different types during his first years of work. This
broadens his experience and knowledge, teaches him more of the
total picture of the company's business, increases his adaptability,
and helps greatly in developing a lasting opinion of the type of work
he really wants to do. His personal study program will obviously

be influenced by his desire to advance scientifically, administratively in R & D, or to transfer to another department.

Many opportunities for training are available with most companies. In nearly all, one of the most important will be on-the-job training, working closely with more experienced people. In addition, many companies have consultants and occasional visiting lecturers and discussion groups in their own organizations. The in-house seminars serve several purposes, one of the most important of which is to give the speaker himself an opportunity to review a subject, organize his own thoughts on this subject, and present them orally to a group. As noted elsewhere, the ability to sell oneself is quite important, and this is a good opportunity for practice.

In addition to these forms of training, many companies encourage participation in college courses, paying at least part of the tuition. Occasionally individuals are selected for training at short, formal courses in specific subjects oriented toward the individual's job. These might include one-week or two-week university training courses in the use of special pieces of equipment or in certain techniques, or might be review courses in major areas of knowledge. They may also include courses taught by company experts.

Frequently participation in these training programs is voluntary (except for the on-the-job training), and the individual should certainly take full advantage of the opportunities. In some cases participation is by invitation only, with each participant having to "earn" the invitation by demonstrating enough merit and potential for growth so that he is selected.

EARNING A PROMOTION

The most important qualification for a promotion is to do one's present job well. The individual should learn all about it and become an expert in that area. He should push his project aggressively (though not objectionably so), make extra effort, and communicate his results well. At the same time the individual should continue to broaden his knowledge so that when a new assignment or promotion comes, he will be equipped to take advantage of that opportunity. These recommendations are applicable, whether one wishes to advance in an administrative or in a scientific route.

In addition to the intelligence and willingness to study and work

required to meet the above suggestions, other personal characteristics are also quite important. Honesty and realism are essential.
This concept of honesty includes the conventional telling of the truth
and reporting the truth, and also includes an active effort to free
one's opinions, evaluations, and conclusions from prejudice and
extremes of optimism or pessimism. Giving credit to others when
it is due is a key feature of honesty.

Each person should have a constructive, helpful attitude toward
others. These characteristics are highly desirable from all viewpoints, whether they be viewed as requirements for successful
leadership, for efficient team cooperation, or for enhancing the
everyday enjoyment of work.

Each one's efforts should be organized for thoroughness and
efficiency, so that the most constructive use is made of time.
Positive efforts along these lines can be a major factor in the
quantity of significant accomplishments made in a lifetime.

Good judgment is probably the one characteristic most needed
in higher levels in an organization. While "good luck" is very helpful
in giving an impression of good judgment, good judgment may also be
expected to be based upon broad, factual knowledge and experience;
realistic evaluation of that experience; intelligent and thorough effort
to place current problems in the perspective of past experience and
information; ability to distinguish the important from the trivial and
emphasize the important; willingness to evaluate alternatives; and
readiness to make a decision and aggressively see it through to a
satisfactory conclusion. While the last of these factors clearly goes
beyond pure "judgment," all are important and related to a degree.

Since promotions depend largely on quality and quantity of performance, good health is another very important factor. Young
people tend to take good health for granted, but one's life style
between ages 20 and 40 is very important in affecting health after 40.
The need for good health after 40 is clear, especially if one considers
the rigorous work schedules and travel demands on our leaders in
nearly all professions. A realization of the need for a healthful life
style, especially including regular exercise, is a key part of controlling one's destiny to the fullest.

Some common troubles which individuals have and which retard
their promotion are indicated below. This listing purposely does not
include the more obvious ones, such as lack of technical training,
laziness, or lack of cooperation.

Dissatisfaction with a present assignment sometimes leads an
individual to poorer performance than he has previously demonstrated.

While it is difficult to maintain excellent performance in a position which is not considered satisfactory, it is clearly evident that poor performance cannot be considered qualification for promotion to a more challenging level. A sharply varying level of performance as the job assignment is changed does not indicate a sufficiently stable personality or interest or self-discipline to permit the individual to handle the greater challenges of a more responsible position (which always includes some activities of less than average interest).

Misrepretantation occurs from time to time and for one reason or another. Regardless of the reason, it is unsatisfactory. The misrepresentation may be intentional or may be unintentional, but in any case does not get across the true picture. Unintentional misrepresentation due to bias or simply due to poor reporting and underselling can do almost as much harm as intentional misrepresentation.

Personality difficulties are obviously sometimes a handicap, particularly to one who would like to advance administratively. While it is not necessary that a good administrator be able to win a popularity contest, he must be able to obtain good results from a team of individuals. There is clearly no single approach to the leadership of such a team which will be successful. Some suggestions of things to do and things not to do are included in the following paragraphs and in the last chapter on "Personal Attitudes."

The young person starting a technical career may focus his sights first on the factors which may help him earn promotions to the group leader or research specialist level, since these represent the first distinct steps up the administrative and scientific ladders, respectively. (See Chapter 3 for descriptions of these positions. Some companies use different titles for equivalent positions, of course.) The following outline may be helpful in providing more specific guides than the more general paragraphs above.

A good group leader should excell in two distinct areas: technical ability in his field and leadership. Emphasis on these two should be roughly equal. His technical ability is usually reflected primarily in the quality and quantity of experimental results from his group rather than from his own experiments. The balance will vary somewhat from group to group. A good research specialist is expected to be at least as good technically but need not have the leadership ability or interest of the group leader.

The following characteristics are desirable for a good group leader. The characteristics associated with technical ability are also desirable for a research specialist. No one would have to have

all the desirable features important for promotion, but one should
have a high percentage of them.

Technical Ability

Upon leaving college the technical person should have a strong
foundation in the fundamental principles which are important in his
field of study, should have a wealth of factual information and know
where to find more on short notice, should know how to make use
of his knowledge, including good experimental ability, and should
have a well-developed desire to learn more. As he progresses in
his line of work, he adds to this a strong competence in the field of
his company assignment, becoming an expert in this area. This
expertise includes knowledge, experimental technique, and an understanding of where his role fits into the overall picture.

In addition, the professional technical person will acquire a broad
understanding of closely related fields and at least a general understanding of other fields which are somewhat related. For example,
if one holds a technical position in a group working on the preparation
of insecticides he needs to become an expert at that, should be quite
knowledgeable about the analytical methods and biological test methods
used to characterize and evaluate his products and about all safety
aspects associated with them. He should also develop a general
familiarity with engineering aspects of large-scale preparation of
his successful products, with all aspects of competitive products,
with economics of manufacture and sale, with ecological considerations, with actual use conditions, and with pertinent legal restrictions
which exist and are under consideration.

Technical ability is not complete without skill at reporting information which has been found or learned. This includes the keeping
of good experimental records in a notebook, the preparation of
summary reports, memos, or letters, and manuscripts suitable for
publication. It is also quite important--probably equally important
for one wishing to advance administratively--that one communicate
well verbally. Such communications will range from informal
conversations to formal lectures to a group of superiors.

Originality is a key feature of the work of a strong professional
technical person. Whether one wishes to consider this a personality
trait or not, it will show as a feature of his accomplishment.
Originality is a characteristic much sought after, is essential for

the "scientist" and highly desirable for the technical administrator.

Some of the more general characteristics that one may expect to find in those with strong technical ability will include initiative in learning and doing, careful planning of programs and experiments, attention to details, reliable interpretation of data, and a critical evaluation of results.

Leadership

The essential judgment of leadership performance will include the quantity and quality of results accomplished by the team consisting of the leader and those reporting to him. The organization of his own and of his group's efforts is a major consideration. A genuine interest in the current and future welfare of his associates, the setting of standards of performance and helping group members to meet them, fairness, and enthusiasm are all factors in good leadership.

The training of personnel reporting to him is one of the major responsibilities of a leader. This will include the indoctrination of new personnel, helping them get started on a technical program, and also helping them adjust easily to the nontechnical aspects of life in an industrial job. His approach to starting a group member on a project should include learning the background and reasons for the importance of the project and explaining these to the person who will work on it. If time permits, and it nearly always does, the technical man should be given an opportunity to study the problem and propose an approach to the solution. The group leader then will want to review the proposal, make additional suggestions, and the two should decide upon a mutually agreeable program. In every case the group leader should be sure the group member knows what he is to do, why the program is undertaken, and when results are expected. An additional part of coaching is a careful review by the group leader, at appropriate intervals, with consideration of all factors. These would include the experimental technique, records, actual data, and consideration as to whether or not the program needs revision. Reports, both verbal and written, need to be given on schedule; the group leader should offer guidance as necessary, both on timing and on quality of the reports.

One of the most important features of good training is the encouragement of originality. The group leader must be receptive to new ideas, both for the technical program and for the administration of the group's activities. The individual should be encouraged to explore his own good ideas whenever possible. If it is judged that an idea has no real merit, the group leader should next review the idea a second time to try again to find merit, and if the judgment is still negative, explain courteously why it does not seem good, giving the originator a chance to offer a rebuttal. The group member should be encouraged to use as much freedom of thought and action as he can handle well.

In training and direction of the group, quality of results needs to be emphasized more than quantity. One can always strive for better planning, better technique, better efficiency, higher quality work; there is a limit to the quantity of effort (not results) which can reasonably be expected.

The administrative requirements of a group leader include the supervision of the work of his group, of course. This may have to be on a day-to-day basis, combined with regular coaching for the less experienced members. It naturally would not be so frequent for the more experienced members. In all cases the group leader needs to be completely familiar with the details of the work done in his group and should exert his responsibility as necessary to see that it is of high quality and that it is reported correctly. While he may delegate certain assignments, he must not abdicate his position on a team which is expected to provide the highest quality results possible. In working with a strong, capable group member he may often be more of a "silent partner," observing, encouraging, providing assistance in getting supplies, equipment, and services, but always aware of details and willing to contribute perspective or a fresh viewpoint when needed.

Each technical employee is usually considered to have the first line of responsibility for his own safety on the job. The group leader is usually charged specifically with the safety of his group. He may fulfill this responsibility by training the individual group members as necessary and insisting that each be his own watchdog on safety. He will, from time to time, need to advise his management that certain new facilities are needed and may help in specifying those needs. He should make himself, his group members, and his supervisors aware of the toxicity aspects of the chemicals with which his group works.

The planning of detailed technical programs will occupy a significant part of the group leader's time. In doing this he will work with the assistant director and director, and also with his group members.

He must learn enough of the company and department objectives to be
sure that his group's objectives and programs are in accord with them.
(This is discussed more in later chapters on selecting and executing
programs, and on management by objectives.) He must also organize
his group's efforts to carry out the programs. This organization
must be such that the programs continue smoothly when he is away
from the laboratory.

Cooperation with other groups in the department and with other
departments is essential. These groups will include some who are
helping supply data and others who will need to use the data generated.
Those needing to use the data, in essence, are "customers"; every
effort should be made to satisfy these customers with the quality,
quantity, and timeliness of the data generated. Inquiries from other
groups deserve a prompt answer, and one should see that there are
no loose ends in the cooperative efforts.

The successful group leader is a good salesman. The first
requirement for this is simply that he have something (his group's
results) well worth selling. The second is that he "sell" it well,
always being accurate, optimistic, positive, and timely in approach,
yet realistic too.

A necessary part of carrying out his job, especially in dealing
with people, is a good familiarity with departmental and company
policies and procedures. While some of this overlaps with the
responsibility of his management and of the personnel department,
the proper knowledge of policies and procedures is still a part of
the daily guidance of a group.

Personal Characteristics and Interests

It is readily apparent that many characteristics of good group
leaders have already been described in preceding paragraphs.
Personal traits should certainly include many of the following: intellectual honesty, loyalty, fairness, conscientiousness, dependability,
organizational ability, good judgment, thoroughness, accuracy,
imagination. He should be inspiring, enthusiastic, and courageous.
He must also be eager to learn and productive. A good memory is a
great asset. He must think, plan, and act.

The successful technical person at any level should be analytical
in thought and should apply this to his own evaluation of himself.
Making a realistic evaluation of his own interests and abilities is a

necessary part of charting his course through life. Similarly, a
realistic evaluation of a job or of any particular situation is necessary
if one is to recognize a good thing when he has it, or to realize that a
change should be made. He should formulate his own goals for life,
develop plans, and train himself so that he can reach his goals.

SALARY ADVANCE

    An individual's salary should be in accord with his ability to
produce results. Consequently, there is a generally accepted salary
range for each classification in an R & D department. Ranges and
actual salaries are usually considered confidential information and
are discussed in specific terms only with individuals. Any individual
who wishes to discuss his salary and his advancement possibilities
should do so with his group leader, his assistant director, or the
director of his department.
    Figure 1 illustrates a typical relationship between salary and time
of experience. It can readily be seen that an individual's salary will
eventually reach the top of the range for his particular classification
and will tend to level off. The only way to continue significant salary

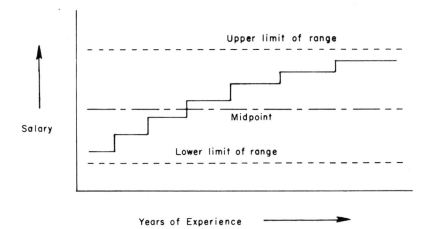

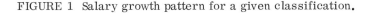

FIGURE 1 Salary growth pattern for a given classification.

advancement is to continue the growth of the individual so that he will
be more productive of results and can move into a higher classification, which will have a proportionately higher salary range. As one
advances in years within a given salary range, particularly as he
passes the midpoint of his salary range, the time interval between
raises may be expected to increase and the size of the raise may
also decrease toward the upper limit of his range. This pattern is
characteristic of all levels within most companies.

Two factors which influence raises, other than salary level within
the individual's range and his own merit, are the general cost of
living and the economic situation of the company. As the national
cost of living increases, there is a general practice of increasing
the salary range for a given classification. In times of economic
difficulty, an individual may expect that the time interval between
raises may be increased, and also the size of raises may be reduced
somewhat.

TERMINATIONS

Companies vary in their organizations, problems, approaches to
problems, and general philosophy; and the makeup of a given company will vary from time to time. As an example, the requirements
of organizing a new company may indicate that one team structure
and approach are necessary, while the running of a well established
company may have completely different requirements. The degree
of orientation toward the marketplace, the degree of isolation of
research from other departments, the percentage of the effort on
fundamental and exploratory research compared to process development, application research, and plant assistance may all vary significantly among companies.

Individuals vary in their own interests, their drive, their ability
to follow a long project, their accommodation for quick change of
orientation, the possibilities for keeping several projects going at
one time, and in other ways.

The company should fit the individual's objectives and interests,
and the individual should fit at least reasonably well with the company's way of doing business. If a reasonable parallelism between
the individual's preference and the company's interests does not
exist after one to three years of employment, the individual may be

well advised to seek another company whose objectives more nearly agree with his own. Such terminations are not a reflection on the individual or on the company and nearly always result in a happier individual eventually.

Occasionally terminations may occur because individuals do not perform satisfactorily. In many cases, this is actually a modification of the above situation. The individual in a different working environment or perhaps even in a different profession which will inspire him more may prove to be much more productive and much happier.

In many companies individual performances are assessed at least once a year, and more often in problem areas. Sincere efforts are usually made to place individuals in positions within the department and within the company so that they can perform well. Efforts are made to identify misfits early, and attention is given to assisting those individuals to perform better. Situations of this sort should be recognized and corrected as soon as possible. It is obviously preferable that poor performers be assisted in finding a job elsewhere before they have been with the company many years. Unfortunately, good performance for five years or more does not always guarantee that the individual will continue to perform well, and in such rare cases terminations could involve individuals with considerable seniority.

It is reasonable to expect that a few terminations will occur each year in any department. If the turnover is greater than about 5%-10% per year, one should suspect the existence of serious problems and seek their identity and correction. If no terminations or transfers occur for several years, such a situation may also reflect a problem, such as unrealistic job evaluations and unwillingness to terminate those individuals whose performance is not adequate or whose future is not reasonably assured in the company.

SUGGESTED READINGS

Later chapters in this book provide more details on many points mentioned here. In addition, the following articles provide a fairly wide sample of views and opinions on career development.

1.   J. Abbott, "Second Careers and the Identity Crisis," Chem. Tech., Nov., 1971, p. 650.

2. Anon., "Affluence, Recognition, Satisfaction", Laboratory
    Management, Dec., 1965, p. 20.
3. F. J. Curtis, "Self Development", Chem. Eng. News., Nov. 3,
    1952, p. 4610.
4. C. A. Hochwalt and N. N. T. Samaras, "The Industrial Research
    Chemist", Chem. Eng. News, Sept. 25, 1950, p. 3296.
5. J. O. Percival, "Increase Your Earning Power", Chem. Eng.
    News, Jan. 25, 1960, p. 10.

Chapter 5

SELECTING AND CARRYING OUT

TECHNICAL PROGRAMS

The essential requirement for success in any technical program
is the proper choice of projects. This is true whether the work is
done at a university, by the government, or in industry. One can
start with an outstanding team of people and excellent equipment, use
the best experimental techniques, and obtain highly accurate data,
but if the result is not worth something the entire effort has been
wasted. It would be far better to do only fairly good work on an
important problem. Naturally, the ideal is to do excellent work on
highly important problems.

The selection of problems in any R & D program will certainly be
most successful if those problems fit into some major area of interest of the organization concerned. For example, in academic
research just selecting a chemical reaction because it is a peculiar
thing and exploring it purely out of curiosity alone, is not a good
approach. On the other hand, if one has a broader concept and fits
this particular problem into a desire to develop a broad understanding of reaction mechanisms, then certainly it becomes much more
desirable. A person who plans a program from a broadly intelligent
viewpoint will achieve much more than the one who just goes here,
there, and yonder as his curiosity of the day leads him.

The same need for selection of important problems which fit an
overall plan is just as true in industrial organizations, of course.
For example, one could develop a product and a process to produce
it simply because an attractive market exists for it. But the mere
existence of a market is not enough to make the production of the
product desirable for any particular company. Is the required
technology one in which the company is already knowledgeable? If
not, the R & D will be slower and/or more expensive than for competitors who already have extensive knowledge in that area. Does
the company already have the sales staff with demonstrated ability
to sell to that market? If not, this will also be an extra hurdle to

79

overcome. These and other considerations, such as raw material position, existing manufacturing facilities which can be utilized, and agreement with the long range plans of the company, should be considered. A quick but careful study could show that the particular product would almost surely be profitable for someone else but not for your own company. On the other hand, the product could be just what you are looking for if you wish to diversify, even with the possible handicaps cited. But to recognize the handicaps ahead of time will contribute greatly toward overcoming them.

Problems which customers present, derived from their use of existing products, are frequently a part of R & D programs, too. If one solves a customer's problem, he has a chance to do two things. First of all, he has a chance to help the selling effort, and that in itself is certainly worthwhile. Quite often he does nothing more than that because the customer's problem is obsolete before he solves it and all he has done is achieve good will. But one can try to be more selective and solve problems which will gain the good will plus generate knowledge that will help eliminate future problems. That is far more desirable.

It seems self-evident that if the R & D program is to have maximum benefit for the organization supporting it, the organization itself must have a plan. This plan should be devoted in part to the immediate future and also to the long range future. It should clarify what the organization is and what it wants to become. The plan must also have the flexibility to meet new challenges and opportunities which have not been foreseen. The important issues must be spelled out as clearly as possible, so that each department contributing to the future of the organization can see what its own role must be.

One of the key issues for R & D is the company's desire for innovations. No company can hope to be first in every new development. The more challenging R & D, of course, is done by those companies which do try to be first in some major innovations and a close second or third in others.

The R & D department (or departments) must be kept informed of the company plan and of modifications as they are made. The R & D program must be formulated to support the organization's plan and must be coordinated properly with all the other departments which are also supporting this plan. This requirement for joint planning and program coordination is one which is difficult to meet. Failure to do so in the past has led to considerable disenchantment with many industrial (and other) R & D programs and departments.

For proper coordination with the company's long range and short

range plans, the R & D department also should have a long range
plan, covering a span of no less than five years, and a much more
detailed action plan for the year ahead. The long range plan may be
relatively brief, with goals described in general terms and without
much detail as to the approach, but matching the company's long
range objectives. The annual plan is the one with which the new
employee is directly involved and which will be the primary subject
of this chapter.

Many approaches have been tried for developing satisfactory
planning and program development systems. The success has not
yet been sufficient that one can conclude that any single approach is
best for all. One of the more promising systems, called by some
"management by objectives," is described in some detail in the next
chapter. Whatever system one uses should lead to a plan for the
organization as a whole, with meshing subplans for each department
of that organization. However, no system, and no set of plans, will
produce good results unless the people involved are dedicated to
achieving good results in a cooperative fashion. The key to success
again becomes people.

HOW IS AN R & D PROGRAM FORMULATED?

Within the framework of the organization's overall plan, several
departments will need R & D help in fulfilling their own programs,
so providing this help will be a significant part of the R & D program.
In many companies the long range part of the organization's plan will
call upon R & D to be the prime source of new products for the future.
(Some other firms may purchase either know-how or other companies
as their main source of new products.) Let us examine some of these
sources of projects more closely, and see how they may contribute
to the R & D program. A simplified illustration follows.

Let's assume our company has a history of producing and selling
goods to segments of the transportation industry. In re-examining
its positions, the board of directors agrees that it should not try to
produce complete transportation units (cars, airplanes, for example).
However, it would like to broaden its range of products for sale, and
especially to be alert to new developments in transportation which
may offer opportunities for new products. A closer look at the
products it now sells shows the following. One group of materials

is closely related to the wheels of vehicles: fibers for the reinforce-
ment of tires, adhesives which are used in tire building (the polymer
division of the company), and shock absorber and suspension systems
(the mechanical goods division). These products are selling well,
but one wonders if there will be the same demand for the same combination of wheels, tires, shock absorbers and suspension systems
in the future. The polymer division is also doing well with the plastic
foam it sells for seat cushions and other uses, but its particular
polymer used as a covering for arm rests and crash pads is in commercial trouble. A competitor has a better product. Can the present
covering material be improved so it is again profitable, or should it
be discontinued? In considering the period 10 to 20 years hence,
what changes will occur in transportation that could make some more
of today's products obsolete? What new opportunities can be generated which will be a part of new transportation systems?

This study leads to a revised plan for the company. It states that
the polymer division should maintain its favorable position in fibers,
adhesives, and foams. (To do so calls for improvements, to stay
equal to or ahead of competition.) This division should phase out its
business in the present polymeric covering materials. The mechanical division should maintain its favorable position in shock absorber
and suspension systems. Both divisions must stay alert to changes
in transportation requirements, and both must search for new products
which will be profitable in the transportation business as it may exist
10 to 20 years from now.

Now let's consider the polymer division's response to this
revised plan. In studying this plan the polymer division's marketing
department sees that it needs help from R & D in three areas: continued technical assistance to customers in solving short range
problems associated with the use of existing products, improvement
in its adhesives when used with a new type of rubber now being
introduced into tire manufacture, and improvement in the flame
resistance of the foam used for seat cushioning and padding in cars
and especially in airplanes. Requests in these three areas are made
to the R & D director.

The manufacturing department of the polymer division is producing its adhesives, fibers, and foams in good quality but needs to
increase its capacity for each by about 20% in the next two years.
There are some preliminary rumors that a competitor has a more
economical foam process, so manufacturing personnel feel they must
have improvements in this too, if they are to remain competitive.
Appropriate requests are made to engineering and to R & D.

Within R & D, the director ponders the long range transportation needs and probable changes to come. He must find a way to be prepared for any changes and to anticipate them if possible. He discusses this with his staff of two assistant directors, their group leaders, and his senior scientists. In addition, he outlines the company's revised plans and the requests from marketing and production. None of the issues is completely new to the staff members, since they have kept well informed on most aspects of the division's business. The decision to withdraw from the polymer covering product area is new but is not unexpected. The staff meeting is closed, with each staff member knowing what part of the company plan, or which requests from an outside department, he is expected to develop a program for.

A short time later the R & D staff is reconvened, and program proposals are reviewed. After discussion, the accepted projects are grouped as follows:

1. Fibers

   A. Project to increase plant capacity by 20% in two years, to be coordinated with engineering and production.
   B. Customer service problems, selected jointly with marketing.

2. Adhesives

   A. Plant capacity increase, same as for fibers.
   B. Customer service, same as for fibers.

3. Foams

   A. Plant capacity increase, same as for fibers.
   B. Customer service, same as for fibers.
   C. Improvement in flame resistance of foams.
   D. Development of a foam system with a thick, tough skin formed as an integral part of foaming, not requiring any polymeric covering layer. (This would partially offset the loss of the polymeric covering material business.)
   E. Project to reduce plant manufacturing cost for foam.

4. Exploratory Research

   A small group is assigned to search for new product concepts in foams, fibers, or adhesives, or in combinations of materials which serve the same function as seats, safety padding, and devices for the protection of passengers in case of the wreck of a vehicle.

5. Long Range Forecasting

One man is assigned initially to study long range trends and changes in transportation, including establishing working relations with marketing, customers, the Department of Transportation, certain universities active in the field, and foreign counterparts.

This program includes problems from other departments within the company, from customers, and those generated within R & D, all related to the company's current plan. Some projects are short range, some intermediate, and some are quite long range in nature.

The program is then developed in more detail, including an outline of the approach to be used for each project, the personnel, new equipment, time, budget money needed, and probability of success for each. The program is outlined in a brief, simple style, as illustrated (in part) in Table 1. Copies of the program outline are sent to each department in the division and to the division management. After a short time for study by others, the program is discussed with representatives of other departments and any differences of opinion are resolved.

The division manager assembles proposed programs and budgets from all departments, checks for suitable coordination and agreement with the overall plan for the company. He compares the total cost of operating the departments with the marketing department's budget for income from sale of goods. If the net profit is suitable he approves the budgets and programs. Copies are provided to the mechanical goods division for communication purposes and to the company president for his approval. The president's approval is the final signal that the plans are satisfactory.

A similar procedure is followed by the mechanical goods division in developing its R & D program. The directors of each R & D department discuss their mutual interests frequently and insist on direct communication between the lower echelons in projects which have some mutual significance.

One of the most important features of program selection is its cooperative nature. Each problem must have potential importance to the company, and each must have adequate relevance to the company's plan. No single person or department has enough information to select all of the best projects and only the best projects. Perfection will not be reached in any case, but the best chance for a strong program will certainly come from a joint effort. Having selected the projects cooperatively, it is now R & D's primary responsibility to develop and carry out the detailed solutions to the problems which have been selected.

A point which is frequently overlooked in the selection of projects is the relationship between importance and time required to develop a commercial solution. Each project should be selected based on its importance at the time the solution will become available, not on its importance at the time of selection. Some customer service and plant assistance problems may be solved in a few weeks to a few months. Some improvements to existing products or processes may be made in a few months to a few years. The commercialization of completely new products or processes usually requires five years or more. Thus, it is obvious that R & D's estimate of timing is highly important, as is the market analysis of the need for a product at some particular time in the future.

BUDGETS

A budget is normally prepared along with the R & D program, as already indicated. Some companies decide how much money they are willing to spend for R & D in a particular year, then develop the program within that budget limitation. Others try to establish what projects should be worked on and what problems should be solved by desired target dates. Then the R & D staff estimates the manpower required to solve those problems by the indicated target dates. These are then arranged in order of priority. From the manpower estimate it is relatively easy to calculate the cost of the program, since each company knows from its own experience the average total cost of one man-year of R & D work. The preliminary budget that results from this approach is then used by upper management, which will combine it with other departmental budgets, including estimates of sales and predictions of manufacturing costs. From all these the net profit is estimated. If this is judged to be too low, the departmental budgets are revised. In the case of R & D the project proposals on the lower

TABLE 1   R & D Program and Expense Outline

Project	Priority	Man-years this year	Target completion date	This year's research expense, $	This year's possible capital, $	Probability of success, %
1. Improve the process for foam A, so that plant capacity will be 20% greater without new equipment.	A					
A. Screen new catalysts.		0.5	April 1	12,000	---	75
B. When one is found, giving 20% faster reaction, evaluate in pilot plant.		3.0	6 mon. later	75,000	---	80
C. Introduce in plant.		0.5	Within 1 mon. after B	12,000	---	80
2. Explore ways of obtaining a foam with mechanical properties equivalent to foam A, but with better flame resistance to pass test D.	A	1.0	Review April 1, re-evaluate desirability of continuing to pass test D	25,000	7,000 (small, heavy-duty mixer)	50

3. Exploratory research, in one or more of following areas: foam, fibers, adhesives, seating, and protective devices.	B	3.0	Within 2 yrs., or re-evaluate desirability of continuing	75,000	---	50

priority problems are dropped or reduced to bring the budget within the range needed to have an adequate profit.

The establishment of priorities on research projects, being an important part of the program selection, should be done as a cooperative effort, with R & D, marketing, production, and higher management participating.

The money spent on R & D, expressed as a percent of sales, varies considerably with different companies and with different industries. Many companies in the chemical industry spend about 3%-4% of the total sales revenue for R & D.

The budget and program are established in terms of the priorities which are set at the beginning of the year. As the year progresses some changes in the priorities and the program are nearly always made. Some of the projects will be seen as less attractive as data are obtained or as customer needs change, others will become more attractive. By the end of the year the department will have spent more money than budgeted in some areas and less in others. The total expenditure will be about as originally projected, unless the budget has been reduced or increased at some time during the year.

More comments will be made about budgets in Chapter 10 on the "Cost and Profitability of Industrial R & D."

A BALANCED PROGRAM

There are several fairly well recognized types of R & D, and a good program should include the input from each type. The following descriptions will indicate what is meant here for each.

"Exploratory research" is that research which is designed to seek something new: new information, new products, or new processes. It is also called "scouting research" by some authors. This type of research, as its name implies, usually explores new territory, with discovery of something useful as its objective. It is analogous to prospecting: the initial object is simply to find the gold mine, to show that it does exist, and where it is. The accumulation of detailed data on features such as a full range of mechanical properties of a product, or full process details on how to make something, will not be a part of exploratory research. Those studies come at a later stage, after it is judged that the exploratory program has found something sufficiently interesting to justify the detailed (and hence more expensive) studies.

"Fundamental research" may be considered to be research which is designed to provide an understanding of a phenomenon. This is quite different from exploratory research. Where the latter seeks the existence of something new, the former takes a much closer look, trying to develop an understanding of a phenomenon which is already known to exist. Fundamental studies may be a part of many or most of the programs in R & D. A company should understand thoroughly its most important processes and products, for it is this understanding that leads to the lowest cost processes, to the best uniformity of quality, and to the optimum level of quality in the company's products. Problems of an unexpected nature are solved much faster if a firm basis of understanding exists. Without this understanding, companies find themselves solving the same problems many times, which in the end is far more costly than doing the R & D right the first time.

"Process development" is a term applied to the R & D study of the best way of making a particular product and of the variables which are important in that process. This study may be started by research, on a laboratory scale. If this is successful, the process may be studied on a larger "pilot plant" scale. This larger scale work is often the assignment of development, with a considerably increased emphasis on the engineering aspects of the process. The proper selection of equipment for the ultimate process is often as important as the selection of starting materials, and it is here that engineering talents become especially helpful. The real goal of the process development program is to provide a complete description of the desired process, including raw material specifications, reaction variables, demonstration of equipment function, and all data necessary for the design of a full scale plant.

"Product development programs" are those which are designed to provide new products for the company to sell. Our hypothetical company may already have versatile equipment for the manufacture of foams, for example. The program which has as its goal the development of a foam suitable for seat cushions but having improved flame resistance would be an example of product development. This type of program may be started by research, in the laboratory, since small scale work is usually faster and cheaper than large scale experimentation. When a suitable product has been demonstrated in the laboratory, its preparation may be scaled up to the pilot plant stage by development.

Product development and process development often go hand in hand, of course. Usually new varieties of existing products will require at least some change in the corresponding processes. Completely new products call for new processes to make them.

In many departments process development and product development are done by the same groups.

"Application research" is the term often given to the program designed to help the company's customers use its products. If our illustrative company wants to sell fibers in the transportation field, it may have to show its customers how to make automotive carpeting, upholstery fabrics, and fabric forms suitable for tire building. These skills, and the assistance to customers, are especially important in introducing new products which will give the customer desired improvements but usually also require some changes in the customer's processes. New "application research" is done by a supplier, to help its customers; if the same work were done by the customer, it would be called "product research" or "process research" by the customer.

Technical assistance to the company's own plants is a normal part of R & D. This role usually falls to development, though research personnel may also be called in as consultants. Plant assistance is especially important at the time of starting a new production unit or of beginning to produce a new product on an existing production unit. Development personnel will usually be called upon to train plant personnel in the operation of a pilot plant prior to the plant start-up and also will be a part of the team of people from R & D, engineering, and production who will start the plant. After the plant is operating approximately according to design, the production department becomes responsible for its continued operation. Development personnel may continue as advisors and occasionally help as troubleshooters but for the most part will return to other projects in the pilot plant stage. In plant assistance, it is R & D's responsibility to see that the available technical information is used properly.

Technical assistance to customers is sometimes handled by the R & D department and at other times is in a "technical service department" which is under the direction of the marketing management. In either case, it is closely analogous to the plant assistance which was just described. The difference is that the assistance is now in the customer's plant, and an even greater degree of diplomacy is required.

Supporting functions of R & D will usually include analytical research for chemical operations and product testing for polymers, fibers, mechanical goods, or consumer products, according to the company's range of operations and products. These functions are essential parts of process and product R & D. One must analyze

and test suitably so that he knows what he has at each stage of a
reaction or of a process, and he must carefully chacterize his final
product. This part of R & D works closely with the plant quality
control department in establishing analytical and test methods. It
may also work with marketing and with customers in helping insure
the suitability of the product for the intended use.

It is not always necessary for any one organization to conduct all
these forms of R & D. For a sound operation, however, the company
should have all of these types of information available to it. Some of
the necessary information may be in the literature, some may be
done by universities, some by competitors, raw material suppliers,
and customers, and some may be contracted to outside research
organizations. R & D-oriented companies usually prefer to do much
of their own product- and process-oriented R & D, plant assistance,
and customer service. In some cases nearly complete know-how is
purchased on certain new processes and products. Almost all companies depend on outside sources for much of their fundamental
understanding; some companies supplement this with excellent fundamental programs of their own.

JUSTIFYING AND SELECTING SPECIFIC PROJECTS

Most companies have more projects available for R & D than the
budget will cover. As a result, some means of evaluating and justifying specific project proposals is needed to permit the best selection
to be made. It is quite desirable to have a surplus of projects available, of course. This insures new projects being available when one
is completed or otherwise terminated. It also means, in principle
at least, that the best are worked on and the less attractive are kept
in reserve.

The smaller companies frequently have a rather informal procedure for justifying R & D projects. The group which will have to
select the R & D program, such as directors of R & D, marketing,
manufacturing, and engineering, will often have good communication
throughout the year and will have a mutual understanding of the
company's overall problems. Selections of projects in such a
situation may be made as a result of brief discussions among those
individuals, taking advantage of the good communication which has
been keeping each one up to date with progress on internal problems,

with the competitive situation, and with changes that customers want.

In larger companies communication throughout the year is usually difficult to maintain: more people have suggestions of projects to work on and more people are involved in decisions; hence, disagreements regarding priority are not so easily settled. To try to resolve such a more complex situation, some of the larger companies require written analysis of the project proposals. This analysis may include a statement of objective(s); the background of known information related to the project; an outline of how the project may be studied; a statement of the timing necessary; a summary of any supporting work by other departments; the patent status; an outline of manpower, expense money, and new equipment (capital) needed for the project; and an analysis of the potential benefits to the company. Such a sheet is outlined in Table 2.

For a detailed analysis of this sort, of course, the person making the proposal must have the help of several departments in supplying the necessary information. R & D would be called upon to estimate the manpower, expense, and equipment part, outline the approach, and estimate the time required to reach the technical objectives. The marketing department or the production department, depending on who would use the results, would contribute to the statement of benefit to the company and of the timing required if the results are to be useful. The patent department should supply the statement on patent status. The department recommending the project would probably supply some of the background information and R & D also would usually contribute.

In this formalized system, the director of R & D or his designate, should study the proposal and attach his analysis of it in writing. His analysis might include the probability of technical success, his agreement or proposed modification of any information given, and a statement of how it could be fitted into the existing program. For example, another project might be scheduled for termination, making available the necessary manpower. More frequently, however, taking on a new project means stopping some other effort, or slowing some other project. A part of the judgment on the new proposal certainly should include a statement of effect on the rest of the program.

In a company following this type of procedure, there will probably be a formal committee which selects projects for the R & D program. They will meet at least once a year, perhaps in the late summer or early fall, to begin establishing a program and budget for the coming year. This committee would collect all project proposals from the R & D staff, marketing, production, engineering, and any other source.

TABLE 2 Sample Research Project Proposal

Submitted by:_____

Date proposed:

   I. Objectives of proposed work:

  II. Status of known information relating to this work:

 III. Proposed method of attack:

 IV. Necessary timing:

  V. Descriptive summary of supporting work by other departments:

 VI. Patent status:

VII. Manpower and Cost:

        Estimate of total man-months required:

        R & D:_____ Other:_____

        Expense cost:

        Special equipment cost:

VIII. Potential benefits if this work attains its objective, and its
       relation to company objectives:

Proposals would be reviewed for their relative importance, their agreement with the company's broad goals, their probability of success, the timing requirements, and their costs. From these considerations relative priorities would be assigned. As many would be worked on as the budget would permit. Those projects in excess of the budget capability would be the ones with the lowest priority ratings.

It is probable that most companies use program selection techniques which lie somewhere between the two extremes cited here for the small, informal organization and for the large, very formal one. Nearly all try to use the same range of project sources, the same types of information for evaluation, and an interdepartmental approach in selecting projects. The best technique for doing this is likely to vary according to the size of the organization, the effectiveness of its day-to-day communication of the overall company business, and the preferences of the upper management group.

Nearly all companies agree that the selection of R & D projects should be a cooperative affair, with participation including R & D, marketing, production, and engineering departments. It seems quite unlikely that the company's technical problems will be solved adequately unless these four departments, at least, contribute. Who else but production people, for example, will know best what their needs are for process improvements in the plant? Who but the engineering department will have the best insight on equipment problems associated with a new process which is expected to reach the plant soon? Marketing representatives meet the customers on a day-to-day basis, and receive all the complaints about the quality of existing products. They often are able to get from customers the projections of what new products are needed to meet new requirements. Thus the marketing department is an essential source of short range projects. The three departments cited are usually very good sources of short range and intermediate range projects related to the company's existing technology, and R & D contributes to these, as well. Occasionally someone outside R & D supplies a good proposal for long range studies, but these most often come from within the R & D group. The projects which are in the nature of an unexpected opportunity that is the outgrowth of a goal-oriented project also usually come from within R & D.

If any one department has overwhelming dominance in selecting the R & D program the result will not usually be satisfactory for long. If production and/or engineering dominate, the R & D program usually becomes a plant assistance effort. After a few years it becomes apparent that no new products are being explored and developed by

R & D, and the company loses its competitive position, with its products becoming commodities.

When marketing departments select all the R & D projects, it is natural that those selections will reflect the pressures on the marketing staff. Those pressures are nearly all short range, caused by customer demands for better quality and lower prices, or by a competitor's success with a new product. There are nearly always so many problems of these kinds that a generous budget can be consumed entirely by them, if no restraint is put on the selection. Without such restraints the R & D department becomes a customer service group only, and all "new" products are "me too" items which are developed late, in imitation of someone else's products.

When all or most of the selections have been made by R & D itself, the results have frequently yielded too many technical successes which were commercial failures. Sometimes outstanding commercial successes have also been apparent. It appears to be the general consensus of management, however, that R & D programs which were not well coordinated with the other departments have not been adequately successful.

In addition to selecting an R & D program on an annual basis, the progress on individual projects is evaluated from time to time during the year. The desirability of dropping a project and of adding a new one, as well as shifting emphasis toward the more successful ones, is more or less continuously being considered. It is rare, indeed, that a program will continue throughout a year on the course which was selected at the beginning of that year. Changes in the program are usually evaluated in much the same way as the original projects were selected, though perhaps somewhat less formally.

At this point it should be apparent why it is important for the administrative staff of the R & D department to be skilled in technical affairs, in understanding the business needs of the company, in presenting their results and project proposals in a clear and convincing way, and in day-to-day communications. All of these skills are needed in finding and selecting the important projects for R & D, which are essential to the future of the department and of the company.

PREPARING THE DETAILED R & D PROGRAM

After the goals or projects of the R & D program have been selected, it is then the responsibility of the R & D staff to formulate suitable approaches or technical plans for reaching those goals. The entire group of detailed plans for all of the goals becomes the detailed R & D program. This program should be carried out expeditiously so as to reach the selected goals, if it is reasonably possible. As progress is made, some plans will have to be altered; and in some cases it will become apparent that the project is not likely to be successful and should be dropped.

Specific R & D projects are usually assigned to a staff member such as a group leader or a scientist. This person will generally be chosen because of his interest in or knowledge of the project, perhaps because work on that project will give him valuable training, or for some other suitable reason. It will then be that individual's responsibility to develop a preliminary technical plan for reaching the goal. If he will do the experimental work himself, he will doubtless prepare the plan himself. However, if he is leading a team of people who will do the experimental work, he should enlist the aid of each technical member of the team in making the plan. Each person will feel more personally involved in the program if he shares in the development of the plan. The participation in planning is also excellent training for the individual. In many cases the team member may know more about his own area of work than anyone else on the team, so his ideas will be highly important.

The development of the initial plan may utilize the steps outlined later in Chapter 7 on "Creativity." It is certainly to be emphasized that creative approaches are highly desired in solving each and every problem in the entire program. As outlined in the discussion on creativity, the problem should be clearly defined, first of all, then related information should be learned, and several possible approaches to the problem should be considered. The best should be selected for the experimental approach.

In many companies the initial plan, as formulated by the group which will do the work, will be reviewed with the assistant director, director, and with other group leaders who may have pertinent knowledge or who have closely related programs. This review provides an opportunity for a broad range of knowledge and experience to be added to the planning, as well as a valuable step in liaison with other interested groups. The resulting discussion often leads to some modification of the initial plan and should result in the "official" or "approved" plan for reaching the goal in question.

At this time the statement of the goal should be made in simple and clear terms and should be discussed sufficiently so that the technical person in the laboratory, the group leader, and higher

R & D management all have the same understanding of that goal.
Each should understand what results are needed, to the extent of
defining the results in quantitative terms whenever possible. The
definition of the goal should also be stated so clearly that the persons
or groups which will use the results, such as marketing, commercial
development, or production groups, will understand it in the same
way.

As an example of a clear statement of a goal, consider the statement of project 2 in Table 1: "Explore ways of obtaining a foam with
mechanical properties equivalent to foam A, but with better flame
resistance to pass test D." It is clear from this that better flame
resistance is needed, and the degree of improvement is specified by
the requirement to pass "test D." It is also clear that this improvement must be made without sacrificing other mechanical properties.

In the case of exploratory research, however (project 3, Table 1),
the goal is stated simply as doing exploratory research in areas of
specific company interest. No precise timetable is set except to
indicate that some useful results should be found within two years.
The R & D management naturally will review and help reorient the
exploratory efforts from time to time within this two year period.

The technical plan for reaching the goal should be outlined and
discussed in such a way that those who are participating, and R & D
management, understand the responsibility and plan of action for
each individual. It is desirable, of course, that other technical
groups which are cooperating have a similar understanding. In
some situations it may not be practical to have the group which will
use the results understand the technical program fully, due to difference in training; but the R & D staff should communicate with the
user and produce results in such a way that the user has a high
degree of confidence in the R & D program and people.

The time of reviewing the initial plan with R & D management
provides an excellent opportunigy for each group member to be sure
he understands why the goal is important. If he does not already
know the reasons for working toward his group's goals he should
ask at this time.

One adjustment which college graduates frequently find somewhat
difficult is this cooperative approach to the selection of a technical
plan. The young Ph.D., in particular, may feel a certain pride in
the initial plan which he proposes and may feel hurt when his carefully developed proposal is not fully accepted. This is one of many
occasions when one should cultivate his objectivity rather than his
emotions. The modification of a plan by more experienced

investigators will nearly always strengthen it. The young scientist or engineer who reaches the stage where he can analyze a problem, prepare a plan for its solution, and have that plan accepted 95%-100% after scrutiny by the R & D staff, has reached a performance level of considerable note.

CARRYING OUT THE PROGRAM

Once the detailed R & D program has been established, the recent graduate is on relatively familiar ground if his training has included independent research. This may be the first opportunity for independent experimental work in unknown areas for those who have not. In either case, he will usually work more or less closely with someone already skilled in the area, depending on his training. The group leader should keep rather close watch on the day-to-day efforts and results, until the individual demonstrates an ability to work with little supervision. In any case, the group leader and other colleagues are available for discussions and will be glad to offer advice and guidance if they are requested. College graduates are not usually expected to have expert knowledge of a company's specific R & D problems. They are expected, however, to have a knowledge of fundamentals, a willingness to learn, and the common sense to ask questions about important things which they do not know.

The development of a good experimental approach takes time and generally is the result of coaching, experimenting, and studying. The group leader and other experienced personnel will help by coaching, often in much the same way that a professor trains his graduate research students. The experience of conducting one's own experimental program is invaluable, provided one does it with an objective of learning and improving his ability as well as obtaining the data which his program calls for. Some study of technique itself is desirable. The published literature provides specific guides in many areas, and a book such as that by Wilson (1) should be read by everyone. He gives excellent guidance on subjects including the choice and statement of a research problem, seaching the literature, elementary scientific method, the design of experiments, the design of operators, the execution of experiments, classification, sampling and measurement, the analysis of experimental data, errors of measurement, probability, randomness and logic, mathematical work, numerical computations, and reporting the results of research.

It is not desirable to add comments here on all the topics covered by books such as that of Wilson. Some, however, seem particularly worth amplifying, as indicated below.

The preparation of the detailed plan most likely included extensive knowledge of prior information related to the goal. Much of this may have been provided rather quickly or sketchily by the group leader or another senior staff member. When faced with carrying out his part of the program, however, the team member should learn as much of that background as he can in as short a time as possible. Money and time have been wasted over and over again by "reinventing the wheel"; to do so again is not to anyone's credit. Guiding the newcomers to the correct literature is one of the areas where the senior work associate should be of special help. He should know the important areas of published literature, selection of books, patents, and company reports toward which to steer the junior colleague. One of the distinct advantages of the group system for R & D is that the group leader and/or other senior group members provide continuity of expertise in areas of the group's specialty.

The strong urging not "to reinvent the wheel" should not be construed as a recommendation to accept the previous literature and experience as a complete limitation for future effort. In contrast, one should always evaluate earlier results in the light of new knowledge, new techniques, and new ideas. The important thing is to avoid repeating earlier work without realizing that one is doing so. A critical review may show that certain earlier work should be repeated, often with refinements or some variations.

Knowing the goal, the plan for reaching it, and having a good background in related work which has been done, one is faced with the selection of the specific experimental approach. This will vary considerably with the nature of the project. In exploratory research one often has to feel his way along, planning the next experiment only after he has completed the current one. The early experiments may be designed simply to show if something can be done. For example, the intent may be to show just that a particular compound may be prepared in a reasonably pure state, without regard to yield, process requirements, or raw material costs. After the feasibility of preparing the desired compound has been shown, the next step might be to make more of it so that it can be purified further and given a screening evaluation for desirable properties, e.g., biological activity if that is the company's interest. As progress is made, considerably more detail will be needed concerning the process for making the desired compound, its purity, its usefulness, and other considerations, as discussed in the next section.

One experimental approach which deserves special mention is the use of statistical design in the selection of experiments and in interpreting the data. Some investigators have a tendency to change one variable at a time, over a wide range of levels of that variable. This is often desirable, especially in the early stages of an investigation. Sometimes in complex systems--e.g., in biological systems--one variable cannot be changed independently of all others, however, and a suitable experimental approach is needed to handle the system. Some other investigators change several variables at once and cannot show the effect of any single variable. This approach is often useful in exploratory work, "leapfrogging" ahead several steps at a time, based on careful mental analysis of the situation. At some time in a fairly advanced program, however, most investigators reach the stage where they need to know the quantitative effects of interactions between variables. The only practical way to do this is with the use of statistically designed experiments. The technique is simple when only a few variables are being changed, each at only a few levels. The mathematical treatment becomes more complex as the number of variables and the levels grow, but very complex designs can now be evaluated with the use of computer programs.

Let us consider that we are studying the process for making a compound which includes a simple esterification step. From some preliminary experiments, plus a study of the literature, we conclude that the most important variables in this step are the catalyst concentration, the temperature of reaction, and the alcohol/acid ratio. A statistical design using these variables, each at three levels, would be that shown in Table 3 (other variables, such as time, would be held constant). Such a design calls for twenty-seven experiments, not all of which may be necessary. Experiments 1, 2, and 3 would show the effect of ratio as the only variable (at one catalyst concentration and one temperature); 1, 4, and 7 would show a temperature response, etc. One might choose to do first the experiments designed to show extreme effects, e.g., 3 (the mildest conditions for good yield, based on acid), 27 (to give the highest yield, based on acid, but perhaps with more side reactions), and a few more in between. These experiments may show which are the next most important to run.

It is possible that results may prove to be simple and one gets all the information he needs well before completing the design. If the results are more complex, and one variable seems to be affecting

TABLE 3 Design of Experiments for Esterification Study

		Alcohol/acid ratio		
		1.10	1.30	1.50
Catalyst Concentration A				
Reaction Temp.	70° C	1	2	3
	90° C	4	5	6
	110° C	7	8	9
Catalyst Concentration B				
Reaction Temp.	70° C	10	11	12
	90° C	13	14	15
	110° C	16	17	18
Catalyst Concentration C				
Reaction Temp.	70° C	19	20	21
	90° C	22	23	24
	110° C	25	26	27

another (e.g., excess alcohol could be complexing with the catalyst, probably more at low than at high temperature), one may wish to complete all or most of the design.

Having completed these experiments, or most of them, the investigator can calculate the direct effect of each variable on the product yield, or purity, or whatever response is being studied. In addition, he can calculate the effect of interactions between any two variables, or even the effect of an interaction among the three variables, as well as the variance (a measure of the degree of experimental error), and the statistical significance of each variable and each interaction between or among variables. The mathematical details of handling such a statistical design have been outlined in simple form by Brownlee (2). He also described other basic statistical treatments of data such as the calculations of root mean squares, the significance of differences between averages, and others. More advanced texts on statistical treatments important to the experimentalist include those of Brownlee (3), Davies (4), Johnson and Leone (5), and Youden (6).

In addition to the more precise treatment of data, the use of statistically designed experiments has at least two other advantages. One is simply the requirement to plan a series of experiments precisely. Using this technique forces one to think carefully about the choice of variables to be studied and the levels of each which should be used.

The other advantage of the design comes in the realm of communication. One can prepare a chart showing the design of experiments, filling in data as they are obtained. When a supervisor or any other interested person comes by and asks "What are you doing today?" or "How is your program coming along?" an immediate and clear answer can be given. Just bring out the chart and say, "I have worked out this design of variables which are believed to be important, and I am evaluating them at the levels shown on the chart. These are the results obtained thus far, and here are the experiments which we will do next." One can tell the whole story in just a minute or two and it will be easily understood. The impression is correctly given that the experimenter has planned carefully and is getting data which can be used to learn the maximum information for a given number of experiments.

Some additional general suggestions concerning the experimental approach are important. As one experiments he should continually re-evaluate his results and his plan to determine if changes are needed in the plan. As results are obtained which seem important, check to see if they can be duplicated. This is especially important in systems where the isolation of variables is difficult, as in polymer studies, biological systems, and other complex types. One should explore a wide range of conditions to find the sensitivity of the process, to see what would happen if one goes too far one way or the other. This knowledge will be valuable for establishing the safety requirements for the process, and also for knowledge of what not to do, and what might be the probable cause when something goes wrong.

One should always be alert for the unexpected. Such an observation is often the key to getting the results desired and also frequently leads to something of equal or greater value than the original target.

Safety for the individual and those close to him should always be an active consideration. The safety rules of the laboratory should be learned during the first days of work and should be observed.

All new operations should be reviewed for special safety precautions before they are started. One should treat all chemicals as if they are hazardous until proven otherwise. Learn what is known about the toxicity and other hazards of chemicals being used. Data of this sort is usually available in standard safety references in the library, for most familiar compounds. The supplier may have additional information. If these sources do not provide a thorough report, Chemical Abstracts should be searched.

Reporting is a regular part of every project. Verbal reports will be given from time to time, as well as interim written reports, and there should be a final report when the project is completed. Reporting will be discussed in more detail in a later chapter.

At appropriate times one should review where he has been, why he has been there, and the results he has obtained. Such a time might be at the completion of a phase of a project, at final completion, or at year's end. Careful review can assess the merits of what has been done, both from a scientific and a commercial viewpoint. Recognition of mistakes made, and their reasons, may eliminate similar mistakes in the future. An inquisitive approach, asking, "If we had a similar problem in the future, how could we solve it better?" should lead to improved planning and execution.

REASSESSMENT OF PROGRAMS AND CONTINUED PLANNING

When a new program has reached its first goal (or "checkpoint") the group leader may feel that it should be reviewed with R & D management, with the intention of deciding to stop or to expand the work, depending on the results to date and the judgment of the team. If the decision is to go ahead, then the program would include a more detailed study. For example, if the program calls for the preparation and evaluation of a particular compound of commercial interest, the following would be considered: searching for the best synthetic route, improving the yield and the purity, using commercially available and economical raw materials insofar as possible, establishing the important variables and the limits of the variables in the preferred synthetic route. During the course of this study more of the desired product would be obtained and more extensive evaluations would be made.

This work should be reviewed informally rather frequently by the group leader and less often by higher R & D management. The emphasis could be shifted at any time, depending on the results. If the study led to a product showing desirable properties, with a potential manufacturing cost which was judged to be reasonable in light of the market needs and the competition, then a more detailed review might follow. The object of this review would be to decide whether to bring development and marketing into the project activity, to keep it in the laboratory until more data were obtained, or to drop it.

If the decision is favorable, and the project is considered suitable for larger scale investigation, the program becomes bigger, more complex, and more expensive. Additional departments normally will begin to take an active role in planning or other assistance. Commercial development or some similar function in marketing will have a strong vote in whether or not the project is scaled up, since the marketing staff should be able to foresee a satisfactory market if the product is to be successful. They may also begin to make recommendations concerning the program to be sure that customers' potential questions on product quality and performance are answered. The engineering department will begin to study the R & D process data, may help design a pilot plant and make more detailed cost estimates, and will help guide the R & D process study toward the most economical process and the use of equipment which is optimum from a cost/performance viewpoint. The patent department should already have been active during the laboratory stage, but now will make more detailed studies concerning possible infringement of existing patents, the filing of suitable patent applications, and resolving any questions or problems concerning patents. The medical department will have given some consideration to toxicity and other safety hazards during the laboratory study, but will now do more extensive evaluations. Short range and long range human toxicity and ecological considerations will be made, with additional testing started as may be necessary.

The R & D program at this stage will usually be a combination of laboratory studies plus extensive pilot plant activities. The combination should provide enough technical information on how to make the product that the process can be defined adequately for the design of a plant, that all important variables are well understood, that analytical methods are available to give process control and product characterization, and that suitable equipment has been demonstrated or that design data permit the assured design of suitable equipment for a plant. During the course of this study, enough of the product should be made so that it is tested thoroughly in the applications for which it is intended. In addition, in cooperation with commercial development or marketing, samples may be provided to potential customers for their evaluation. Such testing by customers is highly valuable in making sure the product is of suitable quality for commercial use.

As a part of the program planning at this stage many companies use a checklist of important considerations, including all those mentioned above, to be sure that nothing is overlooked. The list will contain many standard entries which are suitable for all of the company's products. When considering a specific product, some entries may not be appropriate and will be crossed out. Additional items may be important, especially in the product evaluation area, and will be added. A sample R & D checklist for new fiber development is shown in Table 4. Next to each entry is shown a column where the individual responsible for that item is indicated, along with other entries which are quite important in the coordination of the program.

From the complexity of such a program it is easy to see why many companies appoint a product coordinator who has responsibility for the activities of all the departmental functions involved.

Reviews may be held at various times during such a program, perhaps quarterly, or at other intervals, depending on progress. Changes in the marketplace doubtless will occur, and commercial targets are likely to change. Some of the technical results will be better than expected and others will be poorer. The overall assessment may at any time show that the project is not worth further effort, and it may be terminated. Another frequent occurrence is that the pilot plant phase is temporarily stopped while more data are obtained in the laboratory. The targets often are shifted toward a product somewhat different from that initially envisioned. Only a small fraction of the projects started in the research laboratory reach this expanded scale. A minority of those which do reach this scale are continued on to the plant stage. Obviously the most careful and astute evaluation in the laboratory stage is desired, as are the very best planning and execution in the pilot plant stage, so that relatively few projects go through this very expensive R & D stage unsuccessfully. The expanded R & D program may well cost ten times as much, or more, than did the first laboratory evaluation. Of course, a failure at the plant stage later is even more expensive, often by another factor of five, ten, or more.

When the project reaches the stage that the following aspects are adequately complete, it is ready to be recommended for plant scale operation: the product has been characterized in terms of specifications

TABLE 4 New Product Planning Checklist

	Respon-sibility	Priority	Target date	Review status

I. RAW MATERIALS

  A. Each Purchased
    Raw Material

    1. Vendor(s)
      a. Availability
      b. Price
      c. Specifications
      d. Analytical
        methods
      e. Demonstrated
        suitability
      f. Reproducibility
      g. Problem
        identification
      h. Toxicity

  B. Each Self-produced
    Raw Material

    1. Starting Materials
      (as in A, above)

    2. Laboratory
      Process
      a. Process details
      b. Product char-
        acterization
      c. Product
        specifications
      d. Analytical
        methods
      e. Suitability for
        use
      f. Toxicity

TABLE 4 – continued

	Respon- sibility	Priority	Target date	Review status
3. Pilot Plant Stage				
a. Pilot plant design				
b. Pilot plant construction				
c. Pilot plant start-up				
d. Pilot plant operation				
e. Equipment improvements needed				
f. Raw materials (as in A, above)				
g. Process details				
h. Product characterization				
i. Product specifications				
j. Analytical and test methods				
k. Demonstrated use				
l. Uniformity for intended use				
(1) Factors affecting uniformity				
(2) Demonstration of acceptable uniformity				
m. Reports				

TABLE 4 - continued

	Respon-sibility	Priority	Target date	Review status

4. Patent Status
  a. Company applications
  b. Infringement search				

5. Economic Evaluation				
C. Toxicity and Eco-logical Evaluation				
D. Plant Status				
(Repeat items from pilot plant stage, as desired)				
II. PRODUCT PREPARATION				
A. Process Details				
1. Spinning				
2. Drawing				
3. Additional Steps				
4. Packaging				
5. Test and Analyti-cal Methods				

6. Uniformity
  a. Factors affect-ing uniformity
  b. Demon-stration of acceptable uniformity				

TABLE 4 - continued

	Respon-sibility	Priority	Target date	Review status
7. Reports				
B. Equipment				
1. Design				
2. Installation				
3. Improvements Needed				
C. Patents				
D. Economic Evaluation				
III. PRODUCTION EVALUATION				
A. Fiber Properties				
1. Fundamental Properties				
2. Specification Properties for Primary Use				
3. Properties for Secondary Use				
4. Permanence Properties a. Light exposure b. Bleaching c. Outdoor exposure				

TABLE 4 - continued

	Respon-sibility	Priority	Target date	Review status
d. Hydrolysis resistance				
e. Oxidation resistance				
f. Others				
5. Test Methods				
6. Reports				
B. Uniformity				
1. Test Methods				
2. Correlation with End Use				
C. Application Properties				
1. Dyeing				
2. Finishing				
3. Flammability				
4. Simulated Use Tests				
D. Comparison with Competitive Products				
1. With Existing Products				
2. With Forecasted Future Competitive Products				

TABLE 4 – continued

	Responsibility	Priority	Target date	Review status
E. Toxicity and Ecological Aspects				
1. Re: Humans				
2. Re: Environment				
F. Coordination with Marketing				
IV. END-USE ASPECTS				
A. Screening for Suitable End Uses				
B. Detailed Evaluation in Selected End Uses				
C. Economic Evaluation				
D. Patents				
E. Promotional Literature				
F. Coordination with Marketing				
G. Ecological Aspects				

TABLE 4 - continued

	Respon-sibility	Priority	Target date	Review status
V. PLANT DESIGN AND START-UP				
A. Coordination with Manufacturing				
B. Raw Materials				
C. Process Details				
D. Design				
E. Construction				
F. Start-up				
G. Continued Assistance to Production				
H. Economic Evaluation				
I. Ecological Aspects				
J. Coordination with Marketing				
VI. MARKET INTRODUCTION				
A. Coordination with Marketing				
B. Definition of Initial Product(s) for Sampling				

TABLE 4 - continued

	Respon-sibility	Priority	Target date	Review status
C. Preparation of Samples				
D. Promotional Literature				
E. Customer Assistance				
F. Establishment of Product(s) Suitable to Producer and Customer(s)				
1. Suitability of Process				
2. Product Specifications				
3. Patent Position				
4. Economic Review				
5. Toxicity and Ecological Review				
G. Interim Production of Selected Product(s)				
H. Assistance to Interim Production				
I. Customer Assistance on Selected Product(s)				

which, when met, give a high assurance that the product is suitable
for customer use; the product has been evaluated sufficiently in end-
use applications by the company, a contract research laboratory,
customers, or a combination of these, that it has been shown to be
suitable for the intended uses; the marketing department or commercial development department is convinced the product can be sold at
a profit and at an attractive volume of annual sales for some years
to come; a suitable process for making the product has been demonstrated, giving yields, product quality, and calculated manufacturing
cost (calculated for a plant scale) suitable for sales at the expected
profit; adequate information is available for the plant design; no
patent barriers exist; no safety or ecological barriers exist; the
overall economic evaluation shows a satisfactory profit, expressed
as return on investment or earnings per share of company stock; and
finally, the product still fits with the company's long range plan of
what its business should be. Since long range considerations and
large amounts of money are involved, the decision to go ahead with
plant production is made at high levels in the company's management.
If the amount of money to be spent for the plant is several million
dollars or more, the highest levels of authority, such as a combination including the president and the chairman of the board of directors
will usually have to approve the project.

When the approval has been given to manufacture the product,
plant design will be started by the engineering department or an
outside engineering company, if new production facilities are needed.
Even if the product can be made in an existing plant some changes in
equipment may be necessary. The R & D function at this stage
includes consulting with engineering on the plant design. Prior to
plant start-up the production team will be chosen, and R & D personnel will train the team in the operation of the process, including
actual running of the pilot plant. R & D may continue to provide
large sample quantities from the pilot plant for cooperative work
with customers. Product improvements, and additional uses for
the product, may be sought continually by R & D.

At last the plant is ready. The project moves into the stage
where the real success or failure of the industrial R & D efforts
will be demonstrated. The plant start-up is carried out by a team,
including the production personnel who will have the continuing
responsibility for operation, development personnel who have become
experts at operation of the pilot plant, and perhaps engineering representatives who have helped design the plant. Problems always
arise during the start-up of a plant, but a powerful team of well
trained people can usually solve them fairly quickly.

As soon as product is available from the plant which meets the specifications, marketing or commercial development, with help from the customer service technical group (sometimes a part of marketing, sometimes of R & D), takes the product to customers for their initial testing. Although the customers may have "approved" the product from the pilot plant, they usually want to approve it again from plant production. There is always the possibility that unidentified changes have been made inadvertently in the scale-up.

When the plant is running smoothly, making a product which is within specifications and acceptable to the customers, at a rate close to the design production rate, the start-up team is disbanded. The start-up is declared completed, and the continued operation is now the sole responsibility of production personnel. R & D and engineering personnel return to their departments and take up other assignments. Problems will continue to arise in the plant, however, and more efficient operation is always desired. For these reasons a small number of development personnel will continue to serve as consultants and "troubleshooters" for the plant.

Just as the plant needs continuing help, so will the customers. The technical group giving customer service (marketing or R & D) will continue to assist customers in the use of the product, will help increase the number of customers using the product (jointly with marketing), and will help find new applications for the product.

Only when a new product achieves continued successful use by customers, at a satisfactory profit to the producer, can R & D say that its new product efforts have been successful. "Technical success," in the sense of achievement of difficult technical targets in a professional manner, may have been achieved many times on projects which were terminated before reaching the plant stage. Technical success alone is not enough for the industrial R & D professional, however. His real raison d'etre is full commercial success of his efforts.

The stages in growth of a successful R & D new product program are illustrated in simplified form in Figure 1. In this figure one may consider that the time scale moves from left to right. The time overlap of various stages is shown intentionally, since such overlaps should occur in most well planned programs.

This section has been written with emphasis on R & D programs related to the commercialization of new products, since that is what the majority of industrial R & D efforts is directed toward. Some companies sell processes for making products, some sell plant designs, and some sell services. Each of these can be looked upon somewhat as a "product" (such as a package of information) which

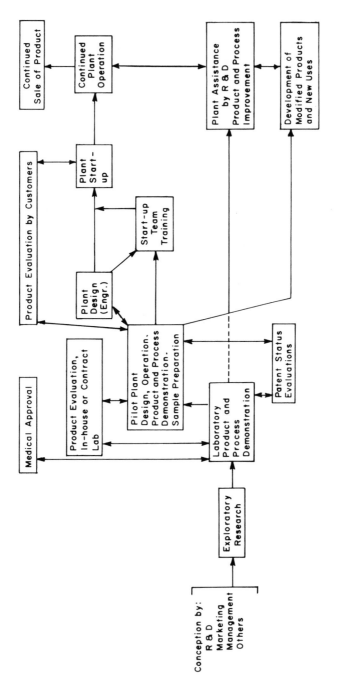

FIGURE 1 Stages of a successful R & D new product program.

is being sold, and the discussion in this section is applicable to a
large extent. Most other R & D projects, even fundamental studies,
can be looked upon as a part of the overall picture of new product
R & D.

SPECIAL PLANNING TECHNIQUES

The technical programs in industrial R & D involve several
departments before they reach commercial success. In programs
of national scope and priority such as those for national defense,
major health programs, and large construction projects, many different companies and government agencies may be involved. As the
project includes more and more groups, the development of efficient
programs, communication, and cooperation become even more
difficult. One of the best techniques which has been found for use
in such uncertain, sprawling, yet urgent situations is that known
as "PERT" (Program Evaluation and Review Technique) (7).
The PERT technique utilizes a diagram showing each significant
step required to reach the project's goal. The diagram normally
consists of a network of circles or rectangles and arrows, with each
circle representing a step, and the arrows connecting the steps that
depend on each other. By following a series of arrows it is possible
to trace through a series of steps, showing the sequence in which
some jobs must be completed before others can be started. A simple
network chart illustrating the principle is shown in Figure 2, for the
major steps previously outlined in Figure 1.
The PERT chart should be prepared in such a way that time
estimates are entered for each of the significant steps. Then by
following the longest time sequence and totalling the time one
establishes what may be called the "critical path." This is the
longest time through the network, and determines the time needed
to finish the project. A delay in this sequence will delay the whole
project, while a delay in other portions will not (unless that delay
is so long as to establish a new critical path).
It is important to remember that estimates of time for each step
are just that: estimates. It should not be expected that every estimate will be met, but revision should be made as necessary. It is
preferable to estimate a range of times, such as optimistic, probable,
and conservative, showing all three time intervals, as in Figure 2.

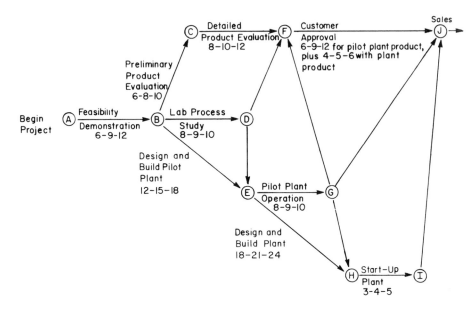

FIGURE 2   Sample PERT diagram for new product innovation
(time in months).

In addition to showing time estimates on each step of the PERT
diagram, one may add other key information if desired, such as
cost estimates and manpower requirements. The names of personnel
responsible for each step are sometimes added as well.

Quite obviously, diagrams of this sort can be very cumbersome
if one tries to show too many steps. The solution to this is to design
them in several layers of detail. The major chart would show the
overall program, with only the most important steps. Each of these
steps then could be the subprogram for another, much more detailed
diagram.

In addition to providing the planning and coordination needed for
efficient progress, these diagrams are excellent tools for communication to all levels. Management can easily see all the important
steps, with estimates of time, dollars, and manpower. The person
responsible for each step is readily shown, so it is clear where
communication concerning that step should be directed. Progress
can be indicated on the chart at regular intervals. Each person on
the program can see quickly where his own function fits in the overall
program, with whom he must coordinate, and what his targets are
in terms of expenditures and time.

Many variations on the PERT style have been used. A very helpful
one is a bar graph style, where each department's function is entered
in a chart in a rectangle, the length of which is proportional to the
time estimated for the step. The steps are all shown in a sequential
manner, so that the total elapsed time and the time overlap of steps
are readily visualized. Such a bar graph is illustrated in Figure 3.

In some situations it is recognized that a particular result must
be obtained by a certain date or it is not worth having at all. For
example, suppose a customer says it must have a component for
pollution control to meet a government requirement by the year 1975.
If you can supply it by then you can obtain a contract for the business.
If you cannot essentially guarantee to supply it by then you must tell
the customer and he will contract for it elsewhere. The planning
problem then becomes one of establishing the necessary steps to

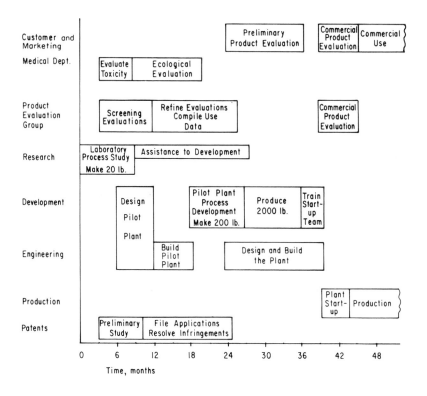

FIGURE 3. Sample bar graph diagram for new product innovation.

reach the goal and determining the time estimated for each step. One must then construct his timetable starting with 1975 and working backward to the present time. The steps must be so arranged that the critical path does not extend beyond 1975, or else the project will not be started.

Although everyone agrees in principle that good planning of projects is necessary, it is remarkable how few are well planned. Apparently there is considerable human reluctance to do one or more of the following: to think a program through in detail from start to completion, to commit oneself to an estimated timetable, to cooperate with other people well enough to permit an overall plan, and to follow a plan after it has been made.

Regardless of the system which is used, good planning is one powerful tool which can be used to improve efficiency and the probability of success. No plan alone will guarantee success. Success will not be achieved unless the project is inherently sound and unless people make it succeed.

REFERENCES

1. E. B. Wilson, An Introduction to Scientific Research, McGraw-Hill, New York, 1952.
2. K. A. Brownlee, Industrial Experimentation, Chemical Publishing Company, New York, 1953.
3. K. A. Brownlee, Statistical Theory and Methodology in Science and Engineering, 2nd Edition, Wiley, New York, 1965.
4. O. L. Davies, Design and Analysis of Industrial Experiments, Hafner, New York, 1954.
5. N. L. Johnson and F. C. Leone, Statistics and Experimental Design: In Engineering and the Physical Sciences, Wiley, New York, 1964.
6. W. J. Youden, Statistical Methods for Chemists, Wiley, New York, 1951.
7. G. N. Stilian, Pert, A New Management Planning and Control Technique, American Management Association, Report No. 74, New York, 1962.

Chapter 6

MANAGEMENT BY OBJECTIVES

In the previous chapter the need for thorough planning by an organization and various specific techniques were discussed. "Management by objectives" was mentioned as a highly valuable system for overall planning. In this chapter we shall consider this system in some detail.

This management system is currently very popular, but one could easily say that it is not at all new. For centuries people have known the desirability of establishing an objective, planning how to achieve it, trying, and evaluating their progress along the way. This in essence is what the management by objectives system is. But we must admit that knowing how to behave is not new, and is relatively easy, while actually behaving properly is more difficult. This system is designed primarily to help do things properly. One of its best features is that it involves every technical person in R & D, including the newest college graduate, in the process. Many new employees will find that their employers do not use a planning system with this name, but the system used will have many features similar to "management by objectives."

Many good references have appeared on this subject, in both journals and books. Particular attention should be called to two by Drucker (1, 2) and one by Odiorne (3). While the titles of these suggest they are written for management, the technical employee who is interested in understanding the place of R & D in the business world and in planning techniques will find them very rewarding.

THE SYSTEM OF MANAGEMENT BY OBJECTIVES

While the scope of management by objectives has already been indicated, it may be helpful to summarize in a different way just what the system is. This is a philosophy and practice of management which systematically utilizes a joint identification of common goals by the individual and his superior, defines major areas of responsibility in terms of results to be accomplished, uses these as a guide for operating the unit or the department, and uses them as yardsticks for appraising the performance of individuals.

In connection with this, the term "management" is used to mean the planning, organization, direction, and regular guidance of an effort so as to achieve a useful result. This concept of management is clearly applicable to a wide range of activities, including business, government, universities, and even one's own personal life.

In applying this system to a business, the first step is for the top management group to establish its area of activity and its assets, define its responsibilities, and set its objectives. With further regard to definitions, a "responsibility" is a statement of a major area in which results are to be achieved. An "objective" is a broad description of results to be achieved on a year-to-year basis if the responsibilities are to be met. The term "goal" is used to describe more specific results to be achieved in a given period of time, contributing toward meeting the broader objectives.

For example, let's consider a company with a long history in technical matters, especially chemistry. The first step would be to establish the responsibilities for such a company. One might tabulate these:

1. Produce and sell certain classes of products and/or services of benefit to people.
2. Create and maintain jobs.
3. Make enough profit to insure the continuation of (1) and (2).
4. Make additional contributions to the welfare of the community and country.

Having established the responsibilities of our hypothetical company, one should then analyze the assets of the organization and might find that they include the following:

1. Money
2. Certain chemical plants
3. Certain basic raw materials
4. Innovative technical personnel
5. Marketing organization oriented toward other producers

From this analysis of one's responsibilities and present position, the next step is to establish the objectives for the organization. In this case, they could logically be:

1. Produce and sell $\underline{X}$ chemicals at $\underline{Y}$ profit during the next three year period.
2. Discover, develop, and sell $\underline{M}$ new chemicals which will bring $\underline{N}$ profit in the next ten year period.
3. Enter two major new nonchemical areas requiring innovative technical approaches within five years.

These are the general objectives of the overall company. Then, progressively, smaller segments of the company, such as divisions and departments, prepare their own objectives and goals in line with the overall responsibilities and objectives of the company.

As an illustration, a division of the company might develop its own objective which would help meet the third broad objective of the company (new major nonchemical areas). Realizing its own technological position in computers and the company's responsibility toward aiding the country in suitable ways, at the same time making a profit so it can continue in operation, the division might propose to adapt its computer control of inventory handling to computerized handling of the United States mail distribution system. Such a system, if worked out satisfactorily, could be licensed to the user, thereby producing some of the profit necessary for the survival of the company.

Any such objective should be accepted only after consideration by all who would be directly concerned. An objective such as this one might well involve know-how and participation by departments such as production (which now has the inventory handling procedure), research and development, as well as engineering (departments which have computer specialists who, perhaps, could define a solution to the problem of mail distribution), and accounting (which would have to enter into the profitability of the operation). Some form of marketing effort, of course, would be necessary to sell the technology to the ultimate consumer. Representatives of each of these departments should participate in careful definition of the objective, the establishment of a timetable for reaching the objective, estimating the cost of achieving the results, and developing integrated plans for achieving the results.

Having established this objective for the division, each department should then set its own goals in line with those of other departments

and also in line with the division's objective. Each should have its
own timetable for getting results.

Some general guidelines for preparing goals are indicated below.

1. Goals should be stated in terms of results to be accomplished.
2. Goals should be challenging but not unattainable.
3. Goals should be stated as precisely as possible, preferably
   in measurable terms.
4. Goals should be stated even though all conditions for their
   accomplishment are not entirely within one's control.
5. Goals should be restricted to important results.

One of the most desirable techniques for setting goals at a particular level involves letting those who will meet a department's
objective propose what their own goals should be in order to reach
the objective and the timetable for reaching them. For example, top
management should communicate its own objectives to lower management levels, asking each lower management to present its own goals
which will permit the overall objectives to be reached. This process
is then continued down through organizational levels to include all the
technical people in R & D, and similarly in other departments. After
the initial proposals of goals and timetables have been made by each
individual, they will be reviewed by appropriate R & D group leaders
and then by the assistant directors and director. Individual and
group goals, timetables, and plans may be modified somewhat to
achieve a coherent, technically sound program for the entire
department. This program is designed to provide the necessary
R & D results to help meet the company's or the division's objectives.
This system of goal setting is illustrated in Figure 1.

It is to be emphasized that the setting of objectives is a multipath
operation. The company may have today an objective of diversifying
in a certain direction. The research scientist may have ideas as to
possible new products in the indicated direction of interest. A successful demonstration in R & D may lead to commercial results which
shape a new set of company objectives for years to come. A more
frequent example of the influence of the technical person on top level
objectives comes in the consideration of the technical possibility of
achieving certain results on a desired time schedule.

Before the R & D program is considered final, one other aspect
of the multipath nature of this system should be fulfilled. The
R & D department does not generate data for its own use but for its
"customers": marketing, production, engineering, and sometimes

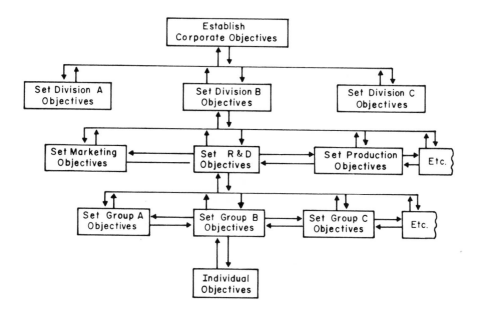

FIGURE 1 Goal setting sequences.

others. To be sure each goal and schedule in the program are correct, they should be reviewed with the department or group that will
use the data. Agreement should be obtained that the goals, when
achieved on schedule, will provide what is needed. Thus each goal
and schedule should have the approval of those who will meet the
goal, the management responsible for the program, and the user
of the information to be gained (Figure 2).

In summary, then we may say that the setting of objectives and
goals involves the following steps:

1. Define responsibilities.
2. Analyze assets.
3. Establish challenging but reasonable objectives and goals, to
    fulfill responsibilities, with a timetable for each.
4. Give each unit which will be called upon to help reach an
    objective or a goal a voice in setting it.
5. Allow each unit which must utilize the results to participate
    in setting the objective or goal.

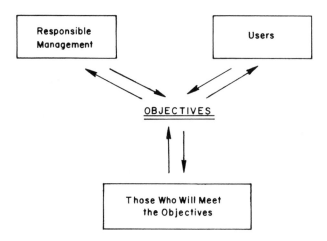

FIGURE 2 Setting objectives and review.

   6. Compare and coordinate the objectives, goals, and timetables
      of all units to be sure that they mesh properly in timing, in
      providing desired results, and in their demands on other units.
   7. Review progress and goals frequently and make adjustments
      as necessary.

The process just described for setting objectives, goals, and
timetables is simply that of good planning, whatever it may be called.
Now let's consider how this operation can be of benefit in communication and coordination. Communication within the organization is
desirable, of course, and what could be better to communicate than
the objectives and goals of the organization, at each level?

One of the current theories of human behavior is that people
basically want to do a good job. A problem that often arises, however, is that they don't really know what is expected of them or what
is needed by their organization. An obvious solution to this particular
problem is to communicate the objectives and goals of the organization
and explain why they were chosen. If the technique of management by
objective is properly followed, there will be objectives and goals for
every level of operation, so that each one knows what is needed and
when, as well as why. People operating under such a system are
likely to feel more secure, to have a better team spirit, and to trust
their organization, since they will have clear reason for believing
that their leaders know where they are going.

Another important feature of the goal-setting process is an inherent part of good communications. If each individual has contributed to the setting of the goals which he must meet, he will almost surely feel like an integral part of the organization. He has been given an opportunity to express opinions, his opinions have been considered, and the good ones which fit the overall program have been accepted. Furthermore, he has been given the opportunity to propose his own timetable, and wherever possible this has been accepted. It actually works out that in many cases the individual proposes too fast a timetable and the manager has to add additional time to it. This type of procedure eliminates much of the opportunity for an individual's feeling that he is just a "number" in an operation, that his opinions are neither considered nor sought, and that he is pushed into a "rat race" over which he has no control.

Again, within the organization coordination is an essential function, and one which can be achieved by the joint preparation of objectives, goals, and timetables. Consider the manager who is responsible for several phases of an operation: if the management by objectives procedure is followed, he has a list of goals, each with a timetable, from each department or section concerned. He also knows the company's overall objectives and timetable. He can easily fit these together into whatever form is convenient for him to see that they are properly scheduled with regard to all aspects of timing. He could have them organized in one of the chart forms discussed in the previous chapter, if desired.

Communication outside the organization is also essential in nearly every case. Nearly all of us are involved in some way with the public, either directly or indirectly. As a result, public understanding and support of our efforts are needed. Communication of objectives is certainly one way of helping the public understand what one is trying to do. While we might think of this as being most obviously true for the politician, it is also quite true for industry, the police force, as well as for our educational system, and very nearly all other forms of activity. Certainly, well thought out objectives which are reasonable and which are thoroughly explained prior to an event can go a long way toward achieving a fair and realistic assessment of the situation by the public. Such an assessment in the long run is essential for real public support.

A third area in which the management by objectives procedure is beneficial is in evaluation. A program, including the results achieved, may be readily evaluated in terms of progress toward previously established goals. Some programs fail, of course. For the future benefit of the organization it is certainly desirable to learn from

this experience of failing. An analysis of the cause of failure, whether
in the selection of the goal, in the work performed in an attempt to
reach the goal, or in the suitability of facilities for permitting achievement of the goal will be essential for a meaningful analysis. It is
also highly valuable to review successful programs and analyze the
real reasons for success, so that more emphasis can be placed upon
factors favoring success in the future.

RIG DOCUMENTS

   In addition to evaluating programs, an individual's performance
can be evaluated in terms of his completion of his goals. In order
to do this in the best way, it is useful to take the system one step
further, adding "indicators" for each goal. Addition of the indicators
is merely the addition of quantitative statements indicating the extent
to which the individual has achieved his goals. (Some prefer to
associate the indicators with the responsibilities, as a measure of
how well these are fulfilled.) We now have three elements for each
person to analyze for himself: his responsibilities, his goals, and
the indicators of how well he has achieved his goals. In order to
take full advantage of the management by objectives system, all
three should be developed by and for each technical person in R & D.
A recommended procedure is to have each one prepare his own
"RIG" document (responsibilities, indicators, goals) for each year.
This is done as a part of the previously described goal-setting
approach to the development of the R & D program.
   Analysis of nearly all technical R & D positions shows the following areas of individual responsibility: the technical program, relationships with others, innovation, personal development, and safety.
Those who have at least one person reporting to them, whether that
one is technical or not, have the additional responsibility of the
development of subordinates. Finally, those in administrative
positions have an obvious responsibility for administration. Each
person should develop one or more goals to match each responsibility,
and one or more indicators to measure the degree of success in
reaching each goal. The goals should be stated very clearly, with
quantitative terms wherever possible. The indicators, in particular,
should be quantitative measures of progress if at all possible. In a

few cases, the indicator may have to be subjective, however, such as
"opinion of my boss."

An illustrative RIG document is shown in Table 1 for someone such
as a director, assistant director, or manager in charge of several
research groups, who is responsible primarily for improvements in
existing products and the discovery of related new products. Table 2
shows a typical RIG document for an R & D group leader, and Table 3
shows one for an analytical chemist in R & D. The technical goals
for each would be developed as previously described and attached as
parts of the documents shown. Illustrative goals, related to the
hypothetical company of Chapter 5, are included. These goals would
be changed annually or more frequently if desired, whereas most or
all of the remainder of the document should be appropriate for several
years. These tables illustrate the RIG principles for typical levels
in R & D functions.

The complete RIG document should also have columns available
for adding comments at the end of the year. One column should be
available for a concise statement of results achieved, compared to
each goal. Another column should have space available for a statement of causes why a goal was not reached, if such was the case
(perhaps the goal was changed, or possibly it proved unattainable
by known techniques).

With the completion of the RIG at the end of the year, the individual is ready to review his performance for himself and also with
his superior. Following that review, he is then well prepared to
draft a new RIG document for the coming year.

PERFORMANCE APPRAISAL

The value of performance appraisals for individuals has been
widely recognized, if not universally used. The individual wants to
and should know how well he is performing in the eyes of his superior
and what he should do to improve. The group leader and other
administrators are not fulfilling their responsibilities unless they
appraise their subordinates' performance and coach them in ways
which will lead to further development of each individual. Good
appraisals are not easy to achieve, however. When these are based
largely on subjective judgments such as a person's industriousness,

TABLE 1 Performance Planning: R & D Managerial Level

Job responsibilities	Indicators	Goals
I. TECHNICAL PROGRAM	1. Achieve at least 7 of 10 major goals on schedule. 2. Achieve at least 50% of 2 additional goals.	1. Goals are detailed in Research Program Proposal. Ten key goals are attached.
II. RELATIONSHIPS	1. Integration of research plans and programs with other sections and departments. 2. Reputation of section with marketing and other departments. 3. Reputation of section in the company.	1. Keep R & D management, other R & D sections, and commercial development informed of plans and progress, at least on a monthly and annual basis, more often on critical items. 2. Communicate and participate with other departments, especially marketing, on a "need to know and/or help" basis. 3. Communicate with, seek help from, and cooperate with other technical departments in the company in guiding and expediting our programs.
III. INNOVATIONS	1. Number of potential new and modified products or processes which have passed laboratory exploratory stage (Goals 1 and 2).	1. Develop commercially suitable products related to but not based on present products for sale in 1975–1980.

2. Number of new and modified products or processes recommended for pilot plant evaluation (Goals 1 and 2).

3. Number and significance of invention disclosures (Goals 1 and 2).

4. Number and significance of patent applications filed (Goals 1 and 2).

5. Number of significant nonpatentable technical innovations (Goal 3).

6. Number of innovations in nontechnical areas (Goal 3).

2. Make significant improvements in present products.

3. Make smaller scale innovations in the daily research and in the administration of research.

IV. ADMINISTRATION

1-3. Existence of five year and one year plans and budget. Stay within budget.

1. Have a five year research plan, revised at least annually.

2. Have a detailed annual research program and budget based on objectives coordinated with R & D, commercial development, and marketing.

3. Staff, equip, and organize to meet the program.

(continued)

TABLE 1 - continued

Job responsibilities	Indicators	Goals
	4. Morale of staff. Number of desirable staff members who have resigned. Number of section contributions to professional functions (publications, lectures, etc).	4. Maintain a professional research atmosphere in the section.
V. DEVELOPMENT OF SUBORDINATES	1. Number of personal discussions held.	1. Personally conduct discussions with each technical man relative to his desires, morale, performance, and recommendations for improvements in the section.
	2. Number attending technical meetings and training programs.	2. Send 50% of technical staff to a professional meeting or training program.
	3. Existence and quality of refresher program.	3. Maintain a technical refresher program during the academic year.
	4. Number of special training courses.	4. Provide special training opportunities where appropriate for individual development.

VI.	PERSONAL DEVELOPMENT	1. Extent of application and customer knowledge gained.	1. Increase familiarity with major product applications.
		2. Knowledge and utilization of other technology in our program.	2. Continue study of earlier and current technical developments related to our products.
		3. Number of professional contributions or activities.	3. Continue participation in professional activities outside the company.
VII.	SAFETY	1. Number of lost-time accidents.	1. No lost-time accidents.
		2. Number of serious accidents.	2. No serious accidents.
		3. Frequency of safety inspections, programs, etc.	3. Have a safety program to include some function monthly.

(continued)

Attachment to Table 1

Research Department Goals

1. Demonstrate a commercially suitable foam process having 20% greater productivity in existing plant equipment, without sacrifice of foam properties.

2. Demonstrate a foam process improvement which gives a 10% reduction in foam manufacturing cost, at equal foam properties (may be done jointly with objective number 1).

3. Demonstrate in the laboratory a foam with mechanical properties equivalent to foam A but with flame resistance sufficient to pass test D; translate to the plant.

4. Demonstrate in the laboratory a flexible foam system having a tough, continuous skin as an integral part of the foam, suitable for automotive padding, not requiring any added protective covering layer; translate to the plant.

5. Demonstrate a process improvement capable of giving a 20% increase in fiber plant capacity within two years.

6. Demonstrate a process improvement capable of giving a 20% increase in adhesive plant capacity within two years.

7. Provide customer service on short range projects selected jointly with marketing, on fibers, adhesives, and foams.

8. Find at least three new products worth extensive laboratory evaluation, in the group consisting of foams, fibers, adhesives, and combinations of materials serving the same functions as seats, safety padding, and safety devices for the protection of passengers in vehicles.

9. Establish a long range forecasting activity related to transportation products of potential interest to the company.

10. Identify at least one long range project related to transportation needs in the next decade and of potential interest to the company.

TABLE 2 Performance Planning: R & D Group Leader

Job responsibilities	Indicators	Goals
I. TECHNICAL PROGRAM AND INNOVATION	1. Written documentations. Achieve at least 10 of the 14 goals on schedule, not more than 2 months late on 3 others.	1. Annual technical goals are attached. 2. Revise goals of the group when necessary to keep objectives in line with the rest of R & D.
II. RELATIONSHIPS	1. Monthly progress reports, memos, and frequent verbal progress reports.	1. Keep manager well informed.
	2. Project reports on all projects within 2 months of work completion. Memos on urgent and minor items.	2. Report research findings.
	3. Percentage of high priority goals achieved.	3. Cooperate with other areas to expedite programs.
	4. Log book and correspondence.	4. Maintain communication with specialty chemical companies.

(continued)

TABLE 2 – continued

Job responsibilities	Indicators	Goals
III. INNOVATIONS	1a. Number and significance of novel concepts. 1b. Number and significance of invention disclosures.	1. Use 10% of working time generating and evaluating novel concepts.
IV. ADMINISTRATION	1. Appraisals filed with personnel. 2. Data transmitted to assistant director. 3. Expenses within budget or higher level authorization to exceed budget. 4. Percentage of high priority goals achieved. 5. Verbal communication with assistant director.	1. Appraise performance of group members. 2. Prepare expense and capital estimates for group. 3. Control group expenses. 4. Assign manpower to meet highest priority technical goals. 5. Make salary recommendations for the members of the group.
V. DEVELOPMENT OF PERSONNEL	1. Existence of documents. 2. Written annual review.	1. All professional employees prepare RIGs. 2. Review RIG documents informally with professionals quarterly and formally at year-end.

3. Meetings attended.	3. Professionals attend appropriate technical meetings at least every 2 years.
4. Courses taken.	4. Group members take special courses where appropriate.
5. Time spent in directing subordinates.	5. Make a conscientious effort to give all subordinates more responsibility.

VI. SELF-IMPROVEMENT

1. Meetings attended.	1. Attend at least 1 technical meeting.
2. Number of activities.	2. Participate in at least 3 professional and civic groups.
3. Utilization of knowledge in technical program.	3. Become knowledgeable in product application technology.

VII. SAFETY

1. Safety meeting reports.	1. All personnel attend monthly safety meeting.
2. Safety meeting reports.	2. Rotate monthly safety program among personnel.
3. Number of accidents.	3. Maintain safe work habits.
4. Housekeeping inspection reports.	4. Maintain clear work area.

(continued)

Attachment to Table 2

Group Leader's Goals

1. Demonstrate in the laboratory a foam with mechanical properties equivalent to foam A but with flame resistance sufficient to pass test D; translate to the plant.

   A. Screen nonreactive flame retardants which are commercially available, in the foam A system; by April 1.
   B. Screen reactive flame retardants which are commercially available, in the foam A system; by April 1.
   C. Evaluate changes in the major resin component of the foam A system, to give better flame resistance at the same mechanical properties, by June 1.
   D. Select the two best approaches, evaluate in machine foaming in molded and slab stock form; by August 1.
   E. Optimize the best system from (D), scaling up to the largest R & D foam machine; by October 1.
   F. Translate to plant production; by December 1.
   G. Prepare draft of sales literature on the properties and uses of the new foam; by December 15.

2. Demonstrate in the laboratory a flexible foam system having a tough, continuous skin as an integral part of the foam, suitable for automotive padding, not requiring any added protective covering layer; translate to the plant.

   A. Explore foam modifications giving collapse of foam structure at the mold surface, giving a tough integral skin; by April 1.
   B. Adapt at least one of the techniques from (A) for use in automotive foam padding systems; by July 1.
   C. Optimize the system selected in (B); by November 1.
   D. Translate to the plant; by December 1.
   E. Demonstrate techniques for coloring the foam skin to match customer requirements; by December 1.
   F. Prepare draft of sales literature on new padding systems; by December 15.

3. Exploratory

   A. Find at least one new foam product or system worth extensive research evaluation; by December 31.

TABLE 3 Performance Planning: Analytical Chemist

Job responsibilities	Indicators	Goals
I. TECHNICAL PROGRAM	1. Meet at least 90% of goals.	1. Goals are detailed on attached sheet (to be changed as requested by Group Leader).
II. RELATIONSHIPS	1. Number of client complaints.	1. Maintain reputation of group by quality of work.
	2. Reputation throughout R & D.	2. Maintain liaison with R & D personnel needing analytical consultation or services.
	3. Reports on schedule.	3. Provide group leader with written monthly progress report.
	4. Reports issued.	4. Issue method reports within 2 months of completion of work.
III. INNOVATIONS	1. Number and significance achieved.	1. Make at least three technical innovations to solve analytical (or measurement) problems not amenable to conventional or known techniques.
	2. Increased efficiency.	2. Make at least one innovation in work procedures or recordkeeping for analytical service to reduce time spent or cost of work

(continued)

TABLE 3 – continued

Job responsibilities	Indicators	Goals
IV. DEVELOPMENT OF PERSONNEL	1. Number completed.	1. Introduce subordinates to at least 2 new techniques by year end.
	2. Meet RIG timetable.	2. Familiarize subordinates with goals and timing via RIG document.
V. PERSONAL DEVELOPMENT	1. RIG document completion, number of reviews on schedule.	1. Prepare RIG document and review quarterly with group leader.
	2. Journals read.	2. Keep abreast of technical literature averaging 10 hr/mo in library.
	3. Attendance at meeting.	3. Attend a technical meeting or short course in 1972.
VI. SAFETY	1. Number of accidents.	1. No lost time accidents or serious injuries.
	2. Number of meetings attended.	2. Attend at least 6 safety meetings.

Attachment to Table 3

Goals for Analytical Chemist

1. Develop analytical methods for iron, nickel, and tin in Foam A,
at 1-30 ppm level, ±3 ppm; by April 1.

2. Develop analytical methods for phosphorus, bromine and chlorine
in flame-retarded foam A system, at 0.5%-15% levels, ±0.1%; by
June 1.

3. Analyze decomposition products from two best candidate flame-
retarded foam A systems, arising from a) thermal decomposition,
b) hydrolysis, and c) combustion; by September 1.

4. Repeat (3) with final system for flame-retarded foam A; by
November 15.

5. Analyze decomposition products from simulated exposure of
flame-retarded foam A to aging on the city dump; by December 1.

6. Provide nonroutine analyses for heavy metals, P, Br, and Cl, as
needed, with no sample delays longer than two weeks.

loyalty, intelligence, etc., they are particularly difficult for all but
the most skilled administrators who have very close knowledge of
the individual being appraised. The management by objectives system, utilizing RIG documents or similar approaches, is a very useful
tool to provide a more easily measurable basis for appraisals. The
main emphasis is on the achievement of mutually selected goals.

It is recommended that the individual's RIG document be jointly
reviewed by the individual and his superior quarterly during the year,
or at other suitable intervals. Most especially, however, the document should be completed at year's end by the individual himself.
He should state briefly the progress and results achieved with regard
to each goal and any underlying reasons for not achieving those which
were not reached. In so doing, he rates himself against his own
goals. Having done this, he reviews his completed document with
his superior. Any differences of opinion should be resolved at this
time and noted on the document.

This jointly completed RIG document forms an excellent basis for
a performance appraisal discussion between the individual and his
superior. Most of the judgment of performance can be based on how

the individual went about reaching his goals. (For more discussion of desirable personal and work characteristics, see Chapters 4 and 12.)

It is readily apparent that this approach to performance appraisal is a joint one, between the individual and his superior. The individual has participated in setting his own goals and time schedules for reaching them. He also makes the initial judgment of his own performance in reaching those goals. In practice, his judgment is often harsher than that of his superior. The superior, rather than being a judge, is more of a coach who helps the individual to reach his goals as nearly as possible, and is a counselor in guiding the individual toward more challenging goals and further development.

No performance appraisal or personal development system is perfect or applicable to all situations. All of them depend upon the willingness of the people involved to try to use them successfully. The RIG system is no exception. Some of the pitfalls are indicated below.

The complete recognition of individual responsibilities is necessary, particularly if the RIG document is to represent the full range of considerations relative to an individual's performance in the current job and his preparation for future jobs of a different nature. Similarly, the proper selection of goals and indicators should cover what is really expected of the individual in all major areas (many minor functions will not be listed). If these are done correctly, then the extent to which he reaches those goals should coincide closely with the superior's actual appraisal of both performance and potential for further development. Ideally the individual should be able to ask, "What must I do to get a promotion?" and receive a meaningful answer. He should be able to formulate with his superior a set of goals, which if met, will qualify him for the promotion (or other desired change). In some cases, it is exceedingly difficult to provide such a clear-cut analysis; but the administrator, in particular, should continually strive for this degree of analytical thinking in dealing with his staff.

The difficulty of achieving goals will vary from one project to another, and the RIG document must not be used simply as a "score card" for raises or promotions. The individual's superior, or other R & D management close to the individual's program, may rightly use the RIG in making an appraisal of the individual's performance. That appraisal may correctly be reviewed by others, e.g., in the personnel department, in connection with raises and promotions, but the RIG should not. There is too much technical judgment involved in deciding how difficult the goals were and the validity of reasons for not reaching the goals in some cases, for anyone other than an expert in the field to reach a judgment on these points.

In some cases the goals may be set so vaguely, or with such an easy-to-achieve level of results, that they lose value in performance appraisal (and more importantly, in the results achieved). This is particularly likely to be true if people feel the RIG is, indeed, used as a score card in personnel evaluations. As indicated before, goals should be set at a difficult but theoretically achievable level. If this is done, most people will not achieve all of the goals 100%, on time. This is especially true in exploratory research and new product R & D. To emphasize these features of goal setting, the R & D management should recognize the same features in their own RIG document preparations, stating that some projected percentage of goals, less than 100%, will be reached (see Table 1).

NONINDUSTRIAL APPLICATIONS

The management by objectives system which has been outlined can be used in total or in part in the management of many functions in addition to industrial operations. Application of this system to the operation of a university, for example, could do much to clarify its role for administration, faculty, students, and the public. A clear statement of responsibilities and objectives would be of great benefit to students and parents who are trying to select a suitable university for attendance. Taxpayers would understand better what their tax dollars are being used for in education. The RIG document could be an answer for those educators who feel that it is not practical to reward teachers on a merit basis because of inadequate standards of measuring performance.

Agencies dealing with the public in sensitive areas, and needing public understanding and support, could make use of this system. The clear communication of goals to the public, with schedules and indicators of progress, would be extremely helpful in our approach toward pollution control, for example.

"Management," in the sense of this chapter, can be applied to one's personal life as well as to the functions of groups. If one wishes to enjoy his life to the fullest and have it be meaningful for others, he will do well to analyze his responsibilities and set goals

and indicators for himself. Individual responsibilities certainly
include one or more for himself, and one or more for others. The
individual should try conscientiously to work out his own responsibilities, as he sees them, and should update his statement of them
at least every few years. Our religions, philosophies, and literature,
which are all rather closely interwoven, provide many guides.

Having identified, at least temporarily, his responsibilities,
goals should be formulated. As in a technical program, they may be
expected to change with time; some may be short range and some may
be long range. A list might include such items as the following:

1. Do the best you can with what you have.
2. Create and maintain a home based on love, trust, cooperation,
   and religious guidance.
3. Do the best possible in one's current job.
4. Broaden one's knowledge and experience in his field of work.
5. Make a contribution to the community.
6. Enjoy a hobby.

Other goals could be selected or other descriptive terms used.
However, a range such as this would certainly guide one in leading
a full life, of real benefit to himself, to his family, and to his community; would insure a balance of interest and activities that would
provide a strengthening and stabilizing background in difficult times;
and would utilize the talents with which each of us has been endowed.

REFERENCES

1. P. F. Drucker, The Practice of Management, Harper and Row,
   New York, 1954.
2. P. F. Drucker, Managing for Results, Harper and Row, New
   York, 1964.
3. G. S. Odiorne, Management by Objectives, A System of Managerial Leadership, Pitman, New York, 1965.

Chapter 7

CREATIVITY

WHAT IS CREATIVITY?

Creativity is an essential feature of research and development.
Indeed, it is a highly desirable aspect of most activities in life and
adds greatly to the pleasure of living. It is found in many forms and
a full spectrum of magnitudes. The Nobel Prize winner in his laboratory, the author of an imaginative book, the artist, the housewife
making an attractive meal from leftovers, the small child at play
with his blocks, the soldier surviving in a hostile jungle--these and
many more utilize creativity for personal enjoyment, to give pleasure
to others, to sustain life, and to help make life the deeply satisfying
experience it can be. It is no wonder that creativity has been a
subject of great interest to many people and that there is a wide
range of literature about it. This chapter attempts to present a
summary with its major emphasis on creativity as it is related to
the industrial scientist and technologist.

Some authors, in writing about creativity, are interested primarily in the mental processes involved, while othere are more
concerned with tangible results. We will consider each briefly.
For our purposes, one useful result-oriented definition is that of
Stein: "Creativity is the process resulting in a novel work that is
acceptable as tenable or useful or satisfying by a group at some
point in time " (1). It is noteworthy that the judgment is made by a
group. In line with this, there is usually surprising agreement
among R & D people when asked to name the creative members of
their organization, even though many have difficulty giving a satisfactory definition of what they mean by creativity. It is also significant that the concept of novelty here means that the work is novel to
the individual or group involved; it does not have to be new throughout

the world. In fact, we often find that major, highly creative break-throughs are made almost simultaneously in several parts of the world.

Hanford, in another interesting article on the subject (2), says that "Originality...is usually achieved by taking a number of dissim-ilar facts which are apparently unconnected and finding some way to bring them into a unified picture. The larger the number of factors which can be brought into focus, the greater the degree of originality."

The definition given by Hanford emphasizes the "synthetic" thought processes in creativity, the combining of known elements in a new way to give a novel result. Analytical thought is also a highly important part of creativity. This thought process leads to a separation of a problem, a composite, or a situation into its component parts, with an examination of the parts to find out their nature, proportion, function, and interrelationships. The analytical thought is most helpful in defining a problem to be solved, a goal to be reached, or the nature and significance of an unexpected discovery. The synthetic thought process may then dominate, combining available knowledge and experimentally obtained data to provide a novel result, thus completing the creative process.

A term which is related to creativity, and often used in industry, is "innovation." This term is used to mean the introduction of some-thing novel, e.g., a new product. As such it includes the creative events as well as the application of more routine techniques in bring-ing the novel item from its first conception to a useful state, such as commercial manufacture and sale.

One of the best reports which gives a feeling for the essence of creativity is the feature article of Time magazine on January 2, 1961. Time had selected the creative research investigator as its "Man of the Year" and specifically named fifteen men from various aspects of science and engineering. The report presents creative research and people in such a way as to give a far better feeling for the real meaning of creativity than any dictionary definition ever will. Some of the comments from individuals were especially illuminating. Willard Libby, Nobel laureate of 1960, for example, said,..."We scientists are the only people who are not bored, the adventurers of modern times, the real explorers, the fortunate ones...*

A few comments by some other Nobel laureates, some of their opinions of themselves and why they have done the wonderfully crea-tive work that they have done, follow. Robert Woodward, professor of organic chemistry at Harvard, is famed for synthesis of quinine, cholesterol, and chlorophyll and for the theory of conservation of

---

*Reprinted by permission from TIME, The Weekly Newsmagazine; Copyright Time Inc.

orbital symmetry. He seeks no practical application for his work but said,..."I am just fascinated by chemistry. I am in love with it. I don't feel the need for a practical interest to spur me..."* And another Nobel laureate at MIT, Charles Stark Draper, an engineer in aeronautics and astronautics, described himself as nothing more than... "a greasy-thumb mechanic type of fellow..."* Another one is William Shockley, of Bell Laboratories, 1956 Nobel laureate for creating the transistor, jointly with two other physicists. In contrast to Woodward's interest without application, Shockley said,..."We simply wouldn't start the research if no application were seen..."*

The lives, interests, and opinions of such individuals show clearly that the highly creative people of the world represent a wide range of types. This supports the view that there is an element of creativity in all of us, even though the heights to which we rise may not include a Nobel Prize. It is hoped that this chapter will help each reader to understand the creative process somewhat better and guide him in making the best of the creative talent which he has.

SOME CHARACTERISTICS OF THE CREATIVE PERSON

Psychologists have studied creativity and creative people for a number of years, and many books have appeared on the subject. One point of debate has been the effect of age, with agreement on some aspects and disagreement on others. Nearly everyone agrees that creativity is manifested at an early age. The imagination of many preschool children is certainly a wonderful thing to enjoy. It is also agreed that judgment comes more slowly, reaching a peak level much later in life than the peak in creativity. Perhaps the best results are achieved when both creativity and judgment are at a considerable level. In any case, high productivity of creative results extends throughout all or nearly all of the working years for many individuals.

It has frequently been said that one is most creative up to about age thirty or thirty-five, with significant novel results declining notably after that. Others have vigorously disputed this. Dennis concluded that the age decade of the forties is the most productive, while the thirties and fifties also are generally very good (3). Berenson has emphasized the value of insight, thought, and stability provided by older personnel (4). Michelangelo and Leonardo da Vinci, two of the world's giants of creativity, were highly productive

---

*Reprinted by permission from TIME, The Weekly Newsmagazine; Copyright Time Inc.

essentially until the times of their deaths at age 89 and 67, respectively.

There are many examples of individuals who have essentially stopped being creative by the time they reached thirty-five. Sometimes the reasons may have been beyond the control of the individual, such as poor health. It is probable that in most cases the individual stopped trying to be creative, due to the burden of too many routine chores which apparently needed doing. The fact that many people have maintained their creativity to an advanced age suggests that most of us can also, at least to some extent. The key to success here is perhaps the conscious effort to do so.

Both psychologists and scientists have tried to identify the significant personal characteristics of creative people. The following are some of the conclusions with which most such students agree. Creative people are highly intelligent and intellectually curious. They ask probing questions, such as "Why did this occur?" and "What would happen if I do it some other way?" They are able to recognize problems and define them clearly and accurately. They put information together in many different ways to reach an acceptable solution to a problem. They tend to be unorthodox, to question conventional ideas, and to resent tight authoritative control by others. They have courage and perseverance and are willing to defend different ideas and concepts with great persistence. Mental restlessness, intensity, and strong personal motivation are common. Although they are restless, their intensity and motivation are reflected in their tendency to be very absorbed in their favorite projects until success is achieved. In this they are goal-oriented, are obsessed with reaching that goal, and are impatient with anything that gets in the way.

Some have suggested that creative people, consciously or unconsciously, depend largely on the synthetic thought processes and may be weak in the analytical aspects. Other students of the subject disagree, stressing the importance of both. The latter opinion seems more valid, in science at least. As will be pointed out later, a careful analysis of the problem to be solved is frequently much of the real foundation for developing a novel solution. Again, the life work of daVinci is a wonderful example of one who was a master at both analytical and synthetic processes.

There is another consideration on which everyone, whether his field of study be religion, psychology, or genetics, agrees. That is, each individual has a limitation as to what he can do. Regardless of the function, whether it is athletics, music, art, or creativity, there will be some relation to a person's age. Without trying to define the

scale or what the units are, it will probably be something like the
relationship shown in Figure 1. Each individual has a range in which
he can operate. The breadth of the range will vary, the scale and
the time will vary, as will the rate at which the individual reaches a
high level, the time during which he maintains his maximum creativity, and the rate at which this falls off. But what we would like to
emphasize is that there are ways to help the individual operate in the
top part of his range, so that with proper training, effort, and opportunity, each one will do the best he can with the talents he has
available.

CREATIVITY IN CONFLICT

   Those who study creativity realize immediately that creativity is
in conflict with many things. Creativity inevitably means change.
If one is going to create something new, whether it be a thoery, a
product, or a way of doing things, almost surely it is going to dis-
place something that already exists, and thus will be in conflict with
what exists. I am sure we have all recognized in ourselves, and
especially in others, that it is a rather common human trait to
respond negatively to change, If somebody presents us too abruptly

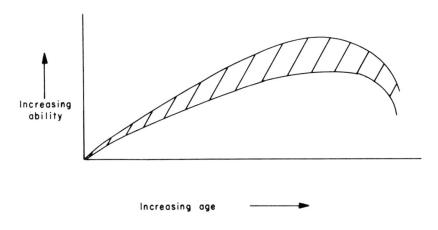

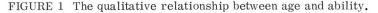

FIGURE 1   The qualitative relationship between age and ability.

with a new idea, many of us react at first by saying, "No," "It won't
work," "It can't be done," or something of that sort. Very often it
is easier to sell a novel concept in smaller steps, but even with this
approach resistance may be expected.

A second form of conflict which is sometimes encountered in
R & D is that between creativity and detailed program planning. Some
managers feel that very detailed planning of a program, extremely
close following of a plan, and very close control are desirable in
achieving results. This may be encountered more often, perhaps,
with management which does not have technical experience. While
this approach is sometimes suitable in the latter stages of an innovative sequence, in extremes it stifles creativity.

Many surveys have indicated that freedom to choose one's research
subject is rated highly as an important element in stimulating
creativity. It is very rare in industry that one is completely free in
making such a choice. Considerable freedom (for productive investigators) is often found within a particular subject area of major interest
to the employer. If the creative person is to be happy with industrial
employment, he will want to find an employer who wants innovations
in subject areas in which that person is already interested or is
willing to become interested.

The demand of relatively routine detail often conflicts with one's
creative interests. Nearly everyone has more which he needs to do
or can do than he has time available to do it. Thus, selections must
be made of what will and what will not be done. For some it is easier
to attend to the day-to-day "necessities" of detail, postponing other
things which are not so urgent, such as reading and thinking. This
is one of the reasons so many "technical managers" lose their technical expertise. It is a tendency which nearly all in R & D must be
aware of, and should resist.

CREATIVITY IN ACTION

Problem Solving

Creativity seems to manifest itself as a novel response to a
desire to do something. The artist may feel the need to create and
so produces his work of art: a painting, sculpture, book, or other

form of art. Sometimes such a response does not include the visualization of a clearly defined goal as one of the first steps. The
exploratory scientist, searching for something new and useful, does
not always have a clearly defined goal other than to search in a particular area of knowledge. In many cases what he eventually finds
is not what he originally considered as a likely result. Most people
in industrial R & D do have specific goals in their experimental
searching, however. One can state these goals in the terms of
problems to be solved, hence techniques of problem solving provide
an excellent guide for the average technical person to increase his
use of creative ability. One successful approach to creative problem
solving is outlined below. Some people appear to have this or a
similar system already "programmed" into their thinking, so that
they develop solutions without consciously going through any such
thought sequence. This outline will not be very useful for such people,
but may be a helpful guide for those who are not satisfied with their
creative problem solving ability, and wish to develop it further.

1. Define the Problem

   The first step in solving a problem is to define it accurately and
reliably. One should be especially alert to the possibility that the
first description of the problem which is received may not be correct,
or simply may not be adequate. If one is formulating a research
program, for example, each problem or goal in it should be stated
in clear terms and in sufficient detail that it has the same meaning
for research management, for those who will solve the problem by
experimental approaches, and for those who will use the results.
This was discussed more fully in Chapter 5 on program planning.
   The following example illustrates a case where a problem was
actually different from its original description. A plastics molder
once complained that a particular thermoplastic which was received
in 250-pound containers was not of uniform quality throughout each
container. This appeared to be the problem, and a suitable solution
would have been to blend the polymer particles more thoroughly
before filling the shipping containers. On closer examination, however, the problem was found to be different. The thermoplastic was
found to be sensitive to hydrolysis during melt processing, if more
than about 0.05% water were present in the polymer. The molder
was opening the 250-pound container several times, each time
removing about 50 pounds of polymer and charging it to the hopper

of his injection molding machine. Relative humidity was not controlled
in the molding area. The rate of water absorption by the polymer
was quite rapid at 60% RH and above. Thus on rainy days, in particular, the polymer absorbed water from the air each time the
container was opened. The first 50-pound sample taken from the
container had about 0.03% water content, but the last sample had as
much as 0.10% water. The injection molding results did vary as
polymer was withdrawn from the shipping container, but not because
the original contents were not uniform. One solution was to keep the
polymer thoroughly dry in the container, during transfer to the molding machine, and in the hopper of the machine. A more practical
solution was to package the polymer in 50-pound units so that each
package was opened just once in filling the hopper of the machine.

Properly defining the problem often requires careful study and
analytical thought. Understanding the true nature of the problem to
be solved is obviously essential. If the problem is one of malfunction
(as the above example), an understanding of the abnormality and of
its cause is necessary. If a single person is to solve a particular
problem, he should be capable of analytical thinking to define the
problem and of synthetic thinking to find solutions for it. If such a
person is not available, it may be necessary to assign a team, with
one or more members who are analytical in approach and others
proposing the solutions.

In the case of a malfunction, one does well to approach the
problem analysis with the aid of Kipling's "honest serving men,"
asking "Who? What? Where? When? How? and in analyzing the
cause, "Why?" It is also quite helpful in really isolating the problem
to ask each of these questions in such a way as to show both what the
problem is and also what it is not. For example, in the case of the
plastic molder cited above, it was helpful to know that the apparent
nonuniformity occurred at one plant but not at other customer plants.
This would show that not all containers were nonuniform within the
container, so that faulty blending was probably not the difficulty.

Numerous detailed examples of problem analysis, especially
where the problem is one of malfunction, are given in the list of
general readings at the end of this chapter, particularly in Kepner
and Tregoe (15).

Somewhat different is the analysis of a problem which calls for
the discovery and development of a new product, compared to one
involving the malfunction of a product or a process. For new product
discovery one must be able to visualize a use for the product which
is compatible with the ultimate cost and with competitive products.

This visualization must not encompass just today's competitive
products and costs, because the new product is not available today.
The analysis must focus on the probable market situation at the time
when the new product does become commercially available, usually
several years in the future. This is discussed in somewhat more
detail in Chapters 5 and 6 in connection with program and goal
selections.

2. Develop Several Possible Solutions

Knowing the problem and what has been learned about it thus far,
one should next formulate several possible solutions. It should be
emphasized that one definitely should strive for several, not just
one approach. Many people make the costly mistake of pursuing the
first approach which comes to mind without having other possible
solutions to compare with it.

This is the stage where one should force himself to answer questions such as "How else can I do it?"; "Can one reach the answer
from a different direction?"; "Would a different combination of
materials lead to the same results?"

The problem solver should propose to himself solutions after the
problem is defined, before he encumbers his thinking by learning the
past history of the subject. This has merit particularly if one is
easily led to install his own "blinders" by studying what has been
done before.

3. Learn Related Information

One learns much about a problem in defining it and in the first
mental searching for approaches toward solving it. After this, one
should go on to learn the background information which is related.
This should be done by studying the literature and company reports
and by discussing the problem with people who already have knowledge
of the subject. This study should lead to more possible solutions.

In some situations even the first possible solution continues to
elude one, no matter how hard he may try to formulate it. When
this occurs one should turn his thoughts elsewhere. Forget the
problem for a time--work on something else. Such a gestation
period often results in an idea popping out at an unexpected time but
with great clarity. "Eureka!" The idea may emerge as if spontan-
eously, fully formed, as patent language once termed "a flash of

genius." This can happen while one is fishing, playing golf, mowing the lawn, or at any other time when the conscious mind is in no apparent way occupied with the problem.

4. Selection and Evaluation

Having mentally worked out several ways of solving the problem, then evaluate the possible solutions, select the best, and test it experimentally. If this is not successful, the problem should be reviewed in light of the new information, alternate approaches again considered, and the best tested.

This outline of four key steps in problem solving is intended to serve as a condensed guide and to stimulate further reading on the subject. Several books are listed in the general readings at the end of this chapter. A study of these will amplify this outline with excellent examples and will certainly add further insight into the creative process.

Brainstorming

Another technique for developing possible solutions to problems is called "brainstorming." To use this technique a group is gathered and a problem is presented to the group. Each one is asked to propose solutions, no matter how impractical they may be. Each suggestion is noted, and no attempt is made to evaluate any ideas at the time. The expectation is that an idea expressed by one person may stimulate a new idea by someone else, so that the group together will provide more ideas than the individuals would separately. In using this approach it is important that no idea, however strange or absurd, should be ridiculed in any way. An open acceptance of all proposals is necessary to avoid inhibiting expression.

When the group appears to have run out of proposals the entire collection may be reviewed. This step may lead to one or two more suggestions. Evaluation can then be made, and the most promising ideas can be selected for experimental study.

Brainstorming does not include opportunity for study and for gestation of thought which are quite valuable. It does offer the advantage of bringing to bear several fresh minds which are not hampered by "knowing" what will not work.

Serendipity

Serendipity is a gift for making unexpected but pleasant discoveries. Quite often in experimental work, perhaps most often in exploratory research, the investigator finds a good result which is different from what he expected. Phrases such as "stumble upon" or "lucky observation" are sometimes used in these cases, but are often most inappropriate. Serendipity, which has often been of major importance, can be favored by the right preparation and approach. Very careful observation clearly will favor seeing the unexpected. A willingness to admit that the unexpected may be real, rather than shrugging it off as a mistake, enhances opportunity. Broad knowledge and a tendency to wonder about the possible importance of a stray observation help greatly in realizing the significance of the unexpected.

Perhaps the most frequently mentioned case of serendipity is Fleming's discovery of penicillin. The discovery of high impact polycarbonate thermoplastics at General Electric has been reported to have been an example of serendipity (5). The flame resistance of "Kynol" fiber, which is excellent in this respect, was an unexpected property (6). The discovery of poly(tetrafluoroethylene) has also been said to have been serendipity (7). These and many other examples exist. One always appreciates the "luck" involved in such a discovery, but again one can help create his own luck with good preparation and the proper approach to his work.

Some Additional Routes to Creativity

The three approaches to problem solving which have been discussed may shed some light on creative activity. A somewhat different view may amplify the understanding of the creative process further. If we ask ourselves how else we can describe routes to successful creative activities we could identify several, some of which are indicated briefly here.

Novel solutions often spring from a consciously planned, detailed search for answers to a problem. For example, it was theorized that flexible polyether-based urethane foams could be made in a direct, one-step process (which would reduce costs), if a catalyst for the isocyanate:hydroxyl reaction could be found which would be many times more powerful than the then-known catalysts. Britain

and Gemeinhardt (8) devised a wonderfully simple screening method
for catalyst testing: they simply mixed the diisocyanate and polyether
which were used in the foam process, without solvent but with a trace
of the catalyst to be evaluated. The time required for the reaction
mixture to solidify in a test tube at 70° C was observed. In this way
hundreds of catalysts were screened quickly. Those which caused
solidification in 4-6 minutes were then evaluated in foaming, and a
commercially successful process quickly resulted.

Asking the question, "How can we do it better?" often leads to
useful discoveries. In the search for catalysts just mentioned, the
conventional procedure was to conduct kinetic studies in solution,
evaluating the effect of a catalyst on the reaction rate constant. This
method would have been very time-consuming, and a mental search
for a better (faster) test method led to the very successful procedure
which was described.

The application of knowledge available in one field of study to
problems in another field has been exceedingly fruitful. In the area
of natural fibers, knowledge that wool develops a crimp because of
a bicomponent structure led to the preparation of the first bicomponent synthetic fibers which are self-crimping (9). Similarly, a
combination of information from the fields of rubber chemistry and
aircraft design led to the "bullet-proof," self-sealing aircraft fuel
tanks. Unvulcanized natural rubber, which closes rapidly after a
high speed perforation, especially when swollen by hydrocarbon fuels,
made an ideal tank liner (10).

Careful observation combined with curiosity is a powerful combination. Polyethylene self-charging electrostatic air cleaners
resulted from this (10). Many people had observed that polyethylene
surfaces attract dust, especially after one tries to rub off the dust.
Finally an engineer conceived of a filter which would be charged
electrostatically by the passage of dirty air through the filter, thus
increasing greatly the efficiency of the filter.

Looking beyond what others have done often leads to new solutions
to problems. For example, in searching for more flame-resistant
plastic foams the burning characteristics of each component of a
polyurethane rigid foam were studied (11). When it was found that
one component, the polymeric isocyanate, was an excellent char
former, the question was asked, "What kind of foam can we make
with a minimum use of components other than the isocyanate?" The
eventual result was a polyisocyanurate foam, using the isocyanate
as essentially the only reactant. The flame resistance of these
foams is outstanding.

Competition is the stimulus for many inventions. A competitor announces a discovery, and the question immediately is raised, "What can we find that will do as well or better?" This was the situation which led to the discovery of polyurethanes and nylon-6. Carothers at duPont had discovered nylon-66, and chemists at I. G. Farbenindustrie in Germany immediately began searching for other fiber-forming polymers which would be competitive. The results were a polyurethane fiber and the highly successful nylon-6 fiber.

Asking the question, "What else can I do with my discovery?" leads to many more inventions. It was in this way that the polyurethane industry grew from a very small fiber use to applications including flexible and rigid foam, elastomers, adhesives, coatings, and flooring materials. The success of this approach is proven by the size of the polyurethane market in the United States in 1971: approximately one billion pounds for all applications.

These examples and discussions show that there are common patterns in most discoveries. Discovery generally comes from a recognition of a need to be fulfilled, or of an opportunity. The concept of a need is self-evident. The opportunity concept was also apparent in the above question: "What else can I do with my discovery?" Discovery almost never, if at all, comes in a "vacuum." Instead, it is a step-by-step advance based on existing knowledge. The same is true of serendipity. The all-important features include one or more of the following: knowing that a problem exists and is worth solving, knowing that an opportunity exists and has possibilities which justify fulfilling, and recognizing the significance of an unexpected event as a solution to a problem or an opportunity to exploit.

DOES INDUSTRY WANT CREATIVITY?

Every company has serious problems in converting creative ideas into commercial reality. The problems are so varied that all R & D people encounter one or more. These difficulties lead to frustration and sometimes even to the thought that industry does not really want creativity. Although there are problems, industry does want and need creativity.

As has already been pointed out, anything new will be in conflict with the established order, and some people will try to preserve the status quo. This may be done because of a "not invented here" syndrome, or for various other reasons. More often than the technical team would like to admit, it is because the new item is just not good enough to be a commercial success.

In spite of the many discouraging hurdles which a new concept must pass before it is fully accepted, the greatest source of misunderstanding for the new employee, relative to innovation, is confusion over what innovations will have a chance of success with a particular company. Industrial R & D desperately needs the creative individual, but nearly always wants his creative talents directed in certain specific areas. Proper direction of creativity is highly important to the success of a company, and to the individual with that company.

Each company has certain goals which it considers commercially important. Creativity is needed at all levels of activity and at all stages of any program designed to reach a goal. These stages may include the original concept of a product, its first demonstration in the laboratory, the development of a process for making it, evaluation of the product, scale-up of the process, plant design, start-up and operation, introduction of the product to customers, and continued marketing of the product. Creativity is not limited to the initial discovery of the product but should be an integral part of the solutions of all problems associated with the entire operation.

The young experimentalist may feel that his ideas can flow only in an unrestricted way, that any limitations which are imposed will stifle his creativity. The author strongly believes that those who feel this way are underestimating themselves and are not analyzing the sources of their ideas. Insight will probably show that their ideas are coming in fields which have been of interest and some study during school. If the same people will apply equal enthusiasm to learning the company's problem areas and concentrate on finding solutions to those problems, they will usually develop an even greater interest in their creative efforts than they had in school.

In spite of obstacles, the opportunity for creativity is always present and the individual must actively seize it. One must have the inner drive to reserve a part of his time for creative effort and for the creative approach to problem solving. He usually has the freedom to take the creative approach if he will, but creativity is not and cannot be "spoon fed".

Objective analysis shows that all types of activity are well populated with obstacles to creativity. This is probably the reason that a strong inner motivation is one feature common to essentially all creative people, regardless of their fields of work.

A FAVORABLE ATMOSPHERE FOR GUIDED CREATIVITY

In order to achieve the "guided creativity" which is essential for profitable industrial R & D, a favorable environment must be maintained. While perfection is not to be expected, the following features should be included in the goals of the department.

Communication up, down, and laterally must be good, in order to define clearly the problems which the company must solve, provide the related background information, show the importance of the problems, and frequently re-evaluate results and programs.

Pressure of a reasonable level, showing the urgency of solving the important problems, is generally stimulating. Excessive pressure and too frequent shifting of urgency (the "yo-yo" approach) are harmful.

Physical facilities are important, but not as important as people.

Fair treatment of people is essential, especially in recognizing merit and in penalizing inadequate performance.

Individualism must be recognized and must not be discouraged. The most creative people often are strongly individualistic and will not perform well if they must conform to an exact pattern. This is a concept which is sometimes difficult for a noncreative manager to grasp.

People with ideas must be encouraged to take risks. A portion of the budget and of the personnel's time must be available to check out the "long shot" ideas, if the potential rewards are significant. The company must be willing to have a considerable percentage of its new product research programs fail, without losing faith.

Broad contacts with stimulating people are highly beneficial. Some should be colleagues, some may be consultants, some may be friends seen at technical meetings.

DO YOU WANT TO BE CREATIVE IN INDUSTRY?

Does each one have the choice as to whether he will be creative or not? The answer is "yes". Everyone has the ability to be creative, at least to some degree. It is somewhat analogous to height: everyone has at least some of it.

Can one teach himself to be more creative? Again, the answer is "yes." Following the suggestions in this chapter can help most individuals to improve their creative performance. Studying one or more of the available books which are completely devoted to the subject will provide additional help.

Can creativity be forced on you? Probably not, but it has been said that "necessity is the mother of invention." Laboratories do not usually try to operate at a pressure level which would be classed as "necessity," though in a few extreme emergencies it has happened. In all, however, creativity can and must be encouraged.

What, then, should the individual do?

First, realize that creativity is wanted. It is wanted in solving all types of problems that are important to your company.

Study. Learn as much as you can about the broad aspects of the company's business and its area of science and technology. Learn what the important problems are, and why they are important.

Force yourself to try creative thinking about one or more of the important problems. Reserve some time for it at regular intervals, such as weekly. Keep trying.

Use the approach to problem solving suggested here, unless you have a better way. The choice of the procedure is not as important as the repeated effort. Try more than one approach: one may work better for you than another.

Think through your ideas, carrying the thought to a logical conclusion. Don't stop with the idea itself. Analyze it to see what will be required to test it. Consider what you would do with the results if the idea worked. What would the results be worth? Could they be utilized practically, at reasonable cost? "Will it work in the plant?" Discussion of the idea and your analysis of it with others can be extremely helpful in understanding fully what the idea is worth and what may be involved in converting it into something useful.

Try exploratory experiments to check your ideas. If you have to work some extra hours to do these experiments, go ahead and do it.

Realize that somewhere along the line you will encounter resistance to new ideas, new products, new concepts. When you do, win over the resisting person or persons to your innovation. Start by having something worth listening to. This may be a well-thought-out concept or the results of some well-executed experiments. Explain your idea and your results to at least a few other department members who are recognized for an open minded approach to the evaluation of new ideas and for their judgment. (It is to be hoped that your group leader is included in this category.) If you can win support from these people you will have strong assistance in convincing other less open minded associates. If this support is not won, perhaps the idea or results do not have much merit. Re-examine them, refine them, and try again.

The person or persons who resist your idea may not even be in R & D. In any case, they should be looked upon as a challenge and a goal to be won. Such people usually are won over to your side if you make a real effort to include them in some way in the innovative process. One good technique is to mention your results briefly, with an explanation of how they might be useful if successful. After a short time give another small progress report. Ask their advice. Get them to participate in the thinking at an early stage. Be sure they are quite familiar with the idea and the results well before they have to make a decision regarding it. Your chances of getting a favorable decision are nearly always much better if the people making the decision are familiar with the subject already. First presenting information on something new at the meeting where a decision concerning it is to be made is asking for a negative reaction.

Don't despair if some of your ideas are shot down. Probably some of them deserved it. Have confidence in yourself, have courage, and persist--always striving to make your ideas, your experimental and mental evaluations, and your presentations better so that they truly are more desirable.

Use the creative approach at all levels of activity, not just to discover new products. Are you having trouble getting your reports out on time? Do you have problems getting along with someone else at work? Is a piece of equipment not functioning properly? Use the same problem solving approach on these and other problems. There is no reason to stop being creative when you leave work, either. Essentially all difficulties in life can be diminished with the right approach. Creativity enriches life in many ways outside the laboratory, as well as inside!

REFERENCES

1. M. Stein, see A. E. Brown, Chem. Eng. News, October 24, 1960, p. 102.
2. W. E. Hanford, Chem. Eng. News, December 8, 1958, p. 70.
3. W. Dennis, J. of Gerontology, 21, 2 (1966).
4. C. Berenson, Laboratory Management, September, 1966, p. 16.

5. P. J. Horgan, Chemtech, October, 1971, p. 639.

6. Staff Report, Textile Industries, December, 1971, p. 43.

7. R. J. Plunkett, The Chemist, July, 1969, p. 289.

8. J. W. Britain and P. G. Gemeinhardt, J. Appl. Polymer Sci.,
    4, 207 (1960).

9. W. E. Sisson and F. F. Moorehead, Text. Res. J., 23, 152
    (1953).

10. H. J. Osterhof, Chemtech., September, 1972, p. 518.

11. J. K. Backus, W. C. Darr, P. G. Gemeinhardt and J. H.
    Saunders, J. Cellular Plastics, 1, 178 (1965).

SUGGESTED GENERAL READINGS

12. S. S. Baker, Your Key to Creative Thinking, Harper, New York,
    1962.

13. W. I. B. Beveridge, The Art of Scientific Investigation, Norton,
    New York, 1950.

14. B. B. Goldner, The Strategy of Creative Thinking, Prentice-Hall,
    Englewood Cliffs, N. J., 1962.

15. C. H. Kepner and B. B. Tregoe, The Rational Manager,
    McGraw-Hill, New York, 1965.

16. L. E. Lloyd, Techniques for Efficient Research, Chemical
    Publishing Co., New York, 1966.

17. D. A. Schon, Technology and Change, Delacorte, New York,
    1967.

Chapter 8

COMMUNICATIONS

The main purposes of this chapter are to stress the importance
of communication, list the major forms used in industrial R & D, and
indicate some key points about each. Many books and articles are
available which provide much more detail on the general subject and
on each form of communication. All technical graduates have had
considerable exposure to both oral and written communication, of
course. In spite of their exposure and the wealth of available literature, many individuals are not good at it, perhaps because they have
not been convinced of its importance.

Can there be any doubt about the importance of good communication?
Can the people of the world ever live together in harmony without it?
Can the people of a country ever understand their own nation without
it? Without communication there could be no education, no cooperative efforts toward common goals, no shared enjoyment of the world
in which we live. Surely the need is clear. Perhaps what is missing
is the realization that each individual's communication is an important
part of the whole.

The essence of communication is conveying your thoughts to
another person in such a way that each of you has the same understanding of the thoughts conveyed. While several methods are available, each process starts and ends with people. Two functions must
be fulfilled: sending and receiving. These simple facts are indis-
putable but are often not considered.

Many who wish to communicate think primarily of themselves or
of the information which they wish to transmit. Very little thought
is given to the person or persons who are to receive the message.
Are they willing to receive it at all? If they try, can they understand
it? Will they know what to do with it? Will they act on it in some
way?

Consider two amateur radio operators who are communicating in
an emergency. The sender must use the same wavelength as the

receiver, and he must send when the receiver is at his set, ready to
listen. The message, when sent and received, must be so worded
as to express the sender's thoughts and the receiver must understand
the sender's thoughts. The message must include a request for
whatever action is needed, and the receiver must confirm that he
understands the desired action and will carry it out. This is good
communication.

In industrial R & D communication is verbal, written, visual, or
a combination of the three. One has no choice as to whether or not
he will communicate, but he does have a choice as to how well he
will do it. Consider your greeting in the morning, for example.
This--or its absence--may tell fairly accurately how well you feel
and forecast how much work you will do that day. Attentive listening
is certainly a form of communicating, too. Going to sleep in a meeting sends its own message. Failure to respond to a request
communicates a distinct impression.

Communication serves a wide range of purposes. Most importantly, it makes results available to those who need them. It is also
an opportunity for the individual to demonstrate to others the value
of his efforts. In providing a good report, whether oral or written,
it is his chance to tell his peers and superiors what he has accomplished. Written reports, in particular, reach beyond one's everyday
range of contacts and also become a permanent record, thus providing
an important opportunity to build one's reputation.

The preparation of a report is valuable training for the author.
In preparing it he must review his work and examine it critically in
an overall context. He has a chance to see if there are holes in it
and usually has time to get more data to fill the gaps. This process
helps him learn better how to organize his work on the next project.
A review of one's notebook often shows the importance of keeping
good records--how often it happens that one's records, when read a
year later, are not as clear and complete as desired! The real test
of record keeping comes when someone must write a report based on
data from several other people's notebooks. An experience of this
sort quickly teaches a group leader to train his people in record-
keeping.

Good technical communication has four essential elements. The
information must be correct, of value, on time, and easily understandable. Other elements may be desirable, but these points are
always of top priority.

The necessity for correctness of information needs no elaboration,
in principle. Many experimentalists agree on this, yet they do not

analyze their data for statistical significance, do not repeat important results to be sure they can be duplicated, and do not know the experimental error in the methods used.

The importance of the value of the information was emphasized in Chapter 5 on the selection of programs. Communications outside the area of technical information should also serve a useful purpose. This may include such wide-ranging items as coaching a new employee, boosting morale, building team spirit, and listening to someone who needs to talk about his troubles. It should not include such time-wasting activities as gossiping and spreading rumors.

The timeliness of needed information was also discussed to some extent in Chapter 5. Other people will use the information generated by R & D, and they usually need it by some fairly definite time. The time scale is more precisely fixed when one is dealing with a manufacturing operation, either in one's own plant or a customer's. In such cases, particularly, it is essential that the report be made on schedule. It is very easy to lose a good customer by promising to correct a problem caused by goods purchased by that customer, simply by not delivering the results on time.

That a communication should be easily understandable again is self-evident. It is not good enough if one can understand the information only after much effort. The report should be understood at the first hearing or the first reading, without the need for repeated study. The goal should be a report which cannot be misunderstood. Anything short of this will waste time for one or more readers or listeners and will lead to confusion.

In evaluating results, people, and departments, the quality and promptness of reports are always major factors. Good reporting is looked upon as primary evidence of good performance; poor reporting, including late reporting, is evidence of unsatisfactory performance.

TYPES OF COMMUNICATION

Communication has been a recurring theme throughout this book. Its essential role in program planning, for example, has been emphasized. It is a key part of all R & D projects--the job is not completed until the results have been communicated to those who need them. It is an intimate part of every work day for each person. The need is constant and the forms are many.

By function, a communication may serve three general purposes.
It may be designed to convey information, and that alone. It may
be analytical in nature, probing for more information to clarify a
problem. Finally, it may be persuasive in purpose, trying to
convince someone of a desired course of action.

In form most communications are verbal, with the second most
numerous being written. Visual aids are often combined with verbal
communications to aid clarity or help maintain interest. Verbal types
will range from informal conversations to highly formal presentations
such as lectures for colleagues at work or at a professional meeting.

Written communications include memos and bulletins distributed
within the company, letters to people outside the company, notebooks
of experimental data, reports for internal use, and publications.
Some guidelines will be given which are suitable for communications
in general, and then specific comments will be directed toward each
major type. The primary emphasis in this chapter is on the sender,
the one who desires to transmit the information. Even though the
technical graduate has developed considerable expertise as a receiver
in earning his degree, a very short section also is included on
receiving communications.

GENERAL GUIDELINES

The English language is our normal choice for communications.
This remarkable language can be clear and very easy to understand.
It can be almost as precise as mathematics. It can also be horribly
confusing if it is not used properly. In technical communications
one does not have to call upon the artistic beauty of the language,
although that is a desirable added attraction. The important features
to strive for are clarity, precision, conciseness, and simplicity, all
contributing to ease of understanding. It is worth remembering that
the technical person must be able to communicate his thoughts to
people who are not technically trained and, hence, are not familiar
with many common scientific terms. One should also remember that
many technical publications and reports will be read by foreigners
who may have only moderate skill with our language. These are all
challenges which can be met successfully.

Some aids in striving for clarity include the use of simple
sentences, short words, and only one thought in a paragraph. Some

excellent examples of flowery and complicated prose can be found in our literature, such as the work of William Faulkner, Thomas Wolfe, and James Joyce. But if one is writing for technical use, <u>Organic Synthesis</u> (<u>1</u>) sets a better style! Each word has a clear, distinct meaning; there are no superfluous words. It is almost impossible to misunderstand what is said in that publication. It represents scientific writing at its clearest.

With regard to the precision of words, the dictionary meaning of a word, not the Madison Avenue version, should be used. Don't exaggerate, but also don't understate a situation. Avoid superlatives, cliches, colloquialisms, jargon, and slang. Make frequent use of a dictionary and a thesaurus.

The particular style which is used should be selected to be compatible with the intended audience. Remember, you must "send" on a wavelength which they can "receive." The more specialized the audience the more specialized may be your choice of words. Most technical writers and speakers err on the side of being more specialized than their audiences, however. It is particularly frustrating to read a report which is so full of unfamiliar abbreviations, code symbols, and acronyms that the meaning is lost to all but those actually working on the project.

It has frequently been said that the two primary causes of poor reports are vanity and laziness. (The same applies to other forms of communication.) Vanity enters when the author will not accept constructive criticism of his manuscript. Too many authors look on their manuscripts as their personal works of art which should be above criticism. Reports can be greatly improved, however, if all suggestions are at least evaluated objectively and the good ones are followed. Laziness manifests itself when one is not willing to expend the time and effort necessary to prepare a good report rather than a mediocre one.

For those who are not lazy, a willingness to revise and revise again will be most helpful. An excellent technique is to write a report or speech well ahead of time, put it away for a few weeks and forget it, then review it. The last reading can be done with a relatively fresh viewpoint and will usually reveal several parts that need revision. A similar review by a critical colleague is invaluable in making sure the communication is all that is desired.

While something close to perfection is a commendable goal, one does not usually have enough time to apply the same degree of effort in preparing all of his communications. There are just too many conversations, speeches, memos, letters, and reports to be prepared. The following is a good general guide for priorities. One is generally least critical of day-to-day conversations, although clarity is still essential in these. Memos and reports within a department are treated more carefully, but not as much so as communications outside a department. People outside will not be as familiar with the background, the language, or the significance of data. The most critical effort is usually reserved for information going outside the company, as in patents, publications, and sales bulletins. Here the audience is wider and less familiar with the information, so misunderstanding will be even easier. Anything which goes into the permanent literature of the company or of the technical world should be prepared with great care and thoroughness.

LETTERS AND MEMOS

In general, a letter is a relatively brief written communication addressed to someone outside the company, while a memo is similar but limited in distribution within the company. Memos usually omit the salutation and complimentary close of a letter but may state the subject and any appropriate reference at the top of the sheet. Most companies use their own standard forms for their memos.

While less formal than official reports, the preparation of letters and memos still needs to follow the same guidelines for ease of understanding, accuracy, and timeliness. When one receives a letter or memo requiring action, a prompt reply should be made, the same day if feasible.

Before a letter is typed for mailing outside the company, it should be checked with one's group leader. He will know the company policy on clearance required for outside correspondence and may also be helpful in reviewing the letter for content. Some readers may be startled to learn that outside correspondence should have some degree of review before mailing. The reasons are simple and valid. Correspondence on company stationery places certain ethical and legal obligations on the company, as well as on the author. Often the ramifications of certain statements may be far more complex than the new employee realizes and the letters should be reviewed by someone with adequate background. In addition, copies of letters should be sent to those in the company who need to know the contents.

The issuing of memos is usually handled less formally. These

again should be shown to the group leader before they are typed,
however. He will indicate who should receive copies, or may pass
it on to higher management, depending on the contents. Copies of
those memos with information of much significance should be given
to the assistant director and/or the director. It is sometimes
embarrassing to one's boss if he learns important results from
someone outside his department when the information originated
within his own department!

NOTEBOOKS

The notebook is a chronological record of experimental work. It
is more than this in some extremely important cases: it sometimes
has to serve as a legal record. For this reason companies use bound
notebooks with pages and directions for use which have been designed
by patent lawyers. The following recommendations are generally
applicable to most companies' needs.

When starting a series of experiments on a project, the goal of
the project should be stated as clearly as possible. The objective
of each experiment should then be described in relation to the project.
Changes in objectives should be recorded as they occur. For each
experiment be sure to list the starting materials used, with source
and lot number if available; the equipment and the procedure used;
all raw data; and calculations, results, and conclusions. The reason
for doing the experiment should be noted, if that is not inherent in
the stated objective. For example, the reason could be to check an
idea originating with the experimenter or it could be that someone
else asked that the experiment be performed. Each page should
contain a title, a page number, an indication of the subsequent page
on which the work is continued, the experimenter's signature, and
the date. The record is much better from a legal viewpoint if someone else who saw the experiment and read the page also signs it as a
witness and dates it. There must never be any question as to whether
a record was added or changed at a later date. To eliminate any
doubt, draw a line diagonally through any unused part of the page,
between the last entry and the signature at the bottom of the page.
If analytical data must be added later, reserve a page for that,
refer to that page, and enter the data there when available.

One should avoid sweeping conclusions of a negative nature in a

notebook. For example, one could desire to prepare a solid polymer
but find that the result was a foam instead. It would be better to
report that a foamed polymer was obtained rather than a solid polymer, instead of reporting that the experiment failed due to bubbling.
If one later desired to file a patent application on the novel preparation of a foam, it would be preferable to have the suggested record
to rely on, rather than the statement of failure.

It should be emphasized again that primary data should be entered
in the notebook. Do not keep notes on scraps of paper and transcribe
these into the notebook. This may improve the neatness but may
also lead to errors in transcription, and will weaken the legal validity
of the notebook. One exception to this is sometimes made when following experimental procedures which have standardized data sheets
available. Data may be recorded on these sheets (especially in pilot
plant work), and the sheets should be preserved. Key information
should be entered in the notebook, and the data sheets may be stapled
into the book at the appropriate place. Analytical reports from
another laboratory, snapshots of equipment, and any other useful
data sources should be pasted or stapled into the notebook to insure
a complete record.

Other information that is appropriate to enter in the notebook
includes pertinent references to literature, patents, company reports
and memos, your speculations concerning your studies, and proposals
for new research.

Each sample which is prepared should be identified with the
notebook page on which its preparation is recorded. A series whose
preparation is on one page may be designated by the notebook page
number, followed by letters to differentiate among samples. This
designation should be used in requests for analysis or any other
treatment to preserve the exact identity of the sample and its correlation with analytical results or other tests.

Most notebooks are designed to include one carbon copy of each
of the original pages. This system permits the experimentalist to
keep either the original pages (bound in the book) or the carbon copies
(removed, punched, and placed in a looseleaf notebook) for a record
in his laboratory. The other half of the record is sent to a central
filing system for retention as a permanent record.

A properly kept notebook makes an excellent legal record (which
will be discussed more in the chapter on patents) and also will make
it easy to prepare final reports. It is the starting point for a wide
variety of communications.

WRITTEN REPORTS

A variety of written reports will be prepared during the course of several years of experimental work. These are designed to present technical results, in an organized form, to those who need the data. These reports also become a part of the company's permanent record, are suitably indexed, and are available for reference. (Memos, even though they may contain experimental data, are not considered a permanent record.) Some of the general types of reports which are used include Short Form Reports, Interim Reports, Final Reports, Tentative Process Reports, and Progress Reports. Other names may be used to describe reports of similar functions, of course. The nature and purpose of each type is indicated below.

The Short Form Report is designed primarily to summarize projects which have not utilized very much experimental time-- perhaps a week to a month. They are similar to the Final Report described below, except several sections may be omitted as not being pertinent. They are also useful for recording briefly unsuccessful efforts of fairly long duration.

The Interim Report is a status report, including experimental data, on a project of long duration. For ease of reporting and reading, and for good communication, it is usually desirable to issue a report on each project every 12-18 months, even though the project may last several years. With such a long project it is not desirable to wait until the end and issue a large Final Report. Instead, Interim Reports are issued at convenient intervals. This report follows the general style of a Final Report.

When a project is completed a Final Report is issued, giving a summary of what was done, conclusions, recommendations for further work, and experimentatal details. Reference is made to earlier Interim Reports, if any exist, and only key elements from those reports would be repeated.

A Tentative Process Report is the R & D proposal of a process for making something. Its emphasis is on procedure, equipment and operation of the equipment. The supporting details of underlying principles of chemistry and physics are found in other reports such as Final Reports. A Tentative Process Report is usually issued before a pilot plant is placed in operation and serves as the initial guide for that operation. A similar report or an Operating Manual will be issued before a new plant process is placed in operation.

Progress Reports are usually short status and summary reports issued at regular calendar intervals, such as each month, every other month, or quarterly. These may be limited to one page for each project and usually give a word description of the status, with relatively few details of data. Their purpose is periodic communication. Their reference value is usually small, since the other report forms described will be more detailed and will appear at logical intervals based on the data available, rather than on a calendar basis.

Many books are available which describe the technique of report writing and the proper use of the English language. For language usage particular reference is made to Fowler (2) and to Strunk and White (3). Some books covering the preparation of reports include those of Hicks (4) and Wilson (5). Hayakawa's book (6) is a particularly interesting treatment of language and its use in communication. The following points relating to industrial reports deserve emphasis.

Every report needs an introduction, putting it in perspective with what is known and what has gone before. While in a memo this may be a reference to a previous request for information, or simply "confirming our conversation of the other day," a slightly longer statement is needed in more formal reports. The objectives should be given in the introduction of a formal report, or a separate section if preferred.

Each report should have a summary, stating clearly but briefly what was done. The main points should be covered. Conclusions should follow this, and again should be very concise. State the most important ones first, to insure the reader's attention.

Recommendations for future action should be the fourth element in the Short Form, Interim, and Final Reports. This section provides the technical team with an opportunity to express opinions as to what should be done next and may extend to action beyond the R & D scope.

These first sections should not require more than two or three pages. They are the parts which will be read by management and should be written with special care. This portion of a report gives the technical person his best chance to show what his efforts have been worth.

Interim and Final Reports have additional sections on the patent status, the experimental details, data, discussion of results, literature references, and acknowledgment of assistance from supporting personnel. A list of notebook pages on which the original data may be found is included in the experimental section. An abstract page is provided, with key words underlined for indexing. The abstract page is sent to those who need to know of the existence of the report, while the full report is sent to those who need the data, and to the library for filing. Short Form Reports include the first four sections, the experimental section, and any others that may be appropriate.

Tentative Process Reports include an introduction, an outline of the process, description of equipment, specifications and analytical methods for raw materials, toxicity, and other safety considerations, and an operating procedure. Key features of the process should be pointed out, with explanations of their importance given.

When the time comes to write a report, be sure to know the subject matter thoroughly. There is no chance for a good report otherwise. Make a clear distinction between the primary data which were experimentally obtained and the conclusions which were drawn from them. Many writers fail in this respect without ever realizing it. An example can be found in reports of rates of reactions between two compounds, A and B, to give product C. The rate of disappearance of A has been measured, and this rate has been reported as the rate of reaction of A and B. Unfortunately, side reactions which could consume A were overlooked. A careful study would have included the rates of disappearance of A and B and of the formation of C. The author must inspect his data carefully and understand the limitations of his experiments so that his conclusions are valid.

Questionable and incomplete areas in the results should be recognized, stated, and opinions about them given. Try to anticipate the readers' questions and provide answers. This can save confusion for the readers and eliminate several exchanges of questions and answers. The reader may wonder, "Did he know that this part of the work is not complete? Why didn't he complete it? What results might he have obtained?" Questions of this kind can be eliminated with careful anticipation.

If writing reports is difficult, the biggest help may be simply the determination to start. Passing that barrier is often the most troublesome part. Collect the information that forms the basis of the report. Organize it in a logical way to provide the experimental section. Revise it, condense it, and organize data into tables and figures. Write the discussion next; compose the introduction, summary, conclusions and recommendations last.

The style of your writing can help greatly in being sure the reader understands the report, enjoys reading it, and develops a favorable impression of you, the author. Tailor the report to the readers' understanding. Avoid jargon and be sure that all code names or symbols are explained the first time they appear. Use precise

language, simple words, and short sentences. Be factual; do not
exaggerate or overqualify.

When the report is completed, set it aside for a few days, if
possible. Then review it carefully. Ask yourself what points you
really wanted to get across and if you succeeded. Review the general
arrangement, the style, grammar, spelling, and abbreviations.
Reporting, like other activities, improves with practice.

Writing a report can be summed up as a process of selecting,
arranging logically, and evaluating the significant facts developed
by the work being reported.

VERBAL COMMUNICATIONS

Verbal communications are fully as important as the written
forms. There may be no written record available for later study,
which is sometimes fortunate, but the listener may keep his mental
impression for a long time. Verbal exchanges are so frequent and
so varied that many people consider planning and delivery only when
a rather formal oral presentation is intended. This oversight leads
to much faulty communication.

Many of the recommendations for report writing apply to verbal
communications as well. In fact, practice in writing one's thoughts
is an excellent preparation for expressing them orally. This is
particularly so when one wishes to express rather complicated ideas
or concepts.

Three types of verbal communications are worthy of somewhat
separate treatment. These are the more or less "everyday conversation" type; short and informal summary statements of progress,
activity, or opinion; and formal oral presentations. The three have
much in common, of course.

Conversation during working hours certainly should include some
pleasantries and personal discussions which are not work-related,
but these should be a minor portion. In work-related discussions,
one sometimes wonders what should be said to whom. In particular,
he may be unsure how far up the administrative line he should initiate
conversations. This will vary with the personal preferences of the
administrators. An open door to an office suggests that informal
visits are welcomed. Other indications will usually be given,
especially in the way an informal visit is received. In general, be

guided by what you think another person needs to know and wants to know, and what will help him. A very few individuals communicate too often; most do not do it frequently enough.

An appropriate time to drop into the assistant director's or director's office would be those when you have just gotten some very good experimental results or some significantly bad ones. If a serious problem becomes apparent in the program, be sure to let your supervisor know promptly. He may be able to help reduce it and certainly should have the opportunity to see how it may affect the immediate future of the program. For visits such as these, organize your thoughts ahead of time, bring along some key data, charts, sketches, or samples, and describe the situation briefly. Give the essence of it and go into detail only if he seems to want that.

In all discussions consider other people's viewpoints. Use tact, be modest, give credit to others when it is due. This approach can do more toward gaining the cooperation of others than almost anything else.

A discussion is not a monologue. Do not monopolize the conversation. Ask questions and listen to the answers. When it is your turn to listen, do so attentively, with the object of understanding what is said. Many people do not listen--they just stop talking. While waiting for the first chance to resume, they concentrate on what they will say next rather than listening. Do not interrupt others. These admonitions are simply suggestions of common courtesy, but they are frequently violated.

You may encounter situations in which you think some action was agreed upon, but the other party does not do what you expected. Try to find out why events did not go as anticipated. The chances are good that the two of you did not have the same understanding of the expected action. Be suspicious of the clarity of your own expression and also of the other person's receiving ability, or the reverse if that fits the situation. You can greatly reduce the frequency of this kind of disappointment by summarizing any action decisions at the end of a conversation and asking if the other person agrees that this summary represents what he and you said.

The second general group of verbal communications consists of short, informal summaries. These may be requested without warning, such as during someone's visit to the laboratory, at lunch, or in an informal meeting. Each person should always be thoroughly knowledgeable about what he has done recently, is doing currently, and plans to do next. He should know why he is doing these things and how they fit with some departmental objective. Finally, he should be prepared at any time to give a quick, accurate, easily understood summary of his work. If this seems difficult, try writing a summary. Revise it again a few weeks later. With a little practice one can formulate an up-to-date summary on a moment's notice. It is a great help to have some kind of chart available to illustrate progress and plans; one example was described in the discussion of statistical design of experiments in Chapter 5. Charts of data or mounted samples are wonderful aids in explaining your work. While these props cannot be available to you at all times, they should be in your laboratory.

When attending a meeting, even if you are not scheduled to speak, consider beforehand whether you could be called upon for an opinion or summary related to the subject of the meeting. If this is remotely possible, give some thought to what you would want to say. Insofar as possible, avoid giving completely extemporaneous statements by using foresight and formulating summaries in advance. Again, in these summaries give the essence of your information without too much detail. Be able to quote supporting data reliably if questioned, however.

At one time or another almost every professional person is called upon to give a formal presentation of his work. Most graduates will have encountered this in school and so will have some acquaintance with it. Not many people do well on their first one or two attempts, but practice adds greatly to the skill of making presentations. Everyone has "stage fright" to a degree, but if you are unduly bothered by standing up and talking to a group, force yourself to have extra practice. Joining a Toastmasters' Club can be of great assistance.

When you must speak formally on some subject, the first thing to do obviously is to collect adequate information on that subject. Study it, select the main points which you wish to convey, and organize the information around these points. Then consider your audience. How much do they know? Do they already know the background, the significance of your subject, and any special vocabulary which may be associated with it? Develop a way to present your information so that the audience can see a relationship between what you want to tell them and something they are both familiar with and interested in. Place the emphasis on communicating with them, not on impressing them.

It is usually helpful to write what you want to say. Study your writing, checking for clarity, ease of understanding, organization, and simplicity of presentation. Revise it along these lines. Practice

an oral delivery and see if you use the allotted time, or if you run
over. Again revise the manuscript so that you can stay within your
time limit. In practice, as in the final speech, the delivery should
be slow enough that you are easily understood. Pause at the end of
certain key sentences for emphasis.

Eloquence, charm, and wit are not essential to a good presentation.
The content of the speech and your manner of delivery are more
important. Amusing stories may be useful as illustrations, but do
not feel any need to start with a joke, or to tell any at all if you do
not do it well. Be natural--put yourself across to the audience as
you are. Show your interest in your subject and your enthusiasm
for it. Be sincere. Involve the audience in some way. Show them
that the information is important to them as individuals. Ask a
rhetorical question occasionally, and pause before you supply the
answer. Use good illustrations whenever possible.

Do not memorize a speech and do not read it. One may follow a
written text, glancing at it occasionally, while still talking to the
audience. Similar use of an outline or notes of key ideas does not
detract from a good presentation. If "stage fright" is particularly
bothersome, it may help one's assurance to have a prepared text or
to have the opening paragraphs typed and available. Read the first
paragraph if necessary. Nervousness usually disappears after the
first few sentences--it is the anticipation that causes more concern
than the actual delivery.

A good way to start is to outline the idea or points which you want
to convey. Then proceed with the main part of the speech. If you
are developing more than one idea it is wise to summarize at the
end of each section which is devoted to a particular idea. Summarize
again at the conclusion. "Tell them what you are going to tell them,
tell them, then tell them what you told them."

If you are using slides, be sure they are legible and understandable.
Project them ahead of time in a room of about the same size you
expect to use for the lecture, and see if they can be read from the
back row. Be sure the slides are numbered clearly (in only one
sequence of numbers) and in order. Check the order with the
projectionist. Try to show the slides in one sequence--changing
back and forth from room lights to slides is annoying to the audience.
If these suggestions seem too obvious, reconsider them when you
attend your next technical meeting!

A dress rehearsal with one or two friends is very helpful. Have
one sit at the front and one at the back of the room. Ask them to be
alert for confusing parts of the speech, enunciation which may not be

clear, and any nervous habits which could distract the audience. Be
alert to the sound level of your voice. If you are using a microphone,
try to stay at a fairly uniform distance from it and speak toward it.
If you are showing slides, speak to the audience, not to the slides.

If you encounter a heckler, don't show irritation or hostility
toward him. Try to work his comments or questions into your talk.
The contrast between courtesy on your part and his approach can only
help you with most of the audience.

Much more information and many enjoyable suggestions concerning speeches and presentations may be found in books such as those
by Monroe (7), Lee (8), and Boettinger (9). Mr. Lee was formerly
the United States Senator from Oklahoma, and wrote from a wonderful
range of experiences.

RECEIVING

Good communication requires both a sender and a receiver. Most
guides on communication emphasize the sending of messages, and
this chapter is no exception. College graduates surely should be
well trained in receiving. A few comments on this equally necessary
part of communication are in order, however.

An "open mind" is always cited as one of the characteristics
developed in a technical education. Unfortunately, it is not always
characteristic of people. Since scientists and engineers are people,
the open mind is more a goal than a reality. It is a worthy goal and
one that each of us should strive for throughout life. When on the
receiving end of a communication, concentrate on understanding
what is being sent. Try to put it in perspective with what you already
know. Scrutinize it critically, testing it for validity. Do not shut it
out just because it is new, different, or unpleasant.

Some people do not receive as much information as they want.
In such a case, don't sit passively waiting for more and fretting
because it does not seek you out. Go after it! Read, participate
in voluntary programs, ask questions. Don't let yourself be lost
in the crowd--initiate conversations, volunteer for some assignment
requiring contact with people, such as seminar chairman. Be a part
of the activities of the department.

Keep your "receiver" in good repair, alert for messages, and
capable of receiving on many wavelengths. You can do this by

staying up to date in your field, by studying new subjects, by learning more about your department and your company, and by continually seeking a total grasp of the programs on which you are working.

REFERENCES

1. Organic Synthesis, published annually and in collective volumes, Wiley, New York.
2. H. W. Fowler, A Dictionary of Modern English Usage, 2nd ed., rev., Clarendon Press, Oxford, 1965.
3. W. Strunk, Sr., and E. B. White, The Elements of Style, Macmillan, New York, 1959.
4. T. G. Hicks, Successful Technical Writing, McGraw-Hill, New York, 1959.
5. E. B. Wilson, An Introduction to Scientific Research, McGraw-Hill, New York, 1952.
6. S. I. Hayakawa, Language in Thought and Action, Harcourt Brace, New York, 1941.
7. A. H. Monroe, Principles and Types of Speech, 4th ed., Scott, Foresman, Chicago, 1955.
8. J. Lee, How to Hold An Audience Without a Rope, Ziff-Davis, New York, 1947.
9. H. M. Boettinger, Moving Mountains, Macmillan, New York, 1969.

Chapter 9

PATENTS

Most university educational programs do little to acquaint the
technical student with the intricacies of patents and patent law. Too
often patents are not considered a major source of information, and
sometimes they are looked down upon as being unreliable references.
At the same time, it is recognized that it is desirable to have one's
name on a patent covering an important invention. While not attempt-
ing to be a treatise on patent law, this chapter will try to provide a
reliable description of patents and their significance from the
technical investigator's point of view.

WHAT IS A PATENT?

The patent laws of the United States are based on our Constitution,
which states in Article I, Section 8, "Congress shall have power to
promote the progress of science and the useful arts, by securing for
limited times to authors and to inventors the exclusive right to their
respective writings and discoveries."

In accordance with this portion of the Constitution, laws have
been passed which permit the federal government to grant "patents"
to protect inventions and "copyrights" to protect works of literature
and of the fine arts. Somewhat related to these is a "trademark,"
which may be registered to protect a name or symbol under which
an article of merchandise is sold. Unlike the patent and the copyright, no originality is necessary for the granting of a trademark
(e.g., Arrow (T.M.) shirts).

A patent may be loosely viewed as a contract between the inventor
and the government, granting the inventor exclusive protection of his
invention for a period of seventeen years from the date the patent is

issued. In return for this protection, the inventor discloses the
nature of his invention to the public. This patent system has contributed greatly to our technical progress, since it encourages
inventors to publish (in a patent) their inventions. This publication,
of course, helps educate others and stimulates other ideas and
inventions.

The patent grants the owner the right to protect his invention
from others, i.e., to prevent others from making, using, or selling
the subject of his claimed invention, but does not grant him the right
to practice his invention. Perhaps this can be explained by using a
fence as an analogy. Builder A can erect a fence around a square
mile of land. Builder B could later fence in a hilltop within this
square mile. The fence put up by B would keep A off the hilltop, but
B could not get to the hilltop without negotiating a passage through
A's original fence. For a real example, U.S. Patent 2,948,691
claims broadly the preparation of polyurethanes from polyethers and
polyisocyanates, while U.S. Patent 2,866,774 claims more narrowly
the preparation of certain polyurethanes from certain polyether
triols based primarily on propylene oxide and polyisocyanates. U.S.
2,948,691 is said to "dominate" U.S. 2,866,774; i.e., anyone wishing to use the invention of U.S. 2,866,774 must have suitable permission to practice the invention of both patents, since he would be
performing an operation claimed specifically in the one patent and
claimed broadly in the other. Also the owner of U.S. 2,948,691
must have suitable permission from the owner of U.S. 2,866,774
to do what is claimed by U.S. 2,866,774. (The unusual fact that the
broader patent was issued after the narrower one was the result of
a complicated and time-consuming interference of the type described
at the end of Section VI. This interference delayed the issuing of the
broader patent.) This situation may appear confusing regarding what
a patent owner can do, but it illustrates that the ownership of a patent
enables one to prevent others from doing what his patent claims.
The situation may become clearer after the subsequent discussion
of what an invention is.

In the United States, patents are issued by the United States Patent
Office in Washington, D.C., a branch of the Department of Commerce.
The Patent Office is directed by the Commissioner of Patents and
includes a large staff of patent examiners and excellent library
facilities. The official publication, listing all patents granted with
an indication of each patent coverage, is called the Official Gazette,
which appears weekly.

Applications for patents are filed with the Patent Office by patent lawyers in a company's patent department or by an outside firm of lawyers that may be hired for the purpose. Close communication and cooperation are needed between the inventors and the lawyer to insure filing the most important applications and filing them in the best form.

Most foreign countries have patent systems with more or less variation from the United States system. Patent lawyers know the specific requirements for handling patent matters in foreign countries, and the technical person entering industry may be guided by this discussion of the United States patent system plus consultation with his company's patent lawyers.

The issuing of a patent discloses the invention covered, so some people have a tendency to keep their inventions as "secrets," not filing suitable patent applications. This practice is generally recognized as dangerous, however. Secrets are sometimes lost, and even more often others will have the same problem and make the same invention in solving it. Thus other inventors could receive a patent on the process, sometimes preventing the original inventor from using his invention (see Sections II, III and V). In any case the original inventor will have lost his chance to prevent others from using his invention.

Similarly, companies are usually not enthusiastic about processes or products which cannot be protected, at least in part, by patents. This has been one of the handicaps in utilizing a considerable number of inventions made in R & D supported by federal funds where the United States government is the owner of the patents. Such ownership usually means that the government will grant a license (a legal form of permission) to use the patents to anyone desiring it, so there is no exclusive protection for the companies so licensed.

WHAT IS A PATENTABLE INVENTION?

Title 35, Section 101, of the United States Code (1952), sometimes called the Patent Act of 1952, states, "whoever invents or discovers any new and useful process, machine, manufacture, or composition of matter, or any new and useful improvement thereof, may obtain a patent therefor, subject to the conditions and requirements of this title."

This section contains the basic elements of the law relating to patentability. It tells us that a patentable invention must be in the

category of a process, machine, manufacture, or composition of
matter, or an improvement in one of these. It must be both new
and useful.

The law further clarifies certain of these criteria. To be patent-
ably new, or novel, it must meet these requirements:

1. The invention was not known or used by others in this country
   before the date of invention (by the one claiming the invention).
2. It must not have been patented or described in any printed
   publication anywhere before the date of the invention or more
   than one year before the patent application was filed with the
   United States Patent Office.
3. It must not have been in public use or sold in the United States
   for more than one year before the patent application was filed.
4. It must not have been abandoned.

These four limitations apply, even though the prior publication,
use or sale was not known to the inventor. The limitation on abandonment perhaps needs more explanation. If a person makes a patentable
invention but shows no intention to file an application on that invention
for many years, it may be considered that he "abandoned" the invention and he cannot get a patent on it. There is no exact definition of
the delay required to be classed as abandonment and this point is
often settled only by the courts.

The classes of subject matter which may be patented may need
some explanation, also. The term "process" simply covers ways
of making things. The manufacturing of fatty acids and glycerine by
the hydrolysis of fats represents a process which received an early
patent. The term "machine" is readily understood, and the term
"manufacture" refers to the product made by some particular process.
A "composition of matter" includes new chemical compounds as well
as two or more substances brought together for some definite purpose,
such as a particular solution, paint, adhesive, or other useful combination not found in nature. Certain plants (biological species), e.g.,
of hybrid types, may be patented. Additionally, a new, original and
ornamental design for an article of manufacture may be patented, for
example a soft drink bottle that meets these requirements.

It may be even more helpful to consider some things which have
been judged not to be patentable inventions. An old, previously known
product which has been synthesized for the first time, e.g., alizarin,
a natural dye, may not be patented (though the process of making it
could be).

One's first thought might be that a discovery is patentable. In
the sense that a discovery is the act of finding something which is

already in existence, such a discovery is not new and therefore not patentable (again, the process of making or using the discovery and apparatus related to the discovery could be new and patentable). Patents cannot be obtained on new elements which are discovered or on laws of nature.

Excellence of workmanship, substitution of equivalent materials, or a change in degree or size, in the absence of unexpected results, are generally not patentable. The invention must not be obvious. The application of normal or ordinary skill and knowledge is not invention. In this case "ordinary skill" is considered to be the skill of one who is thoroughly knowledgeable regarding the subject in question, or as the patent lawyer says, "one skilled in the art." Nevertheless, it is again very difficult to define just what this term means, and the decision is sometimes left to the courts.

In earlier court rulings a term "flash of genius" was sometimes used to indicate an inventive process beyond what was expected of one skilled in the art. The patent law of 1952 largely eliminated the "flash of genius" concept and stated that patentability cannot be ruled out by the manner in which the invention was made. This means that patentable inventions may come from systematic and painstaking research, as well as from sudden inspirations and unexpected observations.

The concept of novelty is rather well defined by law, as indicated above. One does have to know his own date of invention, however, to compare with the legal requirements. The invention date is the date on which the patentable idea first occurred to the inventor or inventors (the "date of conception"). A legally acceptable date of conception must be one which can be proven, however. The inventor's unsupported statement cannot be accepted as proof. A written record that is dated and signed by the inventor, and is also read, understood, signed, and dated by a competent witness is an excellent form of proof.

For the conception date to be legally acceptable in determining priority of invention one must be able to show "reasonable diligence" in demonstrating the invention ("reducing it to practice"). To do this one should proceed to acquire the necessary materials for an experimental demonstration and conduct experiments to illustrate the invention. The exact time interval permitted between conception and demonstration is not well defined; but if a court decides there is a lack of reasonable diligence between concept of the invention and reduction to practice, an inventor will not be afforded the benefit of the earlier conception date. This is particularly important when the question of priority of invention between different parties is raised.

The requirement that a patentable invention be useful (have utility) means that it must be capable of performing some beneficial function alleged for it. The invention must be operative, but it need not be perfect. The invention will not be judged to be useful if it can be used only for illegal or immoral purposes. The issue of utility is not usually raised in actual practice, even though the usefulness may be very slight.

It should be emphasized that a patentable invention must include both the conception and reduction to practice. Conception alone does not constitute a patentable invention. The reduction to practice may be an experimental demonstration or a written description which is filed as a part of a patent application.

WHO IS AN INVENTOR?

An inventor is one who first conceives of a patentable invention and causes it to be reduced to practice with reasonable diligence. (He does not have to reduce it to practice himself.) The conception may be made jointly by a group, in which case the members of the group making the conception are coinventors, if each contributes to the invention in an important way. Coinventors do not have to contribute equally, or simultaneously, to the invention. While these sentences may seem simple and straightforward in meaning, misunderstandings frequently arise concerning inventorship. It is hoped that this discussion will eliminate some misunderstanding for those who are first meeting our patent system on a working basis.

The general requirements which must be met for qualification as a patentable invention have already been described. These give the necessary groups into which ideas or concepts must fall if they are to be patentable, and the requirements for novelty or newness, relative to previously published or commercially used products or processes. These requirements are fairly readily understood, whereas the finer points affecting decisions within one's own organization concerning invention and inventorship are the ones which usually lead to disagreements.

Now let's return to the first sentence of this section, which defines the inventor(s), and consider in more detail several elements of that sentence. While some may say that conception of the invention is the first key in establishing inventorship, it more frequently occurs that the first essential step is to define the invention. This definition is often very difficult to establish and may be quite different from the original idea. For example, suppose that an assistant director (A) conceives of the idea, which is new so far as he knows, of making a useful product from components X and Y. (This could be a new polymer, from monomers X and Y; it could be a new instrument from an irradiating component, X and response-sensing component, Y; it could be a new precision metering pump from a new principle of speed control, X, and a highly accurate delivery system, Y; or many other suitable combinations of two components.) He discusses this with a group leader (B) and a technical member (C) of that group.

Being aware of the need to document the conception, one of the three writes a record of their conversation, stating that the general idea was proposed by A, what other ramifications were discussed by the group, and what plans were made to demonstrate the idea. This record is dated and signed by all three. In addition, someone else who is knowledgeable in the area, but who did not contribute in any way to the idea, reads the record and signs and dates it as a witness.

A quick search is made of the literature to see if the same thing has already been done (no such record was found in this case) and also what related information is available that might be helpful. The necessary starting materials are then ordered and a check is made to be sure that the equipment needed for the demonstration is on hand.

A month passes before the raw materials are received. During this time an urgent problem with an existing product has developed so that C is fully occupied on this problem and has no time to evaluate the idea. Instead, another technical investigator (D) and a technician (E) are acquainted with the idea and asked to try it. The team of D and E works on the idea for a few days, with some promising but not fully satisfactory results. The group, A, B, and D, judges that the potential merit of the idea, if successful, and the results achieved thus far justify more work. For the next six months D and E work on the idea at least one or two days every week, while continuing work on other projects of longer standing. Finally a way is found to combine X and Y to give almost the desired results, and the combination has some advantages which were not originally expected. These unexpected advantages were found as a result of tests requested by D and performed by the product evaluation group (which actually obtained the data showing unexpected performance). In making this combination of X and Y which performed well, D recognized that the combination of X and Y alone performed well for a few minutes but quickly deteriorated. He asked his technician, E, to try the usual stabilizers to see if they would help. Now E was a good laboratory worker with initiative, and he tried not only the stabilizers which were normally used by his group but also some others. He knew from discussions in the lunchroom that a technician in a group working with very different products was evaluating some new stabilizers designed especially to help those products. He asked his friend for a little of each of the new stabilizers and tried them too. Fortunately one of these new types (Z) was better than all the rest, old and new alike. Then it was found that X plus Y combined with a trace of Z would perform very well for long periods of time.

The technical team felt that it had an invention and so informed their patent attorney in writing, giving fairly complete details in a standard form for "reductions to practice." He was asked to study the results to see if an invention did in fact exist, and if so, to give a legal definition of the invention. (Was it X + Y, X + Y + Z, a process for making the combination, a process for solving a problem by the use of the combination, or what?) After a preliminary study of the results, including a discussion with those involved, the attorney decided there was a good chance that one or more inventions had been made. He then conducted a detailed study of previously issued United States and foreign patents and other published literature to see if the same information had been given before.

The attorney found that a combination of X and Y had been mentioned in the discussion part of a foreign patent which issued five years previously, indicating that it was undesirable because of poor stability. No solution to the stability problem had been found, and no claim of the patent mentioned X plus Y. No other information was found on combinations of X and Y, processes for making such a combination, or uses for the combination.

The attorney now was able to consider the following possible inventions:

1. A combination of X and Y: not patentable because it was disclosed in the foreign patent five years earlier. Even though that disclosure was negative in nature, it did show that someone else had the conception, and so that requirement for novelty could not be met.

2. A combination of X, Y, and Z: clearly novel and useful, with no known disclosure anywhere. An application for a composition of matter patent could be filed on this.

3. A process for combining X and Y: the foreign patent had not described the details of how X and Y were combined. The attorney wondered, however, if anything novel had really been done, or if the techniques used were simply copied from other related processes, as anyone skilled in the art would be expected to do. He decided to study the process information more closely to see if any of the conditions had critical ranges required for success, with those ranges being in any way different from other known processes for somewhat similar products. If his superior, the director of research, and the director of commercial development thought that the product XY had some real potential for the future, he would try to file a patent application on the process even if the chance of getting a patent allowed were small.

4. Uses for the product XY: Only a little work had been done thus far in showing the usefulness of the product, enough to meet the utility requirement for patentability of X + Y + Z, but not enough to show novel uses. More work would be done in this area, and he would follow it closely to see if inventions were made here, too.

Having established what the inventions were, the attorney now examined the records and discussed the subjects with all involved to see who the inventors were. His conclusions were these:

1. If the simple combination of X and Y had been inventive, A would have been the sole inventor. This was judged not to be a patentable invention, however.

2. In making the combination X + Y + Z, D recognized the need for a stabilizer and asked E to check certain ones. E did more than this, however; he found a successful stabilizer which was not in the group which D asked him to check. The attorney concluded that D and E were coinventors, since the invention would not have been made without the contribution of each.

3. In studying the records concerning the process, it was found that the original notes of A, B, and C had indicated process conditions which were close to those which worked best and clearly pointed the way to the successful process. It was judged that A, B, and C had each contributed to the suggestions for process conditions; these had not been proposed by only one or two of the three. It was felt, however, that D had made a sufficient contribution in defining the critical conditions of the process so that he was also a coinventor. The application was filed in the names of A, B, C, and D.

It is highly important to have the legally correct inventors listed on a patent application, for several reasons. From the attorney's viewpoint the most important reason is that any patent must be filed in the name(s) of the true inventor(s) or the patent is legally invalid. Finding the correct inventors and giving them credit for their results is also very important with regard to personnel relationships and attitudes, of course.

One other factor came to light in the attorney's study. Being quite thorough, he had asked several R & D people with long records of making inventions, and with good memories, if anyone else in the department or company had ever tried to combine X and Y before. He found that someone (F) in a different section of the department had thought of combining X and Y three years earlier and had recorded the idea in his notebook, but did not reduce it to practice. The issue of inventorship between A and F did not arise in this case, since the foreign patent disclosed the combination. If the combination of X and Y had been found to be patentable, however, would A or F have been the inventor? Clearly, F had the idea first and recorded it. But he did not complete the invention by reducing it to practice. Legally there is no invention without a reduction to practice, so A would have been the true inventor.

In the examples given it is likely that all participants were satisfied with the decisions concerning patent applications and inventors. But the results could easily have been otherwise. Suppose, for example, the combination of X and Y had been patentable and the application was filed with A as the sole inventor. If F did not understand that reduction to practice was a necessary part of invention, he would almost surely have been unhappy. "He had thought of it first, and should have been the inventor. The assistant director pulled rank and got his name on the patent." It is also essential for D to understand that reducing to practice someone else's idea, no matter how laborious, does not qualify as legal inventorship. To qualify he must contribute more than "one skilled in the art," whatever that may mean. Because of the difficulty in defining this term, the benefit of the doubt is usually given in including as a coinventor the professional who "does the work," if there is any basis at all for so doing. There must, however, be some slight identifiable contribution. In our examples, D was included on the second application, although some argument could be made that he took the recommendations of A, B, and C and did only what one skilled in the art should do in connection with that application. (This statement does not apply to the application covering X + Y + Z, of course.)

In the examples given, A showed good judgment as an administrator. When he thought of combining X and Y, he almost surely could have

written a disclosure of the idea which was so broad and so detailed
that it would have pointed the way to the process and outlined the
probable need for stabilizers, as well as many other modifications.
Instead, he called together the people who were likely to be involved
in reducing it to practice and involved them in such a way that their
opportunity for inventive contribution was considerable. In doing it
this way, he realized he might miss getting his name on a patent;
but he also knew that the benefits in terms of incentive for his subordinates and departmental spirit were more important.

The examples used here to help explain the meaning of inventorship are intentionally complex, since many real cases are at least
as complicated. Any difficulty in following the illustrations just
emphasizes that a patent attorney, not a technical person, should
establish what the invention is and who the inventor or inventors are.

RECORDS

Anyone who does work that might eventually lead to a patent should
keep suitable records so that he can prove in court, if need be, any
claims he may make concerning patentability and priority of invention.
The records should show the dates of conception of ideas, steps taken
to reduce ideas to practice, and successful results in experimental
work. Such records can be used to prove the date of conception and
the use of diligence. Three important groups of records are "idea
sheets," notebook records of experimental work, and relatively
formal reports of "reduction to practice" or "invention disclosure."

When an individual or a group conceives of an idea which may be
patentable, a written record should be made of the conception. Some
companies call such records "idea sheets," and expect them as a
formal record, with copies made for the author(s), his supervisors,
and the patent department. Other companies do not officially request
them, but rely on the patent knowledge of group leaders and higher
management to insure that they are prepared and kept by the ones
who believe they have conceived patentable ideas.

The R & D notebook is an excellent place to record ideas. The
page may be given the primary title, "Idea Sheet." A secondary title
describing the idea itself may follow. A description of the idea and
of events leading up to it should be given. Those participating in the
formulation of the idea should be listed, with the contribution of each

if that is clear. Sometimes ideas seem to spring from a conversation
among the members of a group, without any member being solely
responsible. In such a case it is usually right to assume that each
participant shared in the development of the idea, and this should be
stated. Possible ways of demonstrating the idea should be given, as
well as examples of usefulness, if they are successful. Those who
have contributed to the idea should sign and date the page. At least
one, preferably two, people who did not contribute to the idea but
who can understand it should read the idea sheet and sign and date
it as witnesses. A copy should be kept in the notebook, a copy placed
in permanent files (as with copies of other notebook pages), a copy
made for each contributor to the idea, for management, and for the
patent department.

The use of the idea sheet has many advantages. It provides a
primary record of the date of conception. The copy to the patent
department is one indication of diligence and also provides a record
which can be used to help select the correct inventor(s) if someone
else in the company has the same idea independently. The copy to
management lets the boss know that somebody had an idea. He may
also see uses for it that the originators did not. This sharing of the
idea with others is done in such a way that the originators are protected and the idea may spark more new thoughts in other people's
minds.

Efforts to demonstrate the idea should be recorded in the R & D
notebook, of course. Many companies expect the group leader to
read, date, and sign all notebook pages completed by those reporting
to him. This is helpful in strengthening the legal validity of the
notebook as a record. In any case, if it is believed that a notebook
page records a reduction to practice of a patentable idea it should be
read, signed, and dated by one or more witnesses who can understand
it. As added evidence, some companies have a policy that when a
notebook is completed the date of completion should be verified by
a notary public.

The notebook should contain all the experimental details, sketches,
analytical data, literature references, and other information as outlined in Chapter 8, "Communications." One point which many people
do not appreciate until too late is that the experimentalist must know
the compositions of the materials he is using and making. For
example, if a process improvement thought to be patentable involves
the use of a particular catalyst, one must know the chemical composition of the catalyst. A statement that "catalyst 4201 obtained
from the QRS Company was used" is not enough. A patent must

enable another to practice the invention without the need of separate invention. Since QRS Company might change the composition of catalyst 4201 at any time, a legally sufficient disclosure cannot be made without the composition.

In addition to the notebook, it is of utmost importance to have someone other than the presumed inventor actually witness the experiments which constitute a reduction to practice. Such an eyewitness should be someone who can understand the experiments, of course. In very important cases (when they can be recognized in time) actual duplication of the experiment by a witness is very powerful evidence.

The notebook does not have to be neat and attractive to be a good legal record. Clarity of expression and legibility are highly desirable, of course. The content, along the lines indicated above, is the most important feature.

After an idea has been demonstrated the potential coinventors should prepare a short report of "reduction to practice" or "invention disclosure." This report should include a description of what the invention is believed to be; an outline of any prior art which is known, with references; examples of the demonstration of the idea, including experiments, drawings, or other helpful information, with a listing of notebook pages on which the original work may be found; an outline of which individuals contributed to the potential invention and what each contributed; and reference to idea sheets or other records which could help establish the date of conception and the inventors. Copies should go to the patent department, to each listed contributor, and to R & D supervision. Most companies have standard forms for these reports.

Other records may be useful to the patent department in recognizing patentable inventions, so it is standard practice to include the patent department on the distribution list of all formal reports such as interim, final, and progress reports (see Chapter 8). A very knowledgeable attorney may recognize an invention in the contents of such a report when the technical person does not.

PREPARING AND PROCESSING PATENT APPLICATIONS

Patent applications are prepared by the company's patent department and filed with the United States Patent Office in Washington, D. C.

The application includes a brief abstract, then a summary of the invention, a rather detailed description of the invention, examples of the invention, and the claims. Drawings are included when appropriate. This application is prepared based on the information in the report of reduction to practice, on discussions between the patent attorney and the experimentalists, on other reports that may have been issued, and on the attorney's study of the prior art.

Before filing the application the attorney may request that more experiments be made. These may be to show more clearly the distinction between the invention and the prior art, and to more carefully define the invention. In general the patent application and the subsequent patent will be stronger when the invention is thoroughly understood and when all limits of operable conditions are known. Filing an application on a partially developed invention risks the issuing of a defective patent or a weak patent which can be easily circumvented, and opens the way for others to get improvement patents which may be strong and troublesome.

Patent law provides that "Before any inventor...shall receive a patent for his invention...he shall...file in the Patent Office a written description...of the manner and process of making...and using it in such full clear...and exact terms as to enable any person skilled in the art...to which it appertains...to make...and use the same."

The application must not attempt to conceal any vital fact. Courts have held that a patent is void if its disclosure is so indefinable that one skilled in the art cannot practice the invention based on the description given. Many scientists are skeptical of the statements in patents, but patents are not intentionally designed to confuse the reader or conceal the facts. Some confusion may arise because the language of the patent is a mixture of legal and technical practice, not always clear to the technologist. Also, a patent is addressed to others skilled in the art of that patent and may not be written so that someone with only a general technical training can fully understand it. Despite these complications, patents are an informative and useful part of our technical literature, and all good literature searches regarding products and processes should include related patents in the search.

The examples of the patent are the parts which are usually the most easily understood by the technical person. The wording of these most nearly follows the usual style of technical writing. They may be prepared by the attorney, following almost verbatim the examples in the report of reduction to practice.

While the examples may be more easily understood, the claims of a patent are by far its most important part. They define the scope of the invention and of the protection granted. The first claim is usually the broadest and least specific. A series of claims then follows, usually with a general trend toward being progressively narrower and more specific. The most specific claims cover the invention in a way which represents the inventor's surest position, based on the greatest detail of knowledge available to him. All claims must be firmly based on the description and examples given in the preceding body of the patent.

One reason for writing several claims in a patent is to define the invention in several different ways, in order to be sure it is fully covered. There is also the possibility that one or more claims may eventually be found to be invalid, usually the broadest claims. The other, narrower claims could still be valid, however, and give at least some protection to the inventor.

Writing patent claims is a very specialized art and requires considerable practice even by the patent lawyer. The technical person who is quite knowledgeable about patents can join with the attorney to provide the best claims, in most cases. In general, the shorter, simpler-sounding claims are the ones with broad coverage, while the long, detailed claims have more limited coverage. For example, consider the following fictitious claims:

1. A process of preparing an ester comprising reacting an acid and an alcohol.

2. A process of preparing an organic ester consisting of reacting a saturated aliphatic monocarboxylic acid containing two to twenty-two carbon atoms in a straight chain, with a saturated primary aliphatic monohydroxy alcohol containing one to twenty carbon atoms, comprising contacting the acid and the alcohol with an insoluble catalyst containing at least 3% by weight of catalyst of sulfonic acid groups, at a temperature in the range of 90°-150° C, at pressures of 0.1-1.5 atmospheres, for times of 5-60 minutes, while continuously removing the water of esterfication, separating the catalyst from the reaction mixture, and recovering the ester so produced.

A claim of a patent is infringed (see Section VII) only if the infringer does what the claim defines and not if any step or element of the claim is omitted. The first claim above covers any and all processes of making esters from acids and alcohols, regardless of the conditions used, the choice of acid or alcohol, and the addition of any other components such as catalysts or solvents. The second claim covers only the process described--it does not cover a process which is the same in all respects except that the pressure is two atmospheres, for example.

The patent attorney usually prepares a draft of the application and sends it to the inventor(s) for review. Any questionable parts are improved, for it should be both legally and technically correct. Someone in R & D supervision with considerable patent experience will normally review the draft also. He may look at it much as a referee of a manuscript for publication does. From a fresh viewpoint he will ask himself questions such as, "Does it cover the invention as fully as possible? How could I circumvent these claims if I wanted to? Does this suggest improvements which others could patent? Is the technical content correct? Have we disclosed any unnecessary information in the discussion which we did not claim and would prefer not to disclose?"

With all reviews complete, comments and questions settled in the best way possible, the attorney prepares the final draft of the application. He also prepares a "petition," which is simply a request to the United States Patent Office to grant a patent corresponding to the application. An "oath" is included, which states, among other things, that the inventor(s) believes himself to be the first and original inventor of the subject matter. A "Power of Attorney" is prepared, which appoints a patent attorney to represent the inventor(s) before the Patent Office. The inventor(s) signs the oath, power of attorney, and petition (which may be combined in a single page); these are mailed to the Patent Office along with the patent application and a filing fee as required, depending on the number of claims in the patent.

The Patent Office issues a receipt for the application, gives a serial number and filing date to the application, and assigns it to one of the divisions of the Office for study. The filing date is important because the law makes the primary assumption that inventions have been made in the order of their filing dates. That means that until another inventor proves differently, your invention was made before his if you filed before he did.

An examiner in the appropriate division of the Patent Office studies the prior art, i.e., related patents and publications of all kinds. He will find the closest references he can and reject any claims which he believes are described closely enough by these references. He may reject some or all of the claims, then return the application to the inventor's attorney for revision. The attorney and examiner will usually exchange arguments several times by mail, the attorney trying to justify both the number and the scope of the claims. He may even visit the examiner on rare occasions for more detailed discussions. During this process close collaboration between the inventor and his attorney is necessary.

The examiner may finally allow some of the claims, and the inventor with his attorney may settle for those, letting the patent be issued with those claims. The examiner may also reject all of the claims, usually because he says some prior publications "teach" the invention you are claiming, or because he says you have defined the invention in the claims too broadly, covering more than what is supported by the disclosure.

Rejected claims may be referred to a Board of Appeals for further consideration. If the inventor does not agree with the ruling of this Board he may file a suit in the Court of Customs and Patent Appeals or the Washington, D.C., District Court. In most cases it is preferable to reach a settlement with the patent examiner, however, since the Board and the Court find that the examiner was right in about 80% or more of the cases which reach them, and the cost of appeal is considerable.

When the Patent Office finally agrees to grant a patent, perhaps three to six years after the original filing, the inventor or his employer can decide whether he still wants to have it issued or not. If so, the patent department pays a final fee and the patent will be issued by the Patent Office within a few weeks. The Patent Office assigns a chronological number to each patent when it is issued. In addition, the patent will list the inventors; the name of the party to whom the patent is initially assigned, if any; the filing date; the date of issue; and any references cited by the examiner in his consideration of novelty.

The procedure just outlined is the one most frequently encountered when processing a patent application. It sometimes happens, however, that two or more different inventors or groups of inventors file applications on essentially the same invention within a few weeks or a few months of each other. In such a case, the applications are "placed in interference" with each other in the Patent Office, and the different inventors are so notified. The first assumption by the patent examiner is that the application which was filed first represents the earliest invention, and its inventors are termed the "senior party." Those who filed later are termed "junior parties." The junior parties must prove, if they can, that they actually made the invention earlier than the senior party. The burden of proof is stringent, with a requirement to show records of conception and reduction to practice. If the junior parties present enough evidence, the senior party then has to show his records, too. The real inventor is chosen based on the earliest legally acceptable records. It is at crucial times like these that the existence of good notebook and other records, showing conception and reduction to practice, all with due diligence, is highly important.

The granting of a patent does not include a guarantee that it is valid. The Patent Office could make a mistake by not finding all the closely related art or interpreting it correctly. An issued patent may actually be invalid, but someone wishing to prove this may have to pay the expenses of a court suit to do so.

The inventor or his assignee has no rights under a patent application, only under an issued patent. Enforcement of the patent must be by the owner--the United States government has no power to enforce patents other than those it owns.

From this discussion it is easy to see that the filing and prosecution of a patent application is time-consuming for the inventors as well as for the attorney and consequently is expensive. As a result, efforts are made to identify and file the most important inventions first, deferring or even abandoning those considered to have little importance to the company. In many companies a "patent committee," with representatives from the patent department, R & D, and marketing, will assign priorities to ideas and patent disclosures, according to what can be foreseen as the potential importance, probability and cost of successful reduction to practice, and probability of successful issue of a patent. High priority will usually be given to inventions which clearly will be used commercially by the company in the immediate future, to inventions in major R & D programs which are judged to have large future potential, and to very new, significantly different inventions in the company's general area of interest even if no immediate company benefit can be seen. Lower priorities will be given to inventions which represent only small advances in the art, for which no use is predicted in the next two to five years, and to inventions outside the areas of company interest. Some mistakes in judgment are made, but the cost of preparing and processing applications is so high that it is impractical to try to file on every idea that is generated. The setting of priorities, even with the possibility for error, is generally desirable.

WHO OWNS THE PATENT RIGHTS?

The initial owner of a patent is the inventor; with minor exceptions, he is the only one who may apply for a United States patent according to our laws. He may assign his ownership to someone else, however. In industrial R & D essentially all patents are assigned to the employer; and it is the employer who pays the cost of demonstrating the invention, filing the application, and obtaining the patent. The employer, as owner, may reserve the protection granted by the patent for itself, may sell or otherwise transfer ownership in whole or in part to another party, or may license another party or parties to practice the invention.

Disputes have sometimes occurred between employees and employers concerning the ownership of patents covering the employees' inventions. These can be avoided by a written agreement between the employer and employee, defining the rights of each with regard to inventions. Most companies do have such agreements with their employees, stating that patents will be assigned to the employer. This arrangement has been criticized as being unfair to the inventor, but such criticism does not seem appropriate. The inventor is paid a salary and it is part of his job to make inventions. The cost of demonstrating most inventions is great, and the cost of filing and prosecuting the patent application is significant, ranging from several hundred to several thousand dollars. These costs are all paid by the employer.

A variety of methods has been tried in this and other countries to give inventors of important patents some financial reward for their inventions in addition to their salaries. A fair and satisfactory system is difficult to achieve. Sometimes many years pass before an issued patent becomes commercially important. By the time that discovery achieves commercial importance many people other than the inventor(s) have contributed very heavily to the innovation. In such a case, when should the inventor receive extra pay? Should all the others who have contributed so much, perhaps more, to the innovation also get extra pay?

Some systems have provided for royalties to be paid to an inventor when his patent is actually used in plant production. This works well in some cases but not in others. It can happen that a person in a position to control the processes used in a plant shows undue preference for those processes covered by his own patents. This retards improvements in plant processes, among other bad features.

Usually, creative people who make important inventions are rewarded in terms of advancement (either scientifically or administratively, depending on the individual), salary increases, and improved job security. Inventiveness is not the only criterion for these rewards, of course, but it is certainly one which is strongly considered. Until some better system is found, this will continue to be the primary route for rewarding industrial inventors.

INFRINGEMENT OF PATENTS

The owner of a United States patent has the right to prevent others from using his invention for a period of seventeen years from the date of issue of the patent. Practicing the invention of someone else's patent when one does not have the right to do so is called infringement of that patent. If one must practice someone else's invention he should first consider the validity of the patent, since there is always the small chance that the Patent Office made a mistake and issued a patent which was really not valid. Someone highly skilled in both the technical and patent art may make a better search of the literature than the patent examiner did and find prior art which would invalidate the patent.

If the patent is judged to be valid, one has a choice of trying to buy ownership of the patent, obtain a license under the patent, or do more experimental work to find a way to achieve the desired results without using the claimed invention (circumvent the patent).

The degree to which one must differ from (be outside of) the claims of a patent in order not to infringe on it is not clear. In general, if the patent is one which has advanced the art greatly, courts tend to hold that one must operate further outside the claims than if the patent advances the art only slightly. In the fictitious claim 2 in Section V would one circumvent the claim if he used a reaction temperature of 152°C when the claim specified 90°–150°C? Probably not. The probability becomes better at 155°C and very good at 160°C. There is no way of being sure how an individual case will be judged, when differences are small, until one actually has a court decision. Again, the question of infringement is clearly one where the technical person must rely on his patent attorney for advice.

If one deviates from a patent claim only by substituting an "equivalent" component for one in the claim he still infringes on the claim. Here again it is often difficulty to know what "equivalent" means, and judgments may change with time. Early in a series of related developments two materials might not be held to be equivalents, when not much is known about them. Later, with more knowledge and experience, it could be considered that one could be substituted for the other with no unexpected change in results, and the two could then be considered equivalents. Often the discussion in a patent will enumerate many components which the inventors believe are equivalent to the ones actually used.

Another aspect of infringement should be included, "contributory infringement." If one makes and supplies a component to be used specifically in someone else's infringement of a patent, the supplier of that component is engaging in contributory infringement. However, if the component is sold for many established uses other than that which infringes on the patent, then no contributory infringement is involved.

In all practicality, infringement of patents is not considered a problem as long as one infringes on a small scale with no profit from his action. The subject becomes of major concern before starting a commercial production unit, however, and every effort is made to resolve patent questions long before that time is reached.

SUGGESTED READINGS

The following general references are suggested for additional reading.

1.   A. K. Berle, Inventions, Patents and Their Management, Van Nostrand, New York, 1959.
2.   R. A. Buckles, Ideas, Inventions and Patents: How to Develop and Protect Them, Wiley, New York, 1957.
3.   C. D. Tusca, An Introduction to Patents for Inventors and Engineers, Dover, New York, 1964.
4.   J. K. Wise, Patent Law in the Research Laboratory, Reinhold, New York, 1955.

Chapter 10

THE COST AND PROFITABILITY
OF INDUSTRIAL R & D

In the industrial community, R & D is judged in part by its
scientific contribution but even more by its cost and profitability.
This is an aspect of R & D which is not normally taught in
universities and usually requires several years of experience for
the dedicated R & D person to understand and appreciate beyond the
"lip service" stage. The importance of this concept is such, however, that it must be understood thoroughly by all who wish to make
a career which is closely associated with industrial R & D.

Any judgment of the value of R & D is difficult. No universally
accepted rule to follow in such an evaluation is known or offered; but
an attempt is made to illustrate some of the features of cost, profitability, and assessment of R & D programs.

Some of the difficulty of judging the value of research itself comes
from a lack of understanding of just what it is, especially by many of
the people who try to judge it. This may be illustrated by some
informal definitions from a variety of sources. A Nobel laureate
has said, "Research is to see what everybody else has seen, and to
think what nobody else has thought." An industrialist has said,
"Research is when you don't know what you are doing." A finance
executive has said, "There is only one thing I know for certain about
research and that is that it costs money--lots of it."

Our definitions are different: research itself is the discovery and
systematic investigation of phenomena using existing knowledge and
experimental procedure; industrial research is research conducted
by industry with profit as one of its goals. We may add to this the
concept that development is the conversion of useful research results
into commercial reality. Clearly, however, no matter what definitions are used, there is room for misunderstanding, especially by
the nontechnical person, about what R & D is and what to expect
from it.

203

From about 1946 to the early 1960s the general attitude toward
R & D was highly favorable, often unrealistically so. Many management groups did not understand R & D, but because of the technological
successes during World War II, R & D held a revered position.
Companies with no previous experience with R & D felt they had to
have it to compete successfully, and so it was supported with ever
increasing lavishness. Unfortunately, the understanding of the
usefulness of R & D, and how to manage it, did not progress as
rapidly as the expenditures. By the early to mid-1960s management
attitudes were changing. Poorly conceived technical programs,
especially technical programs which were not coordinated with an
overall company plan, were found to be exceedingly expensive and
not commercially rewarding. The status in the mid-1960s was
summarized well by Kiefer in his article, "Winds of Change in
Industrial Chemical Research" (1), and by Kay, "Harnessing the
R & D Monster" (2). R & D expenditures in industry reached a peak
in about 1965, and declined more or less steadily (expressed in
"constant dollars," i.e., corrected for inflation) during the next five
years (3). During this time vigorous efforts were made by both company managements and R & D managements to develop systems for
using R & D more effectively. Previous chapters on selecting and
carrying out programs and on management by objectives illustrate
some of the results of these efforts. The older concept of "hire a
good research person, provide facilities and support, and wait for
results" is no longer considered valid. Direction and encouragement
toward a specific goal that is coordinated with an overall company
plan represents the current approach.

The financial problems of R & D can be illustrated more clearly
with some specific examples. In earlier years the pace of innovation
was far slower, simpler, and less costly. Approximately fifty years
elapsed between Faraday's discovery of the laws of induced electro-
motive force in 1831 and Edison's generator-powered electric lighting
system. Thirty-five years after Maxwell's electromagnetic equations
appeared in 1865, Marconi transmitted wireless signals across the
Atlantic. Eight years after Carothers synthesized polyamides,
duPont introduced nylon. Uranium fission was confirmed in 1939 and
the atomic bomb was exploded in 1945. Bell Telephone announced its
work on epitaxial transistors in the spring of 1960, and a year later a
dozen semiconductor manufacturers began to sell them (4). The last
illustration is an extreme, for the electronics industry is unusually
fast in commercializing new products. Most new products still
require five to seven years from research to production, with some
very complicated or very new products taking longer.

The faster pace of competition, forcing a reduction in the time
for commercialization, has been accompanied by the use of larger
technical teams to help reduce the time, the use of more sophisticated and expensive equipment, increasing salaries and costs of all
services, and broader range of requirements (such as ecological
concerns) which new products must meet. In addition, each new
product in a field must meet and exceed higher levels of competitive
performance than its predecessors did. All of these factors have
led to the greatly increased cost of innovation. This may be
illustrated by the changing cost of successful commercial introduc-
tions of new antibiotic drugs. In 1970 the average cost to bring a new
drug to market was about $7 million, and it required six years from
discovery to commercialization. In 1960 the average cost was just
half as much (5).

In the agricultural chemical field, the situation with pesticide
development is similar. Dow reported in 1972 that one new pesticide
emerged for every 10,000 tested. The time from discovery to commercial use ranged eight to ten years and the cost was more than
$10 million (6). As early as 1962 textile experts were quoted as
saying that it cost $50-100 million to launch a new synthetic fiber
successfully (4). (This range of costs for fibers covers all phases
of innovation, not just R & D.) With such costs it is not surprising
that R & D and company management alike have been concerned that
R & D should be utilized as effectively as possible.

THE COST OF R & D

The cost of R & D and its ever increasing cost are due to many
things. One simple illustration is in starting salaries alone. When
the author entered industrial research in 1947 the starting salary
for a Ph.D. chemist was just under $400 per month. Twenty-five
years later the starting salary for a young Ph.D. was more than
three times that amount. Other R & D costs have gone up similarly.
(R & D is not alone in this respect--most things have increased similarly in cost. Exceptions are those which have had major reductions
in manufacturing cost because of technological improvements, e.g.,
small radios.)

The cost of conducting a technical program can best be illustrated
by showing and explaining a fairly typical budget for an R & D department of 100 employees. (This does not show what the cost is in

terms of the expense for achieving a particular result, of course;
that depends on the value of the program which is selected and the
effectiveness of the efforts.) The budget which is shown in Table 1
may be quite close to reality for some companies, and is at least
illustrative for most others. The actual cost per employee is affected
by many factors which inevitably will vary somewhat from company
to company.

A department with expenses of this sort would be located at a
plant site, so that it could obtain some services such as maintenance
assistance, certain storeroom supplies, and personnel services from
the plant. Of the 100 employees, about 45 would have technical
degrees. The 55 nonprofessionals would be made up primarily of

TABLE 1   Illustrative Annual Budget for an R & D Department of
100 Employees

Item	Expense
Salaries	$1,400,000
Salary overheads	270,000
Travel	50,000
Office supplies	10,000
Outside services	140,000
Maintenance	40,000
Depreciation	160,000
Utilities	30,000
Supplies	240,000
Miscellaneous	40,000
Total	$2,380,000

laboratory assistants, but would also include secretarial, storeroom, and custodial personnel.

Some items in the budget may need clarification. The "salary overheads" include the costs of vacations, pension funds, insurance programs, and such "fringe benefits." "Outside services" would cover expensed costs of building new equipment, relocating equipment, modifying laboratories, etc. The depreciation includes that on the building and on all capitalized equipment.

It is impressive that about 70% is for salaries and salary overheads. Of the other items, the depreciation and utilities are essentially fixed, i.e., cannot easily be reduced as an economy measure. (One could make a small reduction in depreciation if he sold some of his equipment.) The supplies are almost fixed, if one is to carry out the full program. When faced with a need to economize one can delay raises, reduce travel, defer some costs associated with outside services, supplies, and maintenance, and reduce the miscellaneous costs somewhat. By techniques such as this the director can operate nearly a full program, with costs 3%-8% below a "normal budget," retaining full employment. Any reductions beyond that range usually result in a loss of personnel.

In addition to the expense budget which was shown, a large capital investment is required to provide such a department with suitable facilities. The building for such a department would cost at least $2 million. In addition land is expensive, and paved roads and parking lots must be provided. Equipment in the building adds greatly to the cost. A few items will illustrate this. An Instron tensile testing machine may cost $8,000-$30,000, depending on size and attachments; microscopes range from a few hundred dollars to $100,000 or more, depending on type; simple calculators may cost $500, and computers range upwards to the millions of dollars so that most people rent the large ones, rather than buy them; a mass spectrograph will cost at least $35,000. Pilot plant facilities are quite expensive. A small, well instrumented polymerization pilot plant using two 10-gal. reactors costs about $50,000. Large complex pilot plants may cost $1 million or more.

With all costs considered, each employee may require an expense budget of about $24,000 each year, plus a capital investment of $30,000 or more. If the costs are expressed on the basis of professional employees only, (thus including the cost of support by laboratory assistants and others), the expense may be closer to $50,000-$60,000 per year, with capital investment of about $75,000 per professional employee. (The exact costs vary with the company, of course.) Are we worth it?

SOURCES OF MONEY

We spend money at a rapid rate in R & D and require large capital
investments. Where does this money come from? Any company gets
its money from three sources or at least some combination of the
three. One is investment by individuals or other companies--
stockholders. One is by loans, for example, from a bank. Another
is by the sale of goods. Of course the stockholders expect to get a
return on their investments. Somebody is going to give them a return
and they are not going to let you have their money unless you do.
They expect dividends and, hopefully, capital growth. Banks, of
course, expect interest as well as repayment of the loan. The sale
of goods has to provide this money to pay the dividends, to pay the
interest and repay the principal on any loans, and also to provide
enough money to keep the business operating.

Let's look again at the gross income of a company (i.e., money
derived primarily from the sale of goods) to see where the R & D
expense budget comes from. Consider the simple case of a sale of
one dollar's worth of any product. This is the gross income, but is
certainly not all profit. The cost of making the item sold (cost of
goods) might be $0.70. Then there is a group of expense items often
abbreviated "SARE," the combination of selling, administrative,
R & D, and engineering expenses. These, added to the cost of goods,
would be approximately the total cost of operation (a few miscellaneous
costs have been omitted for simplicity). A typical distribution of
these costs, illustrating how the gross income is utilized, is shown
in Table 2 (see also Chapter 2, Table 2 for the highlights of a typical
company financial statement). Here it is assumed that the R & D
budget is 3% of the gross income.

It is easy to see that the R & D budget is a significant part of the
cost of doing business. It is also 15% of the gross profit in this
example. The illustration here is not unusual; the chemical industry
in 1971 spent an average of 3% of gross sales for R & D (3).

How much of a company's gross income should be spent for R & D?
There is no universal answer to this question. A company which is
formed to develop a business from a specific technological break-
through might spend more on R & D for a few years than it receives
from the sale of goods, with the hope of developing products and
markets for them. A well established company, however, will spend
only a small percentage of its gross income for R & D. The drug
industry traditionally has spent a higher percentage than most,

TABLE 2   A Typical Distribution of Income

	Income	Expense	Tax	Profit
Sales	$1.00			
Cost of manufacturing		$0.70		
SARE				
Cost of selling		0.04		
Cost of administration		0.02		
Cost of R & D		0.03		
Cost of engineering		0.01		
Total cost of operation		$0.80		
Gross profit				$0.20
Tax			$0.10	
Net profit				$0.10

ranging about 5%-6% of sales. The rubber industry usually spends
in the range of 1%-2%, and the paper industry spends less than 1%.
The budget is rarely tied precisely to the gross income but is influenced greatly by it. Judgment of how much to spend varies somewhat
with the management group, with the expectation of income for the
years immediately ahead, and with the opportunities which are
available from the R & D effort.

Improvements are needed in the planning of R & D budgets so
that employment is stabilized better. Sudden fluctuations in budgets,
either up or down, lead to employment problems. Most budget
planning now appears to be on a year-to-year basis. Planning on at
least a three year basis would have real advantages for the companies
in terms of employee morale, continuity of excellence of the staffs in
areas of technology important to each company, and in the rate of
progress on major programs. Nothing is so damaging to the morale

of a professional group as a mass layoff of competent personnel because of a budget reduction. Stability can be achieved in most cases if budgets are increased at a rate somewhat less than the growth in income or profits in good years and are held nearly constant in bad years. Small budget reductions can be accepted for a few years without seriously affecting personnel, by not replacing those who leave due to attrition or poor performance and by economizing on controllable expenses.

THE PROFIT EQUIVALENT OF R & D

As was seen in Table 2, the cost of R & D is equivalent to a considerable percentage of the gross profit of a company, 15% in the example given. Another company competetive to that illustrated could reduce its R & D to a bare minimum for survival, say 1% of income, reduce its selling price by 2%, and make just as much profit on an equal volume of sales. If that company's product were in oversupply, it could get a greater share of the total business because its selling price was lower. Which company would fare better in the next ten year period? The R & D enthusiast will of course say that the company spending 3% will do better. But is that really so? How can one be sure? It is not surprising that some companies resort to this tactic in very difficult times.

Let's consider another simple illustration. Suppose one company spends 5% of sales for R & D with a total of 10% for SARE, while another company spends nothing for R & D and 5% for sales, administration, and engineering assistance to the plants. We may expect the company with 5% R & D to have larger sales volume at equal selling prices due to product improvements and better technical service to its customers. But how much larger must the volume be to offset that 5% for R & D? Table 3 shows such a comparison.

In a case such as this the first company must have at least $4 in extra sales for every $1 spent on R & D, just to equal the R & D cost. This example is certainly oversimplified but does illustrate the necessity for R & D to lead to commercial success if it is to be justified at all.

TABLE 3   The Effect of R & D Cost on the Sales Volume Required for
Constant Profit

	Research at 5%	No Research
Sales	$50,000,000	$40,000,000
Cost of Goods (70%)	35,000,000	28,000,000
SARE (10%)	5,000,000	---
SAE (5%)	---	2,000,000
Gross Profit	10,000,000	10,000,000
Net Profit	5,000,000	5,000,000

THE EVALUATION OF R & D PROGRAMS

    Since R & D programs are so expensive, it is inevitable that they
will be evaluated. The principal questions are: By whom?, How?,
and To what end? It is to be expected that those who feel that they
are paying the bill, company management, will do so. In almost
every system the "customer" evaluates what he receives; in this
case the customer of R & D will usually be marketing or production
departments. And finally, R & D personnel themselves will want to
evaluate their own effectiveness. So the "Who," though diverse, is
fairly clear. The "How" and "To what end" are more complex.
    The first attempts at evaluating R & D were directed toward the
general question of whether R & D itself is justified in industry. To
this simple question equally simple answers were given: Look at
the tremendous financial benefits from innovative products such as
nylon, polyester fiber, transistors, computers, the diesel engine,
and the incandescent lamp; look at the high percentage of products
on the market that were not known ten to twenty years ago. Answers
such as these confirm that R & D can be beneficial in principle, but

they are not adequate when considering specific programs. It is readily agreed by managements in technology-oriented industries that R & D is a necessary part of their operations. Valid questions are raised, however, concerning how much should be spent and for what projects. Managements are continually faced with making selections of the best ways to spend their R & D dollars.

In the groping for better means of evaluation of R & D projects, numerous different approaches and criteria have been proposed. A particularly interesting book which deals largely with this subject is that of Seiler (7). The different approaches largely fall into three categories: "quantitative," subjective, and integrative. The term "quantitative" is used to denote the intention, rather than the result, since these approaches at best have been semiquantitative. Each of these groups will be discussed briefly.

In the quantitative group, one of the earliest and simplest attempts was a calculation of the "index of return" (7).

$$\text{Index of Return} = \frac{\begin{array}{c}\text{estimated value of}\\\text{research if successful}\end{array} \times \begin{array}{c}\text{estimated chance}\\\text{of technical success}\end{array}}{\text{estimated cost of the research project}}$$

The two terms which are easiest to agree on are the estimated chance of success and the estimated cost, but both of these estimates are subject to large errors. The estimated value is very difficult to assign.

The obvious limitations of the index of return calculation led to more all-inclusive attempts, such as the "profitability index" (7):

$$\frac{\text{Profitability}}{\text{Index}} = \frac{\begin{array}{c}\%\ \text{chance of}\\\text{technical}\\\text{success}\end{array} \times \begin{array}{c}\%\ \text{chance of}\\\text{commercial}\\\text{success}\end{array} \times \begin{array}{c}\text{annual}\\\text{sales}\\\text{volume}\\\text{in units}\end{array} \times \begin{array}{c}\text{unit}\\\text{sales}\\\text{price}\end{array} \times \begin{array}{c}\text{static}\\\text{market}\\\text{life}\end{array}}{\begin{array}{c}\text{production-engineering} \quad\quad \text{marketing}\\\text{R \& D cost + development cost} \quad\quad + \text{development cost}\end{array}}$$

This calculation obviously is a closer attempt at being quantitative, since all major costs are added, as is the probability of commercial success. Again, however, each term is an estimate. What most people fail to remember is that each estimate of probability should have a probability of error attached to it, and these probabilities of error should also be a part of the total calculation. When done this way, calculated indexes usually have such a high range of error probability that the term "quantitative" scarcely applies.

Subjective evaluations of programs are more commonly used than the so-called quantitative methods. In too many cases the subjective ratings are not based on any careful analysis of the total picture but represent snap judgments and one-sided views. Such types are to be avoided, of course, but they constantly recur. The careful attempts which try to be all-inclusive are likely to be just as "quantitative" as the index of profitability method, and they have the advantage that they are not masquerading under a false impression of mathematical precision. Kiefer prepared a composite checklist for rating projects (1), as shown in Table 4, which is an example of the subjective approach. There is no precise "go" and "no go" demarkation with checklists of this sort, but if a proposed project is rated with mostly "unfavorable" and "very unfavorable" entries, it obviously will not be accepted. Checklists of this sort, modified to suit the particular needs of the company, can help in the comparison of proposed projects.

Many shorter lists may be found in use in various companies. Table 5 illustrates a combination of two checklists used by the author on some projects. The list of questions in the present tense is used at the start of the program and at review times. Questions in the past tense, designated by parentheses, are used in a final appraisal.

The integrative approach to R & D appraisal considers first the total effectiveness of the company as a team. Successes and failures are analyzed in detail to establish the underlying causes and the primary sources of those causes. This is by far the most useful form of appraisal. It perhaps follows that it is difficult, time consuming, and used far too rarely. R & D is only one part of the company team. As was noted in the chapter on selecting programs, the R & D effort can be technically successful but completely wasted if the results are not used. Why were the results not used, did the goal not coincide with company plans? If it did coincide, were the plans poorly prepared, and if so who was responsible? If the goal coincided, the technical results were good, and a competitor made a profit on a similar item, was the problem really in marketing? One of the conclusions frequently reached after such an analysis is that innovation in R & D, the manufacturing capability, and the new product marketing capability are not in proper balance. All must function well if innovation is to be successful.

Some companies have a specific group whose job it is to make appraisals of proposed, current, and completed projects. Others appoint temporary committees to perform this function. In a few cases, R & D departments have their own staff specialists for this purpose. In most cases, however, evaluation is a part-time function of managers in all departments.

TABLE 4 Composite Checklist for Project Evaluations (1)

	Very Unfavorable	Unfavorable	Average	Favorable	Very Favorable
FINANCIAL					
Estimated annual sales of new product					
Time to reach estimated sales volume					
Ratio of annual sales : R & D costs					
Ratio of total costs: annual savings					
Return on sales					
Return on fixed capital					
Return on total investment					
R & D investment payout time					
Fixed capital investment payout time					
Profit in first year of production					
RESEARCH AND DEVELOPMENT					
Chance of technical success					
Technical novelty					
Potential know-how gain					
Relation to company's present know-how					
Time to develop product					
Manpower needed					
Lab and pilot plant equipment needed					
Competitive technical activity					
Patent status					
PRODUCTION					
Process advantage					
Process versatility					
Process familiarity					
Compatibility with present operations					
Equipment availabilty					
Raw material availability					
By-product outlets					
Waste disposal					
Corrosion potential					
Hazard potential					
Freight position					

	Very Unfavorable	Unfavorable	Average	Favorable	Very Favorable
MARKETING					
Product advantage					
Product competition					
Market size					
Market stability					
Market permanence					
Cyclical and seasonal demand					
Number of potential customers					
Market growth rate					
Company known in potential markets					
Compatibility with present products					
Suitable marketing organization available					
Market development requirements					
Promotional requirements					
Technical service requirements					
Time required to become established in market					
Product variations and modification required					
Difficulty of copying or substituting product					
Export potential					
Possibility of a captive market					
Licensing potential					
CORPORATE POSITION					
Relation to company objectives					
Required corporate size					
Advertising or prestige value					
Effect on purchasing other materials					
Effect on present customers					
Operating departments' desire or enthusiasm					
OTHER FACTORS					

TABLE 5 Suggested Checklist for Evaluation of R & D Projects at the Proposal State (and in Final Evaluation)

1. Is (was) the objective properly defined?

2. Is (was) the objective in line with overall company objectives?

3. Is (was) a good program formulated, with suitable checkpoints for interim review and decisions?

4. Are (were) adequate people and equipment available?

5. (Were there adequate interim reviews?)

6. Is (was) there adequate communication with the potential user of the results?

7. Is (was) the technical execution sound?

8. Is (was) the schedule being met?

9. (Was the objective achieved?)

10. Will the results be used when they become available? (Were they used?)

11. Is there a reasonable chance for adequate profit? (Was there a profit?)

Regardless of the method used, it is generally agreed that the probability of a successful appraisal is better if the program is subdivided into small component steps or units and each is evaluated separately. These individual ratings are then used to synthesize an overall appraisal. This step-by-step procedure is more likely to consider all available data and identify unknown areas than is a single attempt to judge the program as an entire unit.

Some additional methods of appraisal of the overall effectiveness of R & D are made, but these are usually secondary in nature. These may include the number and qualitative estimate of value of patents and of publications, and a subjective rating of the laboratory staff in terms of its ability to attract highly desirable employees. The reputation of a department with its peers in the technical world is important to many employees. The primary advantages of a good reputation in the eyes of company management are the assurance provided by outside judges that good quality work is being done and that such a reputation will help attract and keep excellent people.

At this point it may be well to consider the purposes of appraisals. Basically they are twofold. In one case the appraisal is a judgment of past performance (preferably on successes as well as failures) to guide future action. The other type is an attempt to evaluate a project before large sums of money are spent on it, and to re-evaluate as the project continues, to be sure it is still desirable. These appraisals, whether carefully made or not, frequently lead to changes such as reorganizations, firings and hirings, as well as program initiation, expansion, and termination.

Questions sometimes arise as to when project appraisals should be made. The answers are simple. Appraisals should be an integral part of each and every project. The depth of the appraisal should simply be matched to the level of expenditure proposed. Some say appraisals are not necessary at the early low cost, exploratory stage. What most people who make such statements mean is that detailed, in-depth evaluations are not needed at that stage. Exploratory research usually involves the most creative personnel, and limited money is available for it. Good judgment is surely necessary to utilize this talent and opportunity in the best way possible. The exploratory research is designed to discover new products or processes of major value to the company. If it does so, it will be continued and may grow. If it does not produce results, who can blame management for losing faith and stopping it? At the very inception of a project, however small, those involved should ask themselves questions such as "What will it be worth (approximately) if successful?" "What are my chances of success?" "Is it aligned with company goals?"

As a program goes on, it will be appraised informally more or less continually. Specific checkpoints should be planned for review and reappraisal; as the level of effort is increased, the care and extent of appraisal should also be increased. The best possible attempts at quantitative evaluation should be made before major expenditures are approved, such as prior to the building of a pilot plant, a semi-works unit, and a plant for production.

One of the most difficult facets of project appraisal is reaching a decision to stop. R & D people are nearly always optimistic, about their own programs, at least. They eternally expect the crucial solution to be found in the next few experiments. To the relief of everyone, they are sometimes right! The prime responsibility for deciding when to quit for technical reasons lies with R & D management. These people should be best qualified to judge the probability of technical success, utilizing the advice of the people on the project, technical consultants, and their own knowledge. When in their judgment that probability becomes unacceptably low (the level will vary with different projects, of course) the program should be stopped completely or reduced to a small scale laboratory effort. Company management should be advised and concur in the decision.

Projects may also have to be stopped for commercial reasons. The market may have changed suddenly, a competitive product clearly better than your own may have appeared, or other factors may enter. This decision to stop should be made by company management, with the advice of marketing and the concurrence of others involved. R & D should still play a role in this decision--more than one rabbit has been pulled out of a hat at the last minute. The appearance of a better competitive product may spark ideas for improving one's own; changing market needs may create unforeseen opportunities which can be met, even though they are different from the original target.

It should be emphasized that systems of appraisal are not substitutes for judgment. Rather, they are simply methods for organizing available information so that judgments can be made, insofar as possible, based on data. One never has enough data to answer all questions--it is the extrapolation from the known to the unknown which depends so much on mature judgment. Ultimately, the best evaluations are made on the basis of a combination of documented facts, carefully thought out opinions, and judgment.

People have a continuing desire to express complicated issues in simple terms. This is fortunate for most of us, for obvious reasons. It seems possible to do the same thing in the case of R & D evaluations, in part at least. The essence of much of this book can be summarized in the following equation, showing the essential elements of industrial R & D:

Good R & D = good people + good planning + good data + good communication

This combination may also be equated to good jobs for many people and reasonable profits for investors.

REFERENCES

1. D. M. Kiefer, Chem. Eng. News, Mar. 23, 1964, p. 88.
2. H. Kay, Fortune, Jan. 1965, p. 160.
3. D. J. Soisson, Chem. Eng. News, Jan. 17, 1972, p. 7.
4. W. L. Davidson, "The Case for Advanced Technical Programs,"
    pp. 22-28, in AMA Management Report No. 69, "Achieving Full
    Value from R & D Dollars," 1962.
5. Staff report, Chem. Eng. News, May 10, 1971, p. 26.
6. Staff report, Chem. Eng. News, Apr. 24, 1972, p. 20.
7. R. E. Seiler, Improving the Effectiveness of Research and
    Development, McGraw-Hill, New York, 1965; see especially
    pp. 160-161.

Chapter 11

PUBLIC RELATIONS

The previous chapter indicated how expensive it is to conduct
research and development in industry. Any organization which spends
so much of someone else's money needs good "public relations." In
this respect R & D is basically no different from government or a
university.

Most technically trained people give little thought to public
relations. They are oriented more toward the business of getting
data and making things, and are inclined to think of public relations
as something to be left to others who make that their primary
business. It is too often thought that good R & D results will speak
for themselves, with no additional selling effort needed from the
technical team. While this approach may be satisfactory in a few
cases, it is grossly inadequate in most.

Let us consider more specifically what is meant here by having
good public relations. What is it? With whom should the "public
relations" be good? The term "having good public relations" is used
here to mean the process of making others, who need to know,
accurately aware of good results obtained and of the benefits which
may come from them. Those who need to know are in two categories:
those associated with one's business and the public at large. Each
technical person needs to contribute to the public relations which
his department maintains within its sphere of business and, in a different way, needs to contribute to the general public's understanding
of science and technology. The major part of this chapter will deal
with the business-oriented features; the last section will comment
briefly on relationships with the public at large.

It should be clear from this introduction that public relations is
just one particular variety of communication. It is sufficiently
important, however, that a short chapter on the subject is appropriate.

PUBLIC RELATIONS WITHIN THE BUSINESS SPHERE

Within one's own business there are many people and many groups
of people who need to have an accurate picture of what is being done
in R & D. Not all need the same picture. A customer, for example,
needs to know, and is justified in knowing, only that information which
is designed to help him specifically. Many within the company need
to know only a part of the program; others need to have the whole
picture. In every case, however, the R & D staff must strive to
give an accurate picture, i.e., give it in such a way that the other
party (the "receiver") forms an accurate picture. This often takes
more effort than if one R & D group is talking to another, because
most of the people outside R & D are not highly trained technically.

To consider internal public relations more closely, we may begin
within the R & D department itself. When you have significant results,
good or bad, your coworkers should know about them. They may be
able to use these results to advantage in their programs, too.
Discussing your results with others will help develop the spirit of
cooperation that is both personally enjoyable and professionally
desirable. Your supervisors need to know your significant results
so they can assess the progress being made and help guide it in
light of new information.

Fully as important as communicating results within the R & D
department is communication with the proper groups outside the
department. In this category, first of all, is the department that
needs the experimental results. Remember, R & D does not conduct
programs for itself, but for others who need the results. These people
are the R & D customers. They must be kept fully aware of progress.
Extra care must be used in this communication since the "customer"
rarely speaks exactly the same language as R & D. The presentation
must be made in the customer's language, or misunderstanding is
essentially guaranteed. Misunderstandings lead to disgruntled
customers. A great deal of this difficulty leads to a lack of confidence in R & D--a classic case of poor public relations.

Another important group outside the department is the people who
are financing the programs. In practice this means general management and the accounting staff. Management itself does not pay the
bill, but it does have responsibility for profit and therefore for
allocation of money to R & D and to others. Company management
is frequently so far removed from R & D that its judgments are not
based on direct knowledge. Instead, it relies on opinions of the

R & D "customers" and sometimes on the accounting staff. Usually
if marketing and production departments are happy with R & D results,
management will be pleased too. If either of these major R & D
customers is seriously dissatisfied with R & D, there is trouble. If
the difficulties are not worked out in a reasonable time, reorganizations usually follow.

Public relations outside the company, but still within the sphere of
business, are also a part of most R & D departments' responsibility.
To the extent that R & D is expected to work directly with the company's customers, special efforts are justified. Even greater effort
is usually needed to insure proper understanding with a customer
than with a group in one's own company. Close coordination with
marketing personnel is also necessary in all dealings with company
customers.

Communication with one's own profession is also important, both
for personal reasons and for enhancing the department's and company's
professional reputations. Good results that can be published should
be. The technical progress in this country and in the world benefits
greatly from such publications.

Throughout all of this discussion, and in our definition of public
relations, emphasis has been placed on accuracy. One should not
oversell his results. Do not exaggerate. But do not be reticent about
stating good results in a favorable light. Do not undersell. Both
extremes are misleading and are unsatisfactory.

Another feature of our definition of public relations was "results."
These may be of a wide variety. They may include a new process,
some good data that are needed to incorporate into a process, a
proposed program, a new product, the training of individuals, the
analysis of someone's problem, improved customer relations; they
might be something good in any of these areas that the R & D department is responsible for.

The last important term in the definition was "benefits." It is
usually not enough to tell someone outside R & D that one has certain
data. This must be translated for him into his own language, i.e.,
explained so he will understand the significance of the result, rather
than just being given the data. For the salesman, the explanation
might be in terms of solving a customer's problem, of improving
product uniformity, of developing new uses for an existing product,
or of a new product for new markets. For the manufacturing person,
the explanation might be in terms of better product quality, lower
manufacturing costs, or lower capital requirements.

Some general suggestions may be helpful in the approach to public relations. When reporting good results, be generous to all who have contributed. Major advances always depend on the work of many people, and their contributions should be recognized. This is true at times of formal presentations, of course, but is also just as true in those much more frequent day-to-day conversations about a program.

Remember, too, that the day-to-day conversations constitute a large part of the image of the R & D function. The daily impressions build up and are rarely changed much by a big show at a formal review meeting.

A unified approach at times of decision or major review is highly desirable. Anything less--bickering or petty arguments--detracts greatly from a favorable image. When preparing for a meeting of considerable importance, which also involves others outside R & D, the R & D people should work out a unified understanding ahead of time. This does not mean that all have to have exactly the same opinion. It may be that some differences cannot be resolved. In that case, however, arguments should be presented and considered; and any emotions which may be involved should be vented prior to the meeting. In such a case the unified understanding may simply be that several possibilities exist, data are insufficient to select the best, and more data will be needed to permit the selection.

One very important requirement for creating a good impression of R & D is that each person should know what he is supposed to be doing and why. One of the advantages of the management by objectives system, whether called by that name or not, is that each person knows his own goals as well as how they fit into the overall plan for his department and for the company. Regardless of what planning system is used, however, each person should be capable at any time of giving a clear, concise, easily understood statement of what he is doing, why he is doing it, and what his goals are. If anyone cannot do that, he should take it upon himself to get the necessary information immediately!

The two most frequently heard complaints about R & D are probably: "They are working on useless projects" and "They don't know what they are doing." The answer to the "useless projects" complaint is to be found in a cooperative program planning approach, as outlined in Chapters 5 and 6. The other complaint usually arises from the combination of nontechnical critics who do not understand the experimental method, and R & D people who won't take the time to explain properly what they are doing and why. The critic may ask the simple question, "Do you have the answer to the problem?" The R & D person, anxious to get on with the "important" work, answers "No, not yet," and goes back to the laboratory for more experiments. It is not unreasonable that the listener, especially if he has gotten the same answer more than once, concludes the other does not know what he's doing. The proper explanation of the status of a project may be just as important as all the experiments which can be done in ten times the minutes or hours required for a good, clear discussion of where one is in a program, the progress made, and the work which is planned.

The experimental method is a systematic procedure utilizing several steps. The first step is to gather available data related to the problem. Next, the important variables must be found, and the levels at which they are significant must be determined. Then one must learn to control the variables. Finally, one can demonstrate a solution to the problem. Most people do not understand the amount of experimental work required to solve problems and are only anxious for solutions. The technical person must use some of his time educating his customers in the use of the experimental method.

A specific example may help illustrate what is meant here. At one time a raw material supplier received complaints from a customer concerning the ease of burning of a plastic made using one of the company's products. Other customers using the same product did not have the problem, but it could not be dismissed since the customer with the complaint was both large and technically competent. The customer would not identify or supply the other ingredients of the plastic, so analysis of the true cause of the problem was very difficult. Considerable laboratory time was used with no real solution in sight. Faced with loss of the customer, the marketing department became quite upset and called for a meeting on the subject, to include a vice president, top marketing people, and R & D. The implications were clear that R & D did not know what it was doing in this case, even in an area where it was supposed to be expert.

The R & D team asked for enough time at the meeting to give a thorough discussion of the problem, of progress to date, and of plans for the immediate future. The first part of the discussion dealt with the fundamental principles of flammability, including thermal degradation of plastics and the catalytic role of trace materials in affecting both decomposition and burning. The next part outlined the preparation of plastics similar to those made by the customer, the flame resistance of specific formulations, and the obvious effect of certain components on burning. The preparation of plastics by other customers was outlined also, with compositions and the flame resistance performance where known. The burning test methods themselves were explained, including the unique method used by the customer who registered the complaint. The lack of correlation between and among test methods was shown. In each case the discussions were in simple, rather nontechnical language; demonstrations were made to show many points, and data were presented to establish others. Finally, the program for the next month was outlined in detail, showing what each person would be doing, and how that work would contribute to solving the problem.

The meeting adjourned with all having the impression that R & D certainly knew what it was doing; while the answer was not yet in hand, a well-thought-out program was clearly under way. Management and marketing accepted the situation as a difficult one, and were willing to wait longer for a solution. (Happily for all, the problem was solved shortly thereafter, and the company's product was basically improved in so doing.)

The necessary elements in "selling" the benefits of R & D, or of keeping good public relations, are first, good quality of results accomplished and second, good communication of those results to the people who need to know. The technical team readily understands the need for quality of results; it must give similar recognition to the need to communicate on time and in a way which is understood by the people who need the results. R & D is very expensive, and the results must be worth the cost. Don't hesitate to show that it is, indeed, worth that cost.

RELATIONSHIPS WITH THE GENERAL PUBLIC

If a good understanding of R & D is difficult to achieve within one's own company, the problem of generating a reasonable understanding of technology by the general public is even more complicated. Most of the major decisions which affect the future of technology are not made by people whose specialty is technology. Some of the decisions are made by people whose specialty is business administration, finance, or politics. Many of the other "decisions" seem to appear as a result of apparently unrelated or unforeseen developments. If we look upon technology as a tool to use to help us achieve the kind of life we want, those skilled in technology must help explain this tool to the public. In a democracy, at least, it is the public which will try to clarify the life goals that are wanted and hence will direct the utilization of technology toward those goals. The selection of those goals and the means of reaching them is a dynamic, though often sluggish and painful process. The goals will be modified as people's understanding grows. The means available to reach them will change with time, too, partly affected by changing technology and by diminishing supply of certain natural resources. But throughout any desirable changes which are foreseen, technology will continue to be a powerful tool to be used for the welfare of mankind. Proper public relations on the part of the technical community will help insure the best use of this tool.

Technical people must maintain an open dialogue with those whose interests and training are in other fields. This is most important in the areas of politics and education. In the political area, the decisions of the day and for the immediate future must be based on the best possible understanding of all forces and influences, including science and technology. In the field of education, no person's formal training is complete without some acquaintance with the importance of science and technology. Some of those who are being educated today will be the decision makers of the future.

Most companies are aware of the need for communication with the public and encourage technical employees to participate in civic and political activities of their own choosing. Opportunities arise for the presentation of lectures at universities and for informal discussions with students and faculties. These should be looked upon as just that, opportunities. A lecturer at a civic club or a visitor to a university will learn as well as help to educate. He will contribute to the communication which is urgently needed if science and technology are to be properly understood and used.

Chapter 12

PERSONAL ATTITUDES

ATTITUDE MAKES THE DIFFERENCE

The most important and complex instrument in industrial R & D is the individual person. The performance of this person in his work and in his total life depends on many factors. One may list numerous elements which are undoubtedly important, but the first on the list should be personal attitude. How is it that some children of rich and cultured families lead productive lives of benefit to many, while others with equal opportunity degenerate into uselessness? How do some children from the ghettos of the world rise to leadership? How can one farm boy out of many reach the presidency? The attitude of the individual surely plays a major role in the path which each person follows in life.

Attitude is not completely within one's own control. It is a function of both heredity and environment; the individual has no influence whatever over heredity and is limited in his capacity to affect his own mental environment. Nevertheless, each person does have a range within which he can function. Within this range he can influence his own attitude, in much the same way that he can influence his own physical endurance, his store of knowledge, his acuteness of observation, and other parameters of life. Recognition of this ability, and of the desirability of utilizing it, can help each and every person to lead as rewarding a life as possible.

What are some of the attitudes which aid one in making the most of his job in R & D? They are the same ones which will help him make the most of his entire life. One may choose many words and make many lists. Most or all of them will seem obvious or possibly trite. In reality each of us needs to review the obvious from time to time, to test again its validity, to remind us of its continuing importance, and to measure our own performances against the old truths.

As a first consideration, one's overall attitude toward life may be optimistic or pessimistic, happy or sad. The person who starts the day with the feeling that he can do what needs to be done has a good chance of succeeding. The one who starts with the belief that he will fail is usually beaten before he starts. Have you seen what two errors in a row by the opponents, or a "lucky break," can do to the spirit of a ball team? Have you seen a winning rally started by a reliable batter who leads off the last inning with a good, solid hit? These are clear cases where the sudden feeling of "can do," even if it comes late in the day, carries the optimist on to achievement.

The person combining optimism and realism has a far better chance of enjoying life, whatever may befall him, than does the pessimist. Some people look at a sunset and see one of nature's finest glories; others may groan at the prospect of the coming night. Some look at other people and see only their selfishness, pettiness, and meanness; others also see the love for family members, friends, and country, as well as the remarkable generosity of many who give their time, money, and effort to try to improve their communities and help those less fortunate. Some feel there is nothing they can do which is worthwhile or suffer overwhelming boredom; others are challenged by the large and small needs of the people of the world and rejoice at the possibility of helping to develop better cities or new fuel sources or significant medical discoveries or ways of avoiding pollution, as well as tutoring underprivileged children and participating in the many other tasks which urgently need doing. A positive approach, a determination to use each day well and enjoy it to the fullest, may be the most rewarding personal attitude which one can achieve.

Optimism is a more important characteristic for the enjoyment of R & D than for many other kinds of work. Often important programs require months or years of steady effort before even intermediate goals are achieved. The pessimist or the fainthearted will lose interest and confidence along the way, with the result that both he and the project suffer.

One's optimism must be tempered with realism. The time does occasionally come when one must realize that he is on the wrong path, that the probability of success is finally too low to justify further pursuit. This necessary balance of optimism and realism is one of the many such balances which make up what we call good judgment.

Another essential attitude for a successful R & D career is cooperativeness. Cooperation is one of the necessary ingredients

of all teamwork. No all-American fullback ever crossed the goal
line without the cooperation of his blockers. No R & D program
succeeds in reaching commercial reality without the cooperation of
many in R & D, and of even more in marketing, production, engineering, and other departments. A willingness to work with others,
to help others, and when appropriate, to be guided by others is
highly desired and must be cultivated.

Courtesy is one of the ingredients of cooperation. Courtesy is
also a way of showing one's consideration for others. Treatment of
each individual with respect and kindness is one of the highest forms
of courtesy. Daily use of such courtesy contributes greatly to making
each day a pleasant one, each job an enjoyable one. Lack of this
courtesy is what people miss most when they complain about
"dehumanization" of work by technology. It is also one of the major
complaints by underprivileged minority groups. Technology, poverty,
and social class need be no barrier to courtesy. The real barrier
is personal attitude.

Many more elements are joined in one's personal attitudes. Some
of these are grouped in the following sections, with some emphasis
which seems particularly appropriate for industry and for R & D.

LEARN TO RELAX

Knowing how to relax can improve one's enjoyment of each day
and can do much to insure good health years later. Many elements
of current life styles promote tension--one must realize this and
learn to offset those elements by his own attitude. A large portion
of the events of daily living which add to tension are inevitable, at
least by the time they occur. Being caught in a traffic jam perhaps
could be avoided by selecting a different route of travel, but once in
the jam one can do little but wait--the delay is then inevitable. In
such a situation, force yourself to relax and make the best of it.
Treat it as an opportunity for conversation with companions, for
planning a future event, or for pleasant reminiscence.

Many situations at work can lead to tension if you let them.
Disagreements, the necessity to give a lecture, concern over the
outcome of an experiment, worry over illness at home are among
the numerous possibilities. How many are helped in any way by
tension?

To combat tension, first learn to recognize it. Irritable reactions are one definite sign. Are your muscles tense? Try consciously relaxing them, group by group. With practice one can do this quite well. If this effort makes a considerable difference in the state of your muscles, you were tense. Do you feel noticeably more relaxed when some event, e.g., a meeting or a lecture, is over? These are all signs of tenseness which anyone can recognize.

Tension at certain times is completely normal--to be without it would be most unusual. We may assume tension in some limited amount plays a useful role. Like most other things, it is the excess that is dangerous. Tension is one of the personal variables which each of us must recognize as being important, which must be lived with, and which we should learn to regulate to some extent.

Several methods of regulation are available to everyone. For example, watch to see what events cause undue tenseness. After such an event make a conscious effort to relax all over, mentally and physically. Practice will greatly improve your ability to relax and will be more beneficial in the long run than tranquilizers, alcohol, or other artificial crutches. Complete and purposeful relaxation of all muscle groups and of mental processes is a great help in going to sleep, too.

Regular exercise, a balanced diet, and regular sleep are of great benefit in being able to relax. All together help keep the muscle and nervous systems functioning well and able to withstand unusual but temporary stress levels. A sense of humor and the ability to take a detached view of events can help, too. These will often show that a situation which appears to be a crisis is not really one in the long range view. Most such events even have some humorous element if viewed from a little distance, and laughter at some humorous fragment of a sad occasion can do much to help everyone involved. Discussion of these apparent crises with a close friend or member of the family also is invaluable in keeping one's perspective and in keeping tensions within the tolerable and controllable level. A range of interests, too, can provide a desirable temporary escape from the day's problems, something which each of us needs occasionally.

Tension can be likened to the pressure in a steam boiler. As long as the pressure stays within the design limits there is no problem. This is insured by incorporating a safety release valve in the design. If the valve is omitted or is locked shut, disaster is a real possibility.

The author has had the privilege of working for and with several outstanding people who were relaxed at their work yet highly

productive. They did not appear to be in a hurry, had time to talk to
students or colleagues, yet completed a great amount of work. Their
key seemed to be to relax, to concentrate on what they were doing at
the time, and to do it well. When they worked they worked steadily
but with no rush. When the time came to leave work they put it out
of their minds and enjoyed other activities. Their ranges of pleasures
were wide, including people, work, families, travel, sports, and
hobbies. Each interest was enjoyed with concentration, vigor, and
enthusiasm, but without hurry, fuss, or irritation. They know how
to relax at all times.

BE FLEXIBLE

People naturally resist change, but change is inevitable. This
conflict leads to tension and sometimes to more dramatic emotional
responses. But knowledge grows, the needs of people change, industries respond, company organizations are modified, and individual
jobs change, too. We must learn to adapt to change without being
lost as individuals. We must be flexible.

Changes in organizational structure and job requirements may be
large as a company grows. A new, small company may have rather
close association among all key personnel, with each having access
to the total picture of the company's activities. Technology may be
especially important in the day-to-day activities, the development
of markets, and the wooing of customers. Little emphasis may be
placed on long range research, due to the urgent need to develop
enough business to stay alive. As the company grows in size and
security, many changes may be noted. A time comes when there
are too many key people for all to be in close rapport or for all to
have access to the total operation. The entrepreneurial spirit may
not be so much in demand, and technology may play a smaller role.
These shifts in emphasis mean that people must change, too, or seek
other companies which operate in the style that the individuals prefer.

As the company grows it may reach such a size that it is subdivided into divisions or other structures. Where there may have
been one large R & D department before, the reorganization may
create several smaller ones, one for each division. The creation
of several departments may present opportunities and challenges
for some and reduced responsibility for others.

Individual projects may grow in much the same pattern as a company. What starts as a difficult exploratory program for one technical person may soon involve the entire group, then two groups, and soon portions of several departments. The person who did the original work must live with the change from the initial stage, where he had full knowledge and nearly complete control, to the expanded phase, where control may be at the director or general manager level and only a part of the total picture may be available below such a level.

Traumatic changes may occur when a company decides to stop a line of research, cease production of an old line product, or otherwise phase out a segment of its activities. People who have been involved with such an activity, and who have been performing very well, may face serious changes. If they are specialists, their specialty may no longer be needed by the company. If they are managers, there may be no comparable managerial positions open in the continuing areas of activity.

Changes such as the ones cited severely test a person's adaptability. Staying with the company may mean taking a step backward in rank or responsibility, it may mean sharing one's pet project with others and eventually losing control of it, or it may mean one has to "start over" in a new specialty. If none of these alternatives is possible or acceptable, the only choice may be to seek a job elsewhere. Forced changes such as the ones mentioned face everyone in his career, at one or more times. Being aware that changes will come, preparing for them emotionally, and maintaining a broad and firm educational base will make adjustments much easier when they must be made. Knowing, too, that many such changes are a part of company evolution and not personally directed at the individual makes it easier to accept the necessary change.

INDIVIDUALISM

Many people entering industry are apprehensive that they will be forced to lose their individualism. One hears so much about the need for teamwork that he may wonder if there is a suitable place for the individual, as such. Problems of this sort do exist, but a combination of adaptability, quality of performance, initiative, strength of character, and a genuine regard for other people will resolve them satisfactorily in nearly every case. It is clear from this list, however, that the complete egotist will have trouble.

Perhaps the answer to this concern is in the consideration of whether one can work as a team member while still retaining individuality. Yes, one can function as an individual--and this is highly desired--if he is also willing to work with others toward a common goal. He can be a good team member, cooperating and helping others, contributing what he can do best. He must be willing to overlook some "red tape" and grant that others may have ways of doing things which are as good as his own. Sometimes he will need to follow someone else's method rather than his own. But much of the time he can do things his way, as long as it is a good way, not annoying others too much, and as long as he gets results which are useful in reaching a common goal. This is not complete freedom or complete individualism, to be sure. But one will not find these elements complete unto themselves in any job or in any way of life. If we are to live in harmony with others we must be willing to let others have their way sometimes, too. We must be willing to strike a reasonable balance between egotistic desires and accepting some limitations for the benefit of the group.

Just as the complete egotist will have social problems in industry (and elsewhere), so will the person completely lacking in individuality have difficulty in industrial R & D. "Yes men" are rarely wanted. When they seem to be in vogue, the regime that wants them does not last. If a management group purposely stifles individuality, it does not train or attract enough leaders to maintain the business strongly. Even those leaders who do not encourage individuality among their followers are themselves strong individualists. Very few progress, either administratively or scientifically, who do not cultivate the ability to think and act as individuals.

PERSONAL RESPONSIBILITY

Each person, in the joint role of individual and team member, has several responsibilities. These include responsibilities to himself, to his family, to his company, to his community, and to his country. He must maintain a suitable balance of all of his responsibilities.

With regard to himself, the job performance or job requirements should be in accord with his own personal ethics. If there is a conflict, he should try to resolve it within the company, and this can nearly always be done. But if in some company, or with some individual, a conflict cannot be resolved successfully, the person should leave. He should find a different job where he can work in accord with his ethics.

Responsibility for personal development has been a common thread throughout several chapters of this book. Nothing further need be said here.

Responsibility to a family should be a daily matter, maintained in parallel with personal, company, and other responsibilities. Times will occur when a family emergency must take precedence over all others. This is generally recognized, and supervisors are almost universally sympathetic and helpful at such times. These emergencies are not usually the times when families are neglected, however. Neglect is more likely to creep in, undetected at first, until it is a habit which is not easily broken. A person should conciously devote a part of each week at least, if he cannot each day, to nurturing the importance of his family.

A person's responsibility to his company is a clear one. If an individual is going to work for a company, he should support the welfare of that company in a broad sense. He should think, work, and talk for its success. He should support its goals and strive to make it an even better company. This includes working constructively to develop better procedures, policies, and goals.

CHARACTER

The character of an individual may be considered to be the sum of his emotional, ethical, and spiritual components. It is the foundation on which his life's activities rest. It is the measure of his performance in his full range of activities and is most visible in difficult situations. Although the foundation of his actions, it is a dynamic thing, slowly responsive to broadening thought processes and to outside influences.

Like creativity, character may not be easily described or defined but is generally recognizable. People of good character, whatever their station in life, are continually looked to for guidance. Within the limitations of health, it is those of strong character who best withstand the storms of life.

Good character cannot be bought with money, but is far more precious. Limited by heredity, molded extensively by one's early years, it can be modified, strengthened, and honed by steady effort through the years. Challenges, tests, and opportunities are presented to each of us. The way in which we meet and adapt to each one leaves its effect on character.

Good character alone is not a guarantee of promotion in one's vocation, whatever that may be. Combined with intelligence, good health, and the tools of one's profession, however, character is a tremendous asset. Conversely, the lack of it is a great handicap. Unfortunately, the lack of it does not automatically rule out promotions. Peter Drucker, who is recognized as an authority on management, has said, however, that the primary requirement for a good manager is integrity (1). Equating integrity to good character, he wrote, "For it is character through which leadership is exercised, it is character that sets the example and is imitated in turn."

CRITICISM

Criticism is a vital part of life. It is an essential part of learning, and the capability of suitable criticism is one of the objectives of education. One cannot form an opinion about the quality of any work without being a critic. One must first be a critic of himself and secondarily of others. An equally important feature of criticism is the necessity to accept it and respond to it constructively. Both the giving and receiving of criticism are skills which one should study and develop as a part of living and working with people.

Be a Critic

Learn to be a critic, both of yourself and of others. Criticism in its correct use is a careful analysis of quality. We can be good critics only if we are capable of careful analysis and if we know the elements of quality expected in the subject under evaluation. Analysis calls for a fair, objective effort to learn all the significant factors involved in the subject, as well as the extent to which they have been developed and why. An assessment of quality for each is necessary.

Neither step can be done well unless the individual is quite knowledge-able about the subject.

After reaching an understanding of the steps required in criticism, the next move is to achieve an extensive knowledge of the subject to be criticized. While much can be learned by study of the subject, knowledge is generally inadequate without some direct experience; one just cannot fully understand a complex situation without it. The American Indians had a saying, "Do not judge a man until you have walked in his moccasins." There are some practical limitations to this, of course. For example, one does not have to have a disease to know it is undesirable, but a better understanding of just how undesirable it is can come from a personal observation of someone else with that disease. The direct experience needed for good criticism can, in extreme cases, come from first hand contact with the subject, although someone else may be carrying out the activity.

Criticism should not be just a statement of what is wrong or what could be better. While trying to point out areas which need improve-ment, a part of good criticism is also recognizing and supporting those parts which are desirable. Emphasizing only the negative leads to a distorted view on the part of the listener. Unfortunately, this approach is frequently used by those who wish to destroy the subject being criticized, to their own advantage. History has shown that severely biased statements, if repeated often enough without adequately counterbalancing arguments, have been accepted as true, to the ultimate detriment of even large groups of people. Sometimes those who sincerely wish to correct problems have fallen into a closely related trap of emphasizing only what is wrong with a situation. An audience which is not knowledgeable about the subject then reaches the conclusion that everything is wrong, nothing is right. Such a conclusion is usually far from the truth and becomes a major barrier to the correction of the real problems which do exist.

Criticism should be used carefully to help people develop the best qualities which they have and to minimize the effect of the limitations which restrict everyone. The critic should not try to trap others in his own limitations but should try to help others improve their per-formance, utilizing their full range of talents.

The valid purpose of criticism is to help improve a situation, either for the present or for the future. How much improvement should be expected? There is no easy answer. A useful guide, however, is that one should not expect perfection in anyone, and should be more of a perfectionist in criticizing himself than in criticizing others. Criticism should be used sparingly. While

some may be of help, excessive amounts are damaging to morale,
destroy cooperation, and create a state of general distrust. Just
criticism may cause hard feelings at first, but second or third
thoughts usually confirm its validity, and feelings mend. Unjust
criticism, however, is much more difficult to forget or forgive.

Before criticizing someone else it is well to ask oneself some
questions first: Is the criticism really valid? Will it help significantly? Will it hurt someone? Will the benefit more than offset
the hurt?

The Rotten Apple

Some critics carry their efforts so far, and pursue them with
such bias, that they qualify as the proverbial "rotten apple." This
type of performance should not be tolerated long. Efforts should be
made to explain to the individual what he is doing and the effect it is
having. His grievances should be heard, considered, and answered
where possible. More constructive techniques of criticism should
be outlined. Finally, it should be made clear that he should change
his ways or seek employment somewhere else where he will be
more in harmoney with his job.

Reasons for eliminating the rotten apple's performance are
several. His actions can quickly undermine the morale of a large
group. Those who are more gullible may believe him for a time,
with loss of faith in the organization. Some of those being criticized
may respond in kind, heaping one biased exaggeration upon another,
leading to general distrust and wasting considerable time. Others
not in either of these categories will see the damage being done, will
resent it, and will expect corrective action to be taken or they, too,
will begin to doubt the fairness and strength of the leadership. One
rotten apple can indeed spoil a barrel.

This opinion of the rotten apple does not mean, of course, that
constructive criticism should not be encouraged. Quite the contrary.
Carefully thought out criticisms, honestly arrived at, are to be
sought and welcomed. It is only by the constructive efforts of the
staff members at all levels that a department will do its best and
make improvements. Often problems occur in such a way that the
director and other supervisors are not aware of them until they are
of considerable magnitude. Timely criticism by those who see a
problem in its early stages can do much to eliminate or reduce the

size of the problem. This style of criticism is not included in the
"rotten apple" category.

Receiving Criticism

Receiving criticism in a useful way is at least as difficult an art
as giving it. Everyone must learn to live with others' criticisms in
some way, however. In general, the further one advances in his
profession the more criticism he must expect. This is never clearer
than in politics, but it certainly includes industry and all other paths
of life.

The ideal response to criticism is to evaluate it calmly and
objectively, select what part may be valid and act on it, then ignore
the rest. This can be extremely difficult to do. One must cultivate
his own objectivity, willingness to change for the better, tolerance
and understanding of others, and must avoid a "thin skin" which lets
him be hurt unduly by criticism and think that suggestions or different
opinions are meant as criticism. That criticism which the receiver
considers to be unjust is especially difficult to accept calmly and
objectively.

The motives behind criticism are important to the receiver and
how he may wish to respond. Criticism that is clearly intended to
be constructive should be welcomed, studied very carefully, and
responded to in some way. The response may include a change in
activities or an explanation of the reasons behind the action criticized.
In any case, a gracious response and a continued effort to keep such
lines of communication open should be made.

Some criticisms stem from frustration and lack of knowledge,
without more devious intentions being involved. These too, though
often given in unpleasant terms, should be received and alleviated
graciously. Quite often more information, combined with a factual
and sympathetic discussion, will clarify the issue adequately.

Industry, too, has its politics, and criticism is a standard tool
or weapon which is used. In this category the criticism is often
exaggerated and one-sided, and sometimes is quite unjustified. As
an illustration out of the realm of industry, the so-called "missile
gap" between the United States and Russia was raised as a major
criticism by the Democrats in the Presidential campaign of 1960.
The gap, if any, simply disappeared from sight after the election.
Many criticisms in lines of work other than politics are in the same
category.

The best position from which to withstand criticism is one of strength, i.e., of demonstrated performance of high quality. The first defense should be to be sure one's own house is in order before criticism arises. A continual striving for quality of performance puts one in the best possible position to minimize critical comments and to shrug off those unjustified ones that will occur. As a part of this performance, good cooperation and good communication are highly important features. Without these, criticisms will always arise, and will be justified, even though the experimental work may be excellent.

If politics pushes one into a position such that he must defend himself, that defense should be accurate and fair. If criticisms must be directed against others, be sure that they are valid and constructive. While this may not be so dramatic and may appear to suffer in contrast in the short range view, it is the better route in the long run. Every effort should be made to avoid the development of a situation where individuals, groups, or departments become overly critical of each other, creating a chaotic and destructive atmosphere. Such situations must either be calmed by the action of those involved, or reorganizations will be forced as a means of stabilizing the situation. Otherwise catastrophic failure is certain.

FAITH IN THINGS UNSEEN

How many people claim that they can believe only those things which they can see and feel? How many of the same people, when asked what water is, would answer that it is a molecule made from two atoms of hydrogen joined to one of oxygen? Has anyone ever actually seen a molecule of water? There is considerable evidence for this structure, we believe. We have been taught some of the evidence and trust that there is more which most of us do not understand. While accepting this structure, we have certainly never seen it, and most of us have never obtained evidence for it ourselves.

On careful analysis, isn't most of what we "know" in the same category as our knowledge of the structure of water? Most information comes to us on "good authority" and we accept it, occasionally with some moderately critical scrutiny. Even scientific theories, based on experiments which can be reproduced, are subject to modification. None, even of the structure of water, can answer questions such as where did the first water molecule come from, and where is it going?

Each of us, in reality, has extensive faith in things unseen. Each is selective, for reasons of his own, in what is accepted and what is not. The choice may vary with time and experience for any individual, of course.

Faith, and a selection of what to have faith in, have a great deal to do with the breadth, depth, and strength of one's character. Faith, or trust, also has a great deal to do with one's adjustment to his environment and his contribution to it. When there is no trust in other people, for example, destructive criticism flourishes and anarchy stares us in the face. With trust, a degree of serenity can be obtained, with the consequent freedom from worry so that one can do his own job well.

How much trust one is willing to put in others depends upon the individual's own attitude toward people, the record of the other people being considered, and the system in which the group functions. Individual attitudes should take into consideration that no one is perfect and hence perfection is never expected, that most people try to do most things right within the range of vision they have, and that a small percentage of any population is unduly after its own selfish goals. To make the best of such a situation one should be alert for signs of problems, but should approach most situations on the assumption that the other party's intentions are good, even though his viewpoint may be based on a different set of experiences and hence may be somewhat different.

In the hierarchy, many seem to wonder first if leaders can be trusted. The next consideration is for peers or competitors, with the third for subordinates. The integrity of leaders (and of other people) does vary, but it is safe to assume that essentially all leaders obtained their positions with some showing of significant merit. In a particular case, the merit may not be apparent to the observer from below, but it is one thing which should be taken on faith until proven otherwise. Similarly, leaders have to make decisions based on many things. The opinion or the short term welfare of the R & D department, for example, is only one of many inputs which top management must consider. It is often--perhaps too often--judged not possible to explain all the factors going into a decision. Management deserves a degree of faith, however, that they have considered many factors and reached the decision they thought best. These decisions will not always be the best--we must not expect perfection from anyone or any group. The management group is quite critical of itself, however,

and those responsible for many poor decisions do not retain their
jobs long.

In science and in religion each of us realizes that we do not and
cannot have the answers to all questions. We are used to that and
live in reasonable comfort with uncertainties, striving for new
knowledge and for truth but admitting freely and with no rancor that
we will never know everything. We need the same tolerance in our
dealings with people. We should not expect to know everything
behind every decision. Such knowledge would require so much time
in communication and study (to be able to understand the communication from a different specialty) that we would have no time for our
own jobs.

DOES THE GOOD GUY EVER WIN IN INDUSTRY?

One frequently hears "the good guy always loses." It is pertinent
to ask what he is good at and what he is said to lose. Would you bet
on a 100-yard dash champion to win at the 1000-meter freestyle
swimming race? Being a good guy is qualification for judging him
as a good guy.

To "win" in industry does require more qualification than just
being a good guy. If one wishes to achieve acclaim as an industrial
scientist, he needs the qualifications appropriate for that: judgment,
including scientific knowledge, imagination, an ability to convert
ideas into reality, good communications, and other characteristics
already noted in previous chapters. Being a good guy is highly
desirable, but it is not enough in itself to lead to scientific accomplishments. The same general picture is true in the managerial
role, though here character is even more important than for a purely
scientific accomplishment. (This is not to say that the average
manager actually does have either better or worse character than
the average scientist.)

A person can certainly be a good guy and get promotions in
industry if he adds to his desirable character the knowledge, skill
in working with people, imagination, and will to accomplish something worthwhile. He may have to make difficult, even unpopular,
decisions and see them through to conclusion. He may have to fire
someone who repeatedly gives unsatisfactory performances, for
example. He may have to stand firmly in the face of pressure and

criticism. But these things can all be done fairly, with careful study
of the unpopular act before taking it, always basing actions on sound
principles of conduct. Such a person still qualifies as a "good guy."

It is not easy to do the right thing in every situation. Sometimes
a shortcut or a lie may look attractive as an expedient escape from
a problem. Fortunately, however, the path which includes devious-
ness, lying, and other undesirable traits or activities is not an easy
one either. In reality there is no easy route through life. Trying
to do things right has the great advantage of providing self-respect
and the respect of others, which are highly desired and rewarding
prizes.

KNOW YOURSELF

Knowing one's self even reasonably well is an achievement which
may take years to reach. What do you want from life? What do you
want to give to life? What type of person will you be happiest with
as a spouse? What job will you find most rewarding? How far must
you advance in your chosen field to fulfill your expectations? These
are not easy questions to answer.

It was said earlier that the confidence that one can do something
adds greatly to the probability that he will. Nevertheless, such
confidence does not guarantee that the goal will be reached. Others
with equal confidence and greater resources may also be striving
for the same goal and may get there first. One may underrate the
requirements and overrate his own ability and resources. In the
early years of a career one's enthusiasm or ambition may reach
beyond the results achieved, and disappointment follows. Similarly,
underrating oneself can lead to missed opportunities and a lesser
result than might have been. It often happens that a person in his
forties has to readjust his thinking as to how far he can go in his
profession.

A most desirable aspect of knowing yourself is being able to
evaluate a situation (e.g., a job) in terms of how well it permits
you to fulfill your needs and utilize your talents. Some people fail
to recognize a good thing when they have it and are always searching
for that ideal job which probably does not exist for them. Others
drift along in a job where stagnation is almost guaranteed, without
recognizing it in time.

Being able to evaluate a job or any other situation again calls for
being a good critic. One must study, analyze, and evaluate. The
bad features certainly must be recognized and rated, but so must
the good. To concentrate only on the bad is to doom one to frustration
and despair. To see only the good is to live in a fool's paradise which
may collapse at any time. Every situation in life presents us with
good and bad, hazards and rewards. Here again optimism helps,
as does faith that eventually the good will dominate.

Each needs to strive for that rare state of knowledge and fortitude
described by many, especially Reinhold Niebuhr: having the courage
and ability to change what must be changed, the strength and patience
to bear what must be borne, and the wisdom to recognize one from
the other.

BALANCED INTERESTS

A person's emotional, professional, and family stability is in a
much safer condition if he has a balance of interests, rather than a
single, all-consuming passion. Life has its moments of triumph, its
tragedies, and a full range of events between. Even in a job which
is highly rewarding in the total assessment, there will be moments
of disappointment and temporary losses of faith. These can be
weathered far easier if other interests are simultaneously active.

At this point it is assumed, of course, that the scientist or
engineer is sincerely interested in his job and devoting much effort
to it. In addition to providing money to pay his bills, the job is an
excellent outlet for creative desires and an opportunity to be a part
of the complex system that provides livelihood, comfort, and
pleasure for many people. At the same time, a loving family is a
welcome haven, a steadying influence, a source of mutual respect,
love, and enjoyment through the years, and a valuable form of
security against unforeseen troubles. One's family should certainly
receive enthusiastic attention, just as one's job does.

Hobbies provide a relaxing outlet for many desires and energies.
A hobby can be highly creative, to supplement a limited area for
creativity available at work. A fishing trip can be a chance to enjoy
solitude, appreciate nature's glories, or think in a tranquil surrounding.
Gardening can be good exercise, provide the pleasure of watching
nature at work in the growth of plants, and get one out into the fresh

air. Frustrations and tensions can be constructively reduced by a vigorous attack on weeds!

One of a person's interests is sure to have difficulties at some time. If that is his only interest, he is shaken to his deepest foundations. If he has other interests, too, he can find solace and refreshment of spirit in them, keeping him able to meet his challenges better.

SUCCESS

What is success? People seek it, assuming that it will bring lasting happiness. Do the rich have lasting happiness, or the powerful, or the poor, or those who demonstrate great skills, or those who lead a simple, primitive life? Clearly none of these is the key to success. Happiness is not guaranteed to the business tycoon or to the noble savage.

Hosts of people, philosophers, students of religion, members of all walks of life have pursued success, often searching, too, for a definition of just what they might call success. An illustrative range of opinions is worth reviewing. Lawrence Appley, then president of the American Management Association, said that "success is a firm, warm conviction, deep within oneself, that he or she is living a life of real value." Value, to him, was expressed in terms of service to other human beings (2). John F. Kennedy once defined success as the "full use of your powers along lines of excellence." John Milton, the great poet who wrote Paradise Lost, found a new test of his concept of success when he lost his eyesight at age 44. His resolution of the tragedy was expressed beautifully in his sonnet "On His Blindness," which concludes with the moving thought, "They also serve who only stand and wait." The world's religions also provide excellent guides to the nature of success, of course.

A concept of success, if it is a good one, should be applicable to all: rich, poor, talented, those in poor health--everyone. It should represent a scale upon which the self-critic can, at any time, assess his own performance in life. Recognizing errors, faults, and all limitations, he should still be able to judge himself fairly in overall consideration, and say to himself, "Well done," if he meets his idea of success. A suitable definition appears to be the following:

Success is doing the best one can with what he has.

This concept is deceptively simple, but it is very rigorous. It calls for a continual effort to understand what is the best that can be done, in the broadest sense. It calls for an ever resourceful use of the talents and facilities which one has at his disposal. A challenge and a reasonably attainable goal are there for the most powerful, and for the invalid who can "only stand and wait" with patience and courage, providing an inspiration for those more fortunate.

REFERENCES

1. P. F. Drucker, The Practice of Management, Harper and Row, New York, 1954, pp. 157, 378.
2. L. A. Appley, Management News, 38(10), October, 1965.

INDEX